AF539425

THE
EPIC CIVILIZATION

CULTURE AND CIVILIZATION SERIES

THE EPIC CIVILIZATION

Edited by

Dr. R.K. Pruthi

DISCOVERY PUBLISHING HOUSE

NEW DELHI

First Published – 2004

Reprinted – 2026

ISBN: 978-81-7141-863-3

The Epic Civilization

Published by:

DISCOVERY PUBLISHING HOUSE
4383/4B, Ansari Road, Darya Ganj
New Delhi-110 002 (India)
Phone: +91-11-23279245; 23253475; 43596065
Mobile: +91 9811179893 / +91 9871656464
E-mail: discoverybooksindia@gmail.com
orderdphbooks@gmail.com
namitwasan9@gmail.com
web: www.discoverypublishinggroup.com

Printed at:
Infinity Imaging Systems
Delhi (INDIA)

PREFACE

The Ramayana and the Mahabarata are not mere epic. It is a romance, telling the tale of heroic men and women and of some who were divine. It is a whole literature in itself, containing a code of life, a philosophy of social and ethical relations, and speculative thought on human problems that is hard to rival.

In this volume on the epic civilization I have tried to collect interesting accounts on law, economic data, heroic ideal, human relations, with some chronological and bibliographical details of the two epics.

Professors R.S. Sharma, G.C. Pande, Lalanji Gopal, Romila Thaper, K.V. Raman, B.N. Puri, S. Gupta, and B.B. Lal have always been kind and helpful.

Librarians and staff members of USI, ICHR, ICSSR, IIC and Supreme Court have been helpful.

My publisher and his staff at production and printing level have work hard. I thank them all.

R.K. Pruthi

Contents

1 The Rāmāyaṇa: *A Historical Perspective*

It is commonly believed, not only be laymen, but even by scholars well versed in Sanskrit and/or in ancient history that whatever we are told about the places, persons and incidents in the epics is very old, though for the last hundred years and more scholars like Jacobi and Weber had repeatedly said and recently Guruge has pointed out that the social and political conditions depicted in the Rāmāyaṇa-in all its versions-were not very old, and not older than 2nd century A.D.

However these scholars-even Guruge-has not taken the archaeological evidence into consideration, nor discussed the various aspects in a truly historical perspective. Admittedly both these sources are sketchy, very often lacking in verifiable details, still it is these which are available to a culture-historian in India.

Confining our attention to Ayodhyā, the scene of the main story, the questions that we should ask ourselves are:

1. Assuming that the Rāma-story is old, at least going back to 1000 B.C.-1500 B.C. as is believed by some scholars.
   (a) could the description of Ayodhyā as occurring in the Ayodhyā-kāṇḍa be of a city of this period?
   (b) could a king of Ayodhyā, in the heart of U.P., think of marrying a daughter of Kekaya, in the Far off Panjab?
   (c) what were the means of communication between the two countries, as known from the Rāmāyaṇa and as known from other sources?
   (d) what light is thrown on these important questions by stray references to social, political, religious and other events?

No doubt, these questions pertain to the domain of higher criticism. They do not question the competence of the various editors of the Critical Edition. Still there will be occasions in our study where we shall have to disagree with the editors of the constituted text and take the liberty to point out that the text or passages in the Constituted Text might, as they have been related, seem to be in a "bad taste" or inappropriate to the situation, or if these are allowed to remain as they are, then these passages seem to have been interpolated in the *Ur-R,* at a certain period in Indian history as they reflect the social or political conditions of that period.

Ayodhyā in the Rāmāyaṇa is often described as a well developed city. Its various aspects-layout, arterial roads, parks and ponds, various kinds of mansions, some several storied, moat and fortification round the city-will be discussed in some detail, though very often these descriptions are highly conventional and fanciful. However, we shall try to see what truth these are likely to contain.

Ayodhyā in Ancient Literature

Though Ayodhyā later became the capital of Kosala, it does not occur in early Vedic literature. In face, there is no mention of it in the *Vedic Index*. However, according to Law, Ayodhyā is described as a village in *Aitareya-Brāhmaṇa*. VII. 3 and *Śāṇkhāyana-śrauta-sūtra*, XV. 17-25.

These references, if true, fittingly picture the position *of this place, almost at the end of the Vedic Period.* Even otherwise Kosala was one of the last regions to be colonised by the Aryans in their eastward migration or colonisation. It is in this Sūtra (*Śāṇkhāyana-śrauta-sūtra*, XVI. 20-25) *that connexion with Kāśī and Videha is first alluded to.* We shall not enter into further significance of this topic. Suffice if we note that both Ayodhyā and Kosala appear only in Late Vedic Literature.

According to Law (cited above), Ayodhyā was village during Late Vedic times, and he has cited *Aitareya Brahmaṇa* and *Śāṇkhāyana-śrauta-sūtra*. Apparently this reference is not correct, because it is based on a footnote by F.E. Pargiter (JRAS, 1917, p. 52) where he discusses the legend of Śunaḥśepa. The sources mentioned above give this story, but do not *mention Ayodhyā by name*. Hence, it does not find a place in *Vedic Index*, nor in the indices to the works mentioned above. These works only say that he (Rohita, son of Hariścandra) returned to the village (*grāma*) meaning Ayodhyā, because it is understood or implied that Hariścandra who belonged to the Ikṣvāku family ruled at Ayodhyā.

According to the Purāṇas, as collated by Pargiter, Ayodhyā was one of the earliest capitals of Ikṣvāku, one of the first descendants of Manu.

Later, Ayodhyā is mentioned with varying details in the *Rāmāyaṇa* and other Purāṇas.

Not only is Ayodhyā claimed by the Hindus as a sacred place, being the birth place of Rāma, according to Law, it was also the birth place of the First (Ādinātha) and the Fourth Tīrthaṅkaras of the Jainas. Unfortunately I cannot get hold of this book but, if the reference is to the canonical Sūtras then this allusion to Ayodhyā cannot be later than the 4th century B.C.

Reference in late Jain literature have little significance either for the growth or the antiquity of the site. Hence these are omitted.

The first reference is early Buddhist literature to Ayodhyā as well as to Sāketa in Bhddha's time.

Epigraphically, the most important fact is that an inscription from Ayodhyā itself tells us that is was included in the kingdom of Senāpati Puṣyamitra, who had performed two Aśvamedhas during his reign and who is specifically called "the lord of Kosala".

Fa-hien and other Chinese pilgrims note that Ayodhyā was once the seat of Buddhism, though the former also tells us that the Deva temples were in majority.

Ayodhyā-Archaeologically

That Ayodhyā is an ancient site is beyond doubt. There is a mound which spreads along the river, and has been washed away a great deal. There are several other mounds in the interior, known by the prominent personalities of the *Rāmāyaṇa*.

The real problem is how ancient is the site? Does it or will it go back to about 2,000 B.C., as the popular mind thinks to be the Age of Rāma, or will it be only as old as the 7th century B.C. when it was first mentioned in the late Vedic text? On this crucial point, only excavations, both in depth and width, can throw some light. In my first visit, some time in 1967, I had picked up a sherd of the Painted Grey Ware. This, according to Professor B.B.Lal who dug at Ayodhyā in March-April 1975, probably belongs to the late phase of this culture. Hence, provisionally he is inclined to place the occupation of Ayodhyā later than that of Hastināpura and other sites in Haryana and Western U.P.

Whether this late occurrence justifies Lal to place Rāma later than Kṛṣṇa is a moot point. For, in the first place, neither he nor anybody else has conclusively proved that the little data from Hastināpura, even if it belongs to the so-called Mahābhārata sites, proves the existence of Kṛṣṇa at this time. Hence such parallelisms should be left out at the moment. The earlier we lay bare the town plan of Ayodhyā, and its earliest foundation, the better will it be for all interested in these problems.

For our immediate purpose, we can derive little knowledge from Ayodhyā as an archaeological site.

Ayodhyā and its Contacts with the Outside World

A critical study of the *Rāmāyaṇa* implies that we examine in detail how far it was possible for the rulers of Ayodhyā to maintain marriage and other relations with distant in India.

While such relation with kings of Kosala on the south and Videha on the east were quite natural and expected, how far was it possible and why was it necessary for a king of Ayodhyā to marry a daughter of a king of Kekaya, which was situated in the extreme northwest of India?

That this relationship was there cannot be doubted. For, Kaikeyī, a daughter of the king of Kekaya, plays a crucial role in the story. In fact, but for her, the things would have gone on normally and smoothly and Rāma would have been crowned. However, granting this permise is one thing, and understudying its probability is another. For this we have to examine the political and topographical geography of Northern India. Such a study cannot be undertaken without adequate data. Unfortunately, the *Rāmāyaṇa* itself provides very little. Whatever we know, has to be gleaned from three or four chapters (sargas) in the Ayodhyākāṇda. These are:

(a) Ayodhyākāṇḍa 2, 1-9

(b) Ayodhyākāṇḍa 2, 62

(c) Ayodhyākāṇḍa 2, 63-65.

Of these the account in A is least useful. Here we are simply told that Yudhājit, a son of the king of Kekaya, maternal uncle of Bharata, had come to fetch Bharata, the son of Kaikeyī, and Bharata went thither with Śatrughna. No further details-the name of the place where they were to go, or the route, and the mode of transport-are mentioned. Though this may be all right from the point of view of the poet, we miss an opportunity to have some historical facts.

In B we have the following information

1. The Name of Bharata's maternal uncle's residence-Rājagṛha (2.62, 2-6),
2. Names of gifts- kauśeya and ornaments (2. 62. 8), sent by Daśaratha to Kekaya,
3. Crossing of the Gaṅgā at Hastināpura,
4. March *northwards*, through Pancāladeśa and Kurujāṅgala (2. 62. 10),
5. Enter Kuliṅgapurī, after having passed the divine tree Satyāpayacana,
6. Through the Bāhlika,
7. And Sudāmā Mountain,
8. Saw Viṣṇupāda,
9. Vipāśā and
10. Śālmalī, and then entered
11. Girivraja (2. 62. 10-15)

In B I, (M. N. Dutt, Editor [1892] I, p. 382) the names of the places are different to some extent.

1. the name of messengers-Siddhārtha, Vijaya, Jayanta, and Aśekananādana-are given,
2. gift as in B,
3. proceed to Kekaya, by,
4. west Aparatāla,

5. crossed the Mālinī,
6. went north of Pralamva,
7. crossed the Gaṅgā at Hastināpura,
8. arrived at Pancāla,
9. proceeded through Kurujāṅgala,
10. went past the Saradaṇḍa, which,
11. had a tree Satyapāyacaana, with a deity,
12. entered the city of Kuliṅga,
13. passed Teyobibhabana,
14. arrived at Abhikāla,
15. crossed the sacred Ikṣumatī (of the Ikṣvākus),
16. saw Brāhmaṇas versed in the Vedas,
17. went through Vāhlika,
18. towards the mount Sudāman,
19. saw the Viṣṇupada,
20. proceeded a long way, viewing the Vipāśā
21. and the Śālmalī
22. and saw lions, tigers, deer, and elephants,
23. reached Girivraja at night (p. 382).

Return Journey

In C (Critical Ed. 2,65), the details are as follows:

1. Bharata started from Rājagṛha and proceeded eastwards,
2. crossed the Hrādinī and,
3. the Śatadrū,
4. arrived at Cāparaparapatha, after,
5. crossing the river at Elādhāna,
6. crossed the Śilā,
7. passed through the Caitraratha forest from Mahāśaila,
8. rested on the Yamunā, after passing,
9. the Kuliṅga, surrounding the hill,

10. arrived at Jaṁbuprastha, and,
11. the beautiful village of Varutha,
12. and proceeded eastwards,
13. and passed through the Sāla (forest) (2. 65. 9),
14. stopped at Sarvatīrtha, and,
15. crossed the Uttānakā river,
16. with mountain horses,
17. arrived at Hastipṛṣṭhaka,
18. crossed at Lauhityā, the Kapivatī,
19. and the Gomatī at Ekasāla or,
20. Sthānumatī at Ekasāla and,
21. Gomatī at Vinate,
22. and arrived at Kaliṅganagara, and the Śāka forest,
23. saw Ayodhyā (built by Manu).

In C the detail are slightly different

1. As in B, started from Rājagṛha and proceeded eastwards (2.65),
2. crossed the river Sudāma,
3. then the Hrādinī, going westwards,
4. then the Ṡatadru,
5. then on of Eladhāna (i),

(3–5: Bharata's route from p. 335, Ch. LXXI.)

6. arrived at Aparaparvata (2.65.2),
7. crossed the Ṡilā (full of stones?),
8. crossed the Akuravatī,
9. arrived at Agneya Śalyakārasthānam.
10. saw Silāvahā
11. passed the Mahāśaila,
12. entered the Citraratha forest,
13. came to the confluence of the Gaṅgā and the Sarasvatī,
14. entered the forest of Vārundaka lying to the north of Vīramatsya,

15. then crossed the rapidly flowing Kuliṅga and the Hrādinī surrounded by hills and the Yamunā,
16. He and the horses bathed here,
17. entered the forest with *excellent car*. Here lived a number of races,
18. He could not cross the river Gāngā at Aṁśudhāna; he proceeded to Prāgvaṭa and arrived at Kutikoṣṭikā,
19. proceeded to Dharmavardhana,
20. going by the south of Torana,
21. he came to Jambuprastha,
22. arrived in the beautiful village of Varutha,
23. came to Vijihāyana which abounded in Priyaka trees,
24. sojourned at Sarvatīrtha,
25. crossed the river which flowed northwards with mountain horses,
26. arrived at Hastipṛṣṭhaka,
27. at Lohityā he crossed the Kapivatī,
28. at Ekasāla, the Sthānumatī,
29. at Vinaya, the Gomatī,
30. at a forest of Sāla trees near the city of Kaliṅga,
31. crossed the forest at night,
32. arrived at Ayodhyā in the *morning*,

(M.N. Dutt, Section LXXI, pp. 386-89, Cr. Ed. 2. 65. 1-15)

All the versions agree in asserting that Bharata spent seven nights on the journey.

The accounts of these journeys by Bharata from Kekaya to Ayodhyā and from Ayodhyā to this country have not drawn the attention of writers on ancient geography of India. There is no reference to them at all in Guruge, and also in Cunningham's (revised by Sastri), as well as in Dey's, as well as in several writings of D.C. Sircar.

However, as will be shown presently these brief accounts are important from several points of view.

First, the reference to the crossing of the Gaṅga at Hastināpura definitely shows that the poet or poets had composed this portion of the *Rāmāyaṅa* after the foundation of this city.

According to the Dynastic List, it was founded by Hastin, who was 6th from Bharata. Whatever be the exact role and the number of Hastins in the succession list in the Kuru Kula, it would be certainly much later than the time of Rāma and Daśaratha.

Secondly, the capital of Aśvapati, the lord of Kekaya, is called Rājagṛha and Girivaraja. These were, as is well known, also the names of the capitals of Jarāsandha of the Bṛhadratha dynasty of Bihar. Since the latter is definitely known to be contemporary of the Pāṇḍavas and Kṛṣṇa, these Bihar names should be regarded as later, and hence a clear case of toponymic transference, (unless we regard the Rāmāyaṇa references later, when the case would be *vice versa*). Thirdly, the messengers while going to Kekaya, pass through Pancāla and Kurujāṅgala, but in Bharata's return journey no country is mentioned, except the village Varutha, Kalinganagara, and several rivers. Fourthly, messengers had to pass through at least a couple of forests, but Bharata while returning had to cross through only one forest. And this was not a ordinary forest, but was one of Sāla trees. Now this reference, though perhaps casually given by the poet, accurately describes and geographical character of the country.

The Sāla trees even today grow in the Himalaya foothills and south Bihar, western Orissa and western Bengal, and Eastern Madhya Pradesh. For some reason, Bharata had to go to Kaliṅganagara and then enter Ayodhyā that is he must have entered the city from the east and not from the west.

As for the various incidental places and rivers a few can be easily identified. The rest may be correctly located if detailed maps and gazetteers are available.

Among the places, Kekaya appears in *Śatapatha-Brāhmaṇa* X. 6. 1-2; and *Chāndogya-Upaniṣad*, V. 4 (*Vedic Index*, I, p. 188) and is later mentioned by Pāṇini (*Aṣṭadhyāyī* 7.3.2). There too it is an epithet of Aṣvapati. Ayodhyā, however, does not seem to find a place in Vedic literature. Hastināpura also finds no mention, though we have "Hastin" and "Hastipa" (*Vedic Index*, II, p. 502). Ikṣumatī, a river, though associated with the Ikṣvākus in the *Rāmāyaṇa* does not seem to occur as such in the veda.

Vipāśā is mentioned several times in Vedic literature, and twice in the *Ṛgveda*, as Vipāś.

Pāṇini also mentions a river by this name (IV. 2. 74).

However, the form in which it appears in the *Rāmāyaṇa* is post-Vedic (*Vedic Index*, II, p. 300).

Vipāś or Vipāśā is the modern Beas, the Hyphasis or Hypaxis or Bipasis of the Greeks.

Śatadrū: This is the modern Sutlaj, the most easterly river of the Panjab. But in the *Rgveda* it is mentioned twice as Śutudrī. The *Rāmāyaṇa* name hence is post-Vedic, and signifies a river which flows in hundred channels.

Gomati: This name occurs for the first time in the Nadī-Stuti, in the tenth maṇḍala of the *Rgveda* (X, 75. 6). This river is identified with the Gomal, a western tributary of the Indus (*Vedic Index*, I, P. 258). But the name was applied to a river in Kurukṣetra (*Ibid.*), and later to other rivers in the east.

When Bharata crosses the Gomatī (another) at Vinaya, it should be this river, or most probably the present Gomati in Western U.P.

However, most interesting from the point of view of dating this portion of the *Rāmāyaṇa* is the mention of Lauhityā and Kaliṅganagara. While Lauhityā seems to be no other than the Lauhityā in Assam, Kaliṅgaṅagara must be the capital of Kaliṅga or Orissa. This city must have been definitely there in the 3rd century B.C.

While Bharata and the messengers seem to have gone to Kekaya by the southern or south-western route and then proceeded northward, on the return journey, Bharata took the upper or northern route to reach Ayodhyā. Dr. Motichandra also in his excellent discussion on the highways and byeways in ancient India only refers to the route that the messengers took while going to Kekaya's capital from Ayodhyā, but he does not even refer to the route taken by Bharata for returning to Ayodhyā. However, Motichandra does refer to the two routes from Peshawar to the Gangetic plain. The first-the northern one to Lucknow. This passes via Saharanpur, as the present railway line does, and then proceeds further eastwards to Tirhut, Katehar, and Assam. It was this route which Bharata took.

The messengers from Ayodhyā crossed the Gangā at Hastināpura (present Hasnapur), then passed through Kurujāṅgala. Here they saw the Vāruṇī tīrtha and crossed first the Sarasvatī and then Sahardanga (the present Sarhind), and entered the country of Bhuliṇgas and then crossed the Sutlaj and Bias flowing at the foot of the Siwaliks, Thus they reached Sākala (Modern Sialkot) on the river Ajakula (modern Aji). Then by the way of Takṣaśilā they reached Kekaya's capital Girivraja, which Motichandra identifies with Jalalpur also known as Girjhk (after Cunninham). This Jalalpur is about one mile north-north-east of Lahore. Alexander crossed the Jhelum very near this place. However, he offers no comments on this name, nor does he identify all the names of rivers, hills, and plains. Further, from where-what edition- he gets the name Bhuliṅga for Kulinga-we do not know. Much more interesting would have been Motichandra's comments on Bharata's arrival at Ayodhyā via Kaliṅganagara.

Polity

Originally it was intended to write at length on this topic—*Rāmāyaṇa* polity—as well. But I find there is an entire monograph entitled The *Rāmāyaṇa Polity* by Dr. P.C. Dharma, prepared under the guidance of the late Dr. V.S. Srinivasa Sastri. Though it is well done, it is completely uncritical, and the matter is not treated or discussed historically.

Dharma accepts the view that the *Rāmāyaṇa* was composed between the 6th and the 8th century B.C., and therefore all that has been said about political organisations is expected to be not earlier than this date.

In fact, if we view the date gathered from the *Rāmāyaṇa* and juxtapose it with that given in the *Vedic Age*, period by period, we shall find that the *Rāmāyaṇa* polity can on no account be compared with the early Vedic. As best it may reach the late Vedic, about the 6th-7th century B.C., though many things would be as late as the 4th century A.D., as first suggested by Weber.

Similarly uncritical is India in the *Rāmāyaṇa* Age by S.N. Vyas, though it says specifically that objective study is beyond the scope of this work (Preface p. viii).

Dharma in Ayodhyākāṇḍa

By the time Ayodhyākāṇḍa was composed, and as it has been constituted by Dr. P.L. Vaidya, its Editor, we find that Dharma had been well defined or understood in its various aspects, by:

I. The ruler and the ruled

(a) the king

(b) his adviser, particularly the Purohita

(c) citizens (*Paurajānapada*)

(d) forest dwellers or *Ādivāsis*, such as Guha and other Niṣādas

II. Family members as

(a) Father *(b)* Mother

(c) Son *(d)* Brother

(e) Husband *(f)* Wife

Amongst both these major categories and the subcategories in each, it is Rāma alone, the then Sītā to some extent, who stand out most prominently and tell us emphatically what their duty is in their respective capacities as son or husband, and wife. Though the one and the only instance where Guha, the Niṣāda chief, tells us what his duty is no less interesting.

When Rāma and Sītā slept on the bank of the river, before crossing over to go the Citrakūṭa, Guha said that he would wake up all night with his clansmen (*jnātībhiḥ*), because that was his *dharma* (2. 45. 6).

This Guha is later called a *sthapati* (2. 78. 11), and this person held an important position in Vedic Society! Why he is called so, we do not know unless it is because he and his clansmen were boatmakers, as the Nāvāḍīs at Maheshwar on the Narmada are, and not only carriers, who ferried the passengers in their boats, or because, according to the *Sūtras* of Kātyāyana and Āpastamba, *Sthapati* was one who was the local chief of a part of the kingdom. It the latter is the case, this may be regarded as a survival of the Vedic tradition. We can further regard this part of the *Rāmāyaṇa* as at least of the 4th-5th century B.C.

With regard to the king, Daśaratha no doubt consulted the Purohita other advisers, such as the *sabhā*, various limbs of the administrative machinery developed since early Vedic times, still he was supreme and regarded so, as we can gather from the repeated replies and counter replies in the heated dialogue between Rāma and Kauśalyā, Rāma and Lakṣmaṇa, and Rāma and Sītā. Only a few of these passages are quoted here:

Rāma on Dharma

Quotations from the Rāmāyaṇa:

Dharmo hi paramo loke Dharme Sathyaṁ Pratiṣṭhitam/

Dharmasaṁśritam etac ca pitur vacanam uttamam// 2.18.33

Arthadharmau partityajya yaḥ kāmam anuvartate/

evam āpadyate kṣipram rājā Daśaratho yathā// 2.47.13

Adharmabhayabhītaś ca paralokasya cānagha/ tena Lakṣmaṇa nādyāham ātmānam abhiṣecaye// 2.47.26

Pitrā niyuktā bhagavan pravekṣyāmas tapovanam/

dharmam evācariṣyāmas tatra mūlaphalāśanāḥ// 2.48.15

Again Bharata to Rāma:

Jyeṣṭhaḥ śreṣṭhaś ca dharmātmā...

labdhium arhati Kākutasho rājyaṁ Daśaratho yathā// 2. 76. 12

Śāśvato 'yaṁ sadā dharmaḥ sthito' smāsu.../

jyeṣṭhaputre sthite rājan na kanīyān bhaven nṛpah// *2.95.2*

Wife's Dharma:

Bhartuḥ Kila parityāgo ... na kartavyo manasā 'pi vigarhitaḥ.../

śuśrūṣā kriyatāṁ tāvat sa hi dharmaḥ sanātanaḥ// 2.21. 9-10

Again Sitā:

Iha pretya ca nārīṇāṁ patir eko gatiḥ sadā// 2.24.4

Sarvāvasthāgatā bhartuḥ pādacchāyā viśiṣyate/ 2.24.7

Bhartāram anugacchanti bhartā hi mama daivatam/ 2.26.14

Jīvantyā his striyā bhartā daivataṁ probhur eva ca/ 2.21.17

Curiously, while the mother and the daughter-in-law first express surprise, and then intense grief at Daśaratha's meek attitude, Lakṣmaṇa puts up a spirited protest, so much so that he is even prepared to kill or destroy, single-handed, all who participated in this decision.

This has a most dramatic effect, though little known to the masses and even to the scholars, for few have give thought to these incidents.

Some of our so-called young Turks, if they know of Lakṣmaṇa's protest, would welcome it, but what is significant is that neither Vasiṣṭha, the Purohita, nor other advisers, nor the *sabhā* and the citizens seem to have protested at this most unforeseen and indeed heart-rending happening. And these highlight Rāma's oftrepeated sayings that the king is supreme. Probably all these—the Purohita and others—thought as Rāma did, that Daśaratha was bound to implement the promise, if he had indeed given that, however unpleasant the consequences.

Hence Daśaratha's order to Rāma to go to the forest and the latter's acceptance of it as an order from his father and king. And this order Rāma steadfastly obeyed in spit of all persuasions and protests. Rāma thus became an ideal upholder of Dharma, and is described as such.

Later he prides himself as the upholder of the duties of a Kṣatriya, against all odds and consequences. This concept or view is put in his mouth even in the Ayodhyākāṇḍa, so that we may not be taken by surprise when Rāma reaffirms it in the Araṇyakāṇḍa. And one can rightly say that this was the ideal which Valmiki had taken upon himself to illustrate in the *Rāmāyaṇa*.

Just as Rāma typifies a dutiful son, and a subject, and later husband as well, so Sītā typifies by her conduct the ideal Hindu wife. A wife's place is always with the husband wherever he be—in a palace or in a forest. And when Rāma, in spite of all these expressions of love and duty, is not inclined to allow her to accompany him, she gives the threat of committing suicide by taking poison, by drowning, or by immolation in fire. And, I think, it was this threat which she had to give twice which worked. Later when Sītā meets the aged Anasūyā, wife of Atri, the latter gives the same advice, viz. that an Aryan wife has *in all circumstances* to regard her husband as the paramaṁ daivatam (2.10. 9-24).

It is this very ideal which Kauśalyā has to follow, for she was also desirous of accompanying Rāma to the forest. But the latter said that her duty—Dharma—was to remain with Daśaratha.

And we see the re-affirmation of all these, but particularly of the law or the principle of primogeniture in the family of the Ikṣvākus. And Bharata thus refuses to be crowned but proceeds to bring back Rāma to Ayodhyā, and, when the latter is unable to oblige him, he brings back his *Pādukās* and installs them on the throne. Bharata thus exemplifies yet another aspect of Dharma, the duty of a brother, and the implicit obedience of family's long-standing tradition (2.76. 10-13); the expression *anāryajuṣṭam asvargyam* (2.76.13), which reminds us of the similar expression in the *Gītā*, implies that anything else is contrary to the Aryan way of life, and one that will not permit one to attain Svarga. Hence we may characterize this as the "Age of Obedience".

Gods: Indra and Viṣṇu:

Besides a few allusions to Puṣya Yoga, to Daivajnas, and to ill-omens, the only reference to the worship of gods is found in a few verses which tell us of the daily life of Kauśālyā. In this connexion it might be noted that neither Daśaratha nor Rāma nor *anybody else goes to any public place of worship*, such as a temple when it is decided to coronate Rāma. This might suggest that no public temple had come into existence at that time, or that whatever was done, was done within the four walls of the King's Palace.

For, the allusions to the worship of Nārāyaṇa by Rāma with his wife (2.6.1), and also to the fact that both of them slept on a bed of Kuśa grass in a temple (*Āyatana*) of Viṣṇu, and then dressed in the *kṣauma* clothes bowed before Madhūsudana (2.6.7), seem to imply that all the activities were performed, prior to the coronation, at home, in their own residence. The references to the so-called temples (caityas) are of a general nature (2.6. 10-12).

Earlier we are told that Kauśalyā meditated on Janārdana after performing *prāṇāyāma* (2.4.33).

From a larger point of view these are the only names of Viṣṇu that we get in this kāṇḍa. Few as they are, names like Govinda, Gopāla, or even Krṣṇa indicating Viṣṇu's identification with "Child Kṛśṇa" are significantly absent.

Another important pointer about the date of the composition of the Ayodhyākāṇḍa is that at this time the total number of gods was believed to be just 33 and not 33,000. Kaikeyī could not invoke a larger number to witness the promise affirmed by Daśaratha (2.10.21). When Rāma, in spite of Kauśalyā's request and Lakṣmaṇa's forceful speech, decides to go to Daṇḍaka, Kauśalyā invokes at the time of performing auspicious only Sādhyā, Viśvadeva, Marut, Dhātā, Vidhātā,

Puṣā, Aryamā, Soma, Bṛhaspati, Nakṣatras, Graha, besides Indra and Garuḍa who helped in bringing Amṛta. In this list we find some Vedic deities, Indra and Garuḍa, and also the great god Skanda (2.22.2-5). Indra's worship was becoming less popular, but his *Ketu* (pillar or flag) has been referred to several times. And we know that these pillars were in existence in about the first century B.C. in parts of Rajasthan and Madhya Pradesha. A fleeting reference to such pillars helps to date the Kāṇḍa in this period or later. The foregoing list of gods is fairly large, and is suggestive of two facts, namely, the faint survival of the Vedic tradition, as well as of the emergence of the newer cults and deities, such as Skanda. Surprisingly nowhere is there any reference to Śiva, nor to Kārttikeya and Gaṇesa. Thus we may conclude, as far as this evidence of gods is concerned, that the time when this portion was composed seems to be the end of the Vedic, and the beginning of the early historic period, when gods like Skanda were just becoming popular. The numismatic evidence would date this period to about the 3rd century B.C. It is about this time that we have the earliest remains of temples first from Nagari, then Vidisha and Mathura. Unfortunately the one discovered at Ahicchatrā, as far back as 1944-46, has not been fully exposed.

Omens and Astrological and astronomical incidents:

Ayodhyākāṇḍa contains a few allusions to omens and astrological and astronomical incidents. These should be discussed in a historical framework, so that we may know where to place the Kāṇḍa, or the sections or verses which mention these things.

Of the most frequently referred to occasions, is the fact that it was (a) Caitra and (b) Puṣya Yoga, and therefore ideal time for Rāma's coronation.

Then suddenly Daśaratha had bad dreams. He speaks of Daivajnas (astrologers), who had foreboded dire events, because. "The Star of my life has been afflicted by terrible planets like the Sun, Mars and Rāhu" (2.4.18). The idea of *Śubha* (auspicious) and inauspicious (*aśubha*), I think, is ingrained in the human mind alone. Possibly animals, insects, etc, have no faculty of this nature, though they might learn to avoid things—food, places—which harm them, just by instinct.

Man goes a step forward. He stores these impressions in his memory. Repetitions of such events make him associate these events with this or that climatic phase, or the time of the day or night. A right explanation is rarely available immediately. But human mind seeks an explanation. Thus come into existence superstitions.

A brief survey of Vedic literature, right from the *Ṛgveda*, shows that, even at that time, whatever be its exact period (1500 B.C. or much earlier), the idea about things or events auspicious and inauspicious was there'.

In the *Ṛgveda* (VIII. 88.4) there is a reference to *sudine* (good day). *Taittirīya-Saṃhitā* (6.1.4.4) speaks of a person who gives up his vow of silence on the rise of Nakṣatra.

However, the belief in *grahas* (planets), particularly Rāhu and Ketu, cannot be traced back to this period, that is the early Vedic period.

'Graha is mentioned first in the *Śatapatha-Brāhmaṇa* but here it is said to refer to the Sun, and to denote a power exercising magical influence. According to the *Vedic Index*, the question whether the planets were known to the Vedic Indians is a vexed question. Even now, 60 years after the publication of that very useful work, and the discovery of the Indus Civilization, we have not made much progress.

While there is no reference to Rāhu, Ketu in the sense of the 'meteor' or 'comet' 'occurs in the late *Adbhuta Brāhmaṇa*.

There is no reference to Rāhu or Ketu in Pāṇini, as would appear from the exhaustive study by the late Dr. V.S. Agrawala.

It is also interesting to note that in the section "Divisions of Time" (Chapter III: Social Life), there is no reference to Tithi or Day, either as *vāra* or *vāsara*. Though *vāsara* occurs in the Vedic literature, *vāra* does not. Hence even Shankar Balkrishna Dikshit, who wrote on *History of Indian Astronomy* more than 80 years ago, had to admit that the division of the month into days was not an Indian conception. It had come into existence by the time of *Yājnavalkya-Smṛti*, though the seven *grahas* were known by the time of Atharva-Jyotiṣa. In fact, a definite mention of the day, as Sen Gupta showed later, occurs in a late 5th century inscription from Central India.

Dikshit has also shown that the beginning of the year was with Caitra, and that the month of Caitra was more auspicious than other months and had connexion with Puṣya Yoga.

With regard to the seven day week, Kane, after an exhaustive review, has to say that the evidence is not conclusive that the Indians had seven day week from the Vedic times; at the same time he well points out that the Indians did not borrow the concept or system *en bloc* from the Greeks or the Chaldeans.

As far as the epigraphical evidence is concerned, we cannot cite any record earlier than the Eran Stone Pillar inscription of Budhagupta of the Gupta Era 165 (i.e. A.D. 484). This mentions Thursday and 12th *tithi* of the light half of Āṣāḍha.

Kane then reviews the literary evidence. Here the fact that the *Pancasiddhāntikā* while summarizing the *Romaka-siddhānta* mentions Monday; then Garga, dated at the 1st century B.C., refers to the seven day week from Sunday to Saturday; and then after taking into consideration some other evidence, Kane concludes, "the above references furnish a *terminus ad quem* for India's knowledge of the planetary week days (viz. first century B.C. -first century A.D.)". The *terminus a quo* cannot be stated with certainty.

He then cites a few other theories about the days of the seven day week in India, but has to conclude at the beginning of this section that the Indians had the elements of the week day and developed it by 'coming' into contact with the Babylonians, Syrians (and we might add the Romans).

Now this is an important concession, when we examine the *Rāmāyaṇa* historically. For we are told several times that Daśaratha thought of Rāma's coronation, because it was Caitras and because it was in conjunction with Puṣya (Puṣyayoga). (Though one wonders why, in spite of all these auspicious signs, the whole thing went wrong, completely wrong, completely sabotaged!!)

Dikshit had to say that certain things in the *Rāmāyaṇa* were later than the Vedic and Vedāṅga. So far I have not found any reference to *divasa* or *vāsara* or Rāhu and Ketu in Kauṭilya's *Arthaśāstra*. Nor is there a reference to the Puśya Nakṣatra as one which is the favourable Nakṣatra for coronation. But all these and the term 'Daivajna' occur in the *Bṛhat Saṁhitā* of Varāhamihira. And this astronomer-cum-astrologer is fairly well dated to the end of the 5th and the beginning of the 6th century A.D.

And this at present should be regarded as he lowest limit to which we could place all the references to omens and superstitions based on astrology. Of course, by further study of all the passages at present relegated to appendix, we might be able to detect a few more, and also depending upon the version in which these occur, connect these up with the superstitions at present current in each major region, such as Bengal or Kashmir or Nepal. This, however, entails an independent study, which however has to be taken up if our epics and Purāṇas are to be studied from point of view of Higher Criticism.

In the Critical Edition of the Bālakāṇḍa we are only told (1.17.5) that Kauśalyā gave birth to Rāma, who had half of Viṣṇu's personality (*mahābhaga*) in him. Bharata had one-fourth, Lakśmaṇa-Śatrughna had also inherited one-fourth of Viśṇu's personality. Then one version gives the astronomical details of Rāma's birth, viz. that it was in the 12th month on the 9th *tithi*. Aditi nakṣatra, in Karkaṭa Lagna. These verses have been omitted from the Critical Edition.

After-death Ceremonies:

In the Ayodhyākāṇḍa, there are three occasions when a reference is made to the ceremonies performed by the near relatives of king Daśaratha.

1. Immediately after Daśaratha dies (2.59) and until Bharata returns, the body is immersed in oil, 2.60. 12-14.
2. After Bharata returns from Kekaya, 2.70, 2.71, 1-9 and 11-23.
3. When Bharata with his three widowed mothers meets Rāma, Lakṣmaṇa and Sītā.

On the last occasion, they perform what is called *Jalakriyā* (2.95. 21-33), Lakṣmaṇa is asked to fetch Iṅgudipiṇyāka and *cīra* (fresh bark). And then Sītā is asked to proceed first, followed by Lakṣmaṇa and Rāma. They all go to a *tīrtha* on the Manadākinī. There pure water, with Aigunda *piṇyāka* mixed with ber fruit, was offered on a bed of Darbha (Grass). This is something like *śrāddha* ceremony, and characteristic of the situation was the offering of Iṅgudi and jujube fruits, because this was the normal food of Rāma, Lakṣmaṇa and Sītā (*yadannaḥ puruṣo bhavati tadannās tasya devatāḥ* 2.95.31).

Pending Bharata's arrival, Daśaratha's body was laid in a vessel containing oil, but not actually embalmed, as the words indicate: *tailadroṇyāṁ...saṁveśya jagatīpatim* (2.60.12) and later *uddhṛtaṁ tailasaṁkledāt... bhūmau niveśitām* (2.70.4). It would be interesting to find parallels to such a custom at any time in India, or elsewhere.

For the immersion of the body, not only a large vessel, preferably of metal (copper/bronze) or wood and not pottery (for the latter absorbs a lot of oil, as our experiment with a small oil lamp showed) is needed and sufficient quantity of oil, at least two maunds or half a quintal. But this no primitive society can provide. These can be had only at a fairly advanced stage of civilization.

After I wrote this, I found to may great surprise and joy that the death ceremony undertaken after Bharata's arrival was of the usual Hindu type. The body was placed on a bier and taken in a procession, scattering or distributing gold and all kinds of clothes to poor persons. And the fire was prepared out of all kinds of scented woods. Then followed recitation of Sāma by Brāhmaṇas. What is noticeable in this description is the reference to people going to the burning ghāt on the river Sarayū in litters and conveyances, suitable to their status (*śibikābhiś ca yānaiś ca yathārhaṁ tasya yoṣitaḥ* 2.70.19). All the wives of Daśaratha and other women had also accompanied the dead body. Then was observed the 10-day period of mourning.

The practice of immersing the dead body in oil is mentioned by *Satyāṣāḍha-śrauta-sūtra* (29.4.29) and *Vaikhānasa-śrauta-sūtra* (31.23), as cited by Kaṇe, prescribes that if an *āhitāgni* died away from his people his corpse should be laid down in a tub or trough filled with sesame oil and brought home in a cart.

It is interesting that the word for the receptacle—tub or trough—in the *Śrauta-sūtras* is *droṇa*. As far as this occasion is concerned, the people at Ayodhyā had to wait for Bharata, so in the end, the result was the same. The age of these Sūtras is not *very old,* about 4th century B.C.

More interesting is the description in the *Mahāparinibbāna Suttanta.* This also is a work of about the 3rd century B.C. and here we are told that the Buddha's body was wrapped in new cloth, cotton wool, etc., and placed in an oil vessel of iron which was covered with another vessel of iron. Then the funeral pyre was built of all kinds of perfumes and the body placed on it.

Here again the reason for immersing the body seems to have been the time taken for wrapping so many types and quantity of cloth, and getting all sorts of perfumes.

What is of significance is the reference to a vessel of iron, exactly as I had anticipated. Another inference may be legitimately drawn, viz. that this immersion is possible when so much oil, whether of *tila* (sesame) can be easily procured. And this was perhaps so in Eastern India.

With regard to the reference to the carrying of Daśaratha's corpse on a palanquin (*śibikā*), it was again according to the practice recommended by later Vedic texts and Smṛtis.

However, the fact that not only the corpse could be carried in a cart, but even the mourners could accompany it in various kinds of conveyances is interesting. It was perhaps out of necessity, because usually the cremation took place on the river bank, and this was at a distance. And if the women of all sorts of status could to accompany the corpse, then procession had to be made for them. However, all these gradually disappeared, so much so that women were completely prohibited from going to the cremation ground.

Road-making:

When Bharata decided to go to Citrakūṭa and request Rāma, Sītā and Lakṣmaṇa to return to Ayodhyā, he was accompanied by a large army. Apparently there was no road for an army with all sorts of vehicles between Ayodhyā and the Gaṅgā (though we are told that Rāma had left in a chariot and after three days' journey reached the Saṅgama).

Either the author who composed (added) the *sarga* (chapter 74) did not know of this, or we are to assume that there was some kind of road for a small *ekkā* (one-seat cart), so popular until recently in U.P.

Anyway, here is an excellent example of how interpolations might take place. But more than that we learn how new tracks were made in unknown unchartered areas. Indeed, it reminds us of the modern army commander, blasting out roads through hills and forests, and building bridges over rivers, with the help of sappers, miners, and diggers (*bhumipradeśajnāḥ*), *khanakāḥ, yantrakāḥ*, wood-cutters (*vṛkṣatakṣakāḥ*), well-diggers (*kūpakārāḥ*) and architects (*sthapati*) or 'local lords.'

These and others levelled roads, filling up cavities, and removing hillocks, building bridges (*babandhur bandhanīyān*) and even planting trees where there were none (*a-vṛkṣeṣu deśeṣu*).

And lo! in a short time a fine road, decorated with flags and festoons and sprayed with sandal-scented water was ready. With all preparations completed Bharata started on an auspicious *muhūrta*.

Few writers on the Rāmāyaṇa or the town/city in ancient India have ever noted these verses in the Critical Edition (2.74.1-13), which admirably describe what a progressive state should have. The various artists, technicians, craftsmen and engineers who have been mentioned with actual work they did would do credit to a modern municipal corporation and Public Works Department.

Sandals:

It is well known that when Rāma refused to return from Citrakūṭa, and Bharata threatened to fast unto death, Rāma agreed to return after his 14 years' sojourn in a forest, and for the duration gave Bharata his *pādukās* (sandals). These sandals were not of ordinary type: grass, wood or leather. While the actual material with which these sandals were made is not mentioned, we are told-and this appears in all the versions—that these were studded with gold.

Now there is nothing surprising to learn that kings in those days wore gold-studded footwear. While, in many cases, this may be regarded as an exaggeration, there is no doubt about the existence of such things, because we have gold-embroidered sandals of the young Tut-ankhamen from his grave in Egypt.

But what is worth inquiring is how Rāma happened to have such gold-studded sandals with him, at Citrakūṭa. He had left everything behind, and gone as a hermit, in bark clothes. Only Sītā was allowed to keep her ornaments, and she had donned bark garments over her silk sari!!

So this incident of the sandals is a later interpolation, while one edition, that used by M.N. Dutt for his English translation, mentions that Rāma gave the gold-studded sandals as demanded by Bharata, the Critical Edition says that Bharata (suddenly) produced such gold-studded sandals, and asked Rāma to put them on and then return them to him. And Rāma wore them for a second, and gave them back to Bharata.

In this connexion it would be interesting to examine the growth of the concept of 'Footprints.'

In Vedic literature there is little of image-worship, though we are told of the "three steps of Viṣṇu". However, nowhere is there any indication that the footprints of a divine person or a sage, or, in their absence, the sandals worn by such a person, were ever worshipped.

In our present knowledge this concept was first introduced or popularized by the early Buddhists. When they were forbidden by Buddha to worship him in a human form, the devotees, as is usual in India and many countries, began to worship his relics, and immortalize incidents in his life. Thus we have "Buddha's footprints", besides scenes from his life, in several early Buddhist monuments, such as Sanchi, Bharhut, Bhaja, Karla, and stūpas like Amaravati and Nagarjunakonda.

So this incident of Bharata getting the *pādukās* of Rāma and worshipping them could have been introduced not before the 3rd century B.C. Then while recasting the Ayodhyākāṇḍa the sandals were studded with gold. For certainly Bharata could not worship ordinary footwear!!

When I pointed out this in an article, the substance of which was earlier relayed by *Sāmāchar*, some scholars pointed out that Bharata knew that Rāma would not return. So he haa taken the gold-studded *pādukās* with him. Then he "suddenly" produced these sandals when Rāma advised him not to fast unto death, but to return to Ayodhyā. According to this version, included in the Critical Edition, Rāma put on these sandals, then took them off, and gave them back to Bharata. However, this whole scene seems to have been concocted in the 2nd century A.D. and interpolated later in the *Rāmāyaṇa*.

Ayodhyā:

Whatever be the nature of the first or the earliest Ayodhyā, a village or a city, its description, as it appears in the Critical Edition of the *Rāmāyaṇa*, is of a well laid out city, with arterial roads—a *rājāmarga* or a *patha*, fortification all round, and in addition a ditch *parikhā*. Within the city, there were various kinds of buildings: *harmya, prāsāda, veśma,* and *vimāna*. Some of these were seven or eight stories (*aṭṭalaka*) high.

There were checkposts (*gulma*), parks and gardens, besides drinking houses (*pāna-gṛhas*), houses for recreation (*krīḍā-gṛhas*). There were shops or bazars, where all sorts of things could be had, and the godown stocked with paddy. The merchandise was brought from far and nearby ox-drawn carts as well as on camelback.

No detailed description of a single house is available, nor any inkling given as to how these were built—with mud or mudbricks, *pakka bricks*, and lime or stone. Nor are we told how they were roofed: with tiles or simply thatched. Some houses had at least terraces from where the residents could see the procession passing through the main highway.

What is interesting in the description is, and this very few writers seem to have noted, that not only the houses or palaces had several rooms, some of which could be approached seated in a chariot, but that all the three queens of Daśaratha and Rāma lived in *separate* houses. Rāma's residence particularly was not near, adjoining to that of Daśaratha, but at some distance, so that when he was called by Daśaratha, a chariot had to be sent for him.

Whether all this description is of really existing city or much of it is imaginary, we have the see—indeed examine—with all the evidence from India and abroad, particularly Western Asia; when—at what time—could such a city have existed in India, or in the Gangetic valley to be particular? Little thought has been given to such question say previous authors who have written on the *Rāmāyaṇa* Age". Confining our attention to India, we have to say, with Mohenjodaro, Harappa and Lothal before us, that Ayodhyā could have had arterial roads and fortification. A moat is also not impossible with the perennial waters from the Sarayu.

The city could have had a number of small and large houses with two or three or more rooms. There could have been other things as well, besides parks and gardens.

At Mohenjodaro some houses had two storeys, and probably all of them had flat roofs or terraces. This is possible in a dry climate of Sind, but not in Central U.P. where Ayodhyā was situated.

The question now remains of very tall houses with seven or eight storeys, some of which had Kailāsa-like towers or *Śikharas*.

Either these descriptions are completely imaginary or they are based on fairly tall structures that existed in Eastern India, either in the form of stūpas or temples, and residential houses with at least two or three storeys. Unfortunately no city-site, except Taxila and Nālandā, had been excavated in India from which we could form some idea of the tallest residential houses in ancient India, leaving out stūpas and temples. As far as the structural history of temples is concerned, there were no temples with *tall śikharas* before the 6th century A.D. And even these *śikharas* might be compared with Kailāsa as far as the conical nature of their structure is concerned but, not in height.

Now Fa-hien, who visited Ayodhyā in the 5th century A.D., did see a Buddhist stūpa, Whereas two centuries later, Hiuen Tsiang (Yuan Chwang) noticed more than 100 monasteries with thousands of Mahāyāna and Hīnāyana Buddhists, and only 10 Deva temples.

This is the lower limit to which we could ascribe the description of a highly developed city in the *Rāmāyaṇa.* Those, who do not like such a low dating, will have to be satisfied with the other limit, which cannot be earlier than the 3rd century B.C. For, the earliest stūpas, as far as known today, belong to this period. It is at this time that we have the earliest representation of storied houses, with men and women peeping out from small windows in the extant panels of the gateways of the stupas at Bharhut and Sanchi.

As far as the layout of the city with arterial roads is concerned, we have some idea from the Mauryan Taxila excavated by Marshall. This is not at all encouraging. Unlike the later well laid out Sirkap, the roads—indeed lanes—are zigzag, and not straight and well laid out. Nearer home, Kauśāmbī could have provided the best evidence. Unfortunately it is not yet horizontally dug. But probably this site, as well as Ahicchatrā, and so many others in the Gangetic valley, besides Ayodhyā itself will not give a better picture of town planning in Mauryan India. To say anything of Ayodhyā before this period, or its reputed Pauranic antiquity, be it *Tretā* or *Dvāpara Yuga*, dated to 5000 B.C. and beyond, would be pure speculation. However, if the excavations so far conducted in India, outside the Indus Valley and the Panjab are any guide, the earliest houses at Ayodhyā—whatever be that period, perhaps not earlier than the 8th-9th century B.C., if the account in the *Aitareya Brāhmaṇa* is indeed correct and a true description, viz. that is was a village, even in the time of Hariścandra, one of the Pauranic kings—could not be better than mud huts, exactly as we see in the villages near Ayodhyā today. Possibly, and *I say this with great hesitation,* a hint to this effect is contained in the description of Kauśalyā's body covered with dust (*pāṁśu*) as she falls down unconscious on hearing Rāma's banishment to the forest. Though we are nowhere told how the houses were built, such covering with dust is not possible, *not expected*, in a well-made floor, of a house built with *pakka* bricks or stone. Hence this unconscious reference possibly tells us that the houses were nothing but mud huts in the earliest Ayodhyā.

The (conception of the) provision of separate houses or palaces for Daśaratha's three queens, and also for Rāma and Sītā, and the existence of the guilds of craftsmen, barbers, musicians, merchants and traders, and the facts that respectable women never exposed themselves to public view, that women were usually confined to the inner apartment, that when they went out, they moved in palanquins or other conveyances which were adequately covered with veils or curtains — all this again suggest a highly developed social organization and social values which we do not normally expect at a very early period.

Unfortunately, both scholars and laymen are used to reading classified description of these ancient cities, as they appear in Purāṇas and epics, given by writers as generalized accounts. Hence we all are accustomed to imagine that Dvārakā, Hastināpura, and Ayodhyā were so fully developed as given in the epics or their generalized accounts, But an integrated picture, reconstructed with all available evidence, is bound to the different, and certainly very disappointing to our scholars and laymen alike. For few of these are aware of the centuries of development that lie behind these full-fledged descriptions of cities.

An exhaustive survey of 74 excavated sites, including the well known epic sites such as Hastināpura, Ahicchatrā, Kampil, Kauśāmbī, Kanauj, Rajgir, Pāṭalīputra, Vaiśālī, and Śrāvastī, all yielding the Painted Grey ware, black and red ware, the Northern Black polished ware, and iron showed that everywhere the earliest house were made of mud or mud brick, and the floors occasionally plastered with lime. It was only in the late phase, dated by typical finds and C-14 dates to period after 500 B.C., that burnt bricks were used.

The same is the story, regarding fortification. All earlier constructions were made of mud or mud bricks. And the alleged brick rampart at Kauśāmbī was probably an embankment, and certainly late because it has not been stratigraphically co-related with any habitational phases in the city itself.

Similar conclusion is suggested by the few details of the way how these royal residencies were furnished. While all kinds of ornaments of gold—*hiraṇya* and *suvarṇa,* -besided those of diamonds and pearls, which both men and women wore, are mentioned, there are references to seats or chairs of gold, even cots and chariots, and costly coverlets for the bed.

So much wealth can be produced only by trade and commerce, and perhaps conquest in war. As we know our history *now,* such a flourishing state was ushered in about the 1st century B.C.—A.D. with the regular establishment of trade with the Roman world, both by sea and land, after the formation of the Kuṣāṇa and Roman empires. Thus, at present, on the basis of our integrated study, the following stages in the development of Ayodhyā may be suggested.

1. A village or a small town, as stated by the *Aitareya Brāhmaṇa,* c. 800 B.C.-1000 B.C., dependent on stock-breeding, hunting and agriculture—specially paddy.
2. Slightly larger town during the time of Buddha (Ajātaśatru). Economy—not much different from that in (1).
3. Further growth, under Aśoka when some stūpas and monasteries might have been built.
4. A city under Puṣyamitra, when one or two *aśvamedha* sacrifices were performed after defeating the Yavanas, as suggested by epigraphical evidence. Palaces and earliest temples built at this time. It was at this stage that we can expect a *regular* contact between Ayodhyā and other cities in Eastern India and the distant Gandhāra either by the Lower Gaṅgā or the Upper Gaṅgā routes. Though it is possible that, when Candragupta Maurya drove out Alexanders' outpost and concluded fresh treaty with Selecus Nikator, this distant country must have been under the political hegemony of Pāṭalīputra.
5. Further development under the early Gupta kings, It is at this time that a larger number of Deva temples, as seen by Hiuen Tsiang a few centuries later, must have come into existence. The city must have assumed the form as described (of course with much exaggeration) in the *Rāmāyaṇa.*

It must have been apparent, that if this was the likely development of Ayodhyā, then the present *Rāmāyaṇa*, even the Critical Edition, gives one sided picture of the city. Of course, this is expected and natural. There is no reference to the Buddhists and Jainas, who, we know from their literature, as well as from Chinese travellers, did live in the city, as early as the 5th century B.C.

It is hoped that the excavations which are being conducted at Ayodhyā since 1975 by Prof. B.B. Lal will throw more positive light. Probably a proper surface exploration alone could tell us how large was the extent of the ancient habitation. No doubt, it was more long than broad, and considerable portion must have been eroded away by the river. Even then, such a survey should be useful.

Meanwhile, what one can be sure of is that the original habitation—whatever be its true nature, a village, a city or a town,—was surrounded by Sāla trees and was well stocked with paddy as these are truly indicative of the ecology of the region. Perhaps the Sāla trees do not grow in the vicinity today. Possibly this tree-line has receded further eastwards, but the two references to Sāla forests and trees in the Ayodhyākāṇḍa indeed belong to the earliest stages of the composition of this Kāṇḍa.

As far as the socio-religious and astrological and astronomical references or practices are concerned, we see a steady growth, almost paralleling that of the settlement. The worship or invocation of the Vedic deities like Aryamā, Indra, and Pūṣan by Kauśalyā is indeed a legacy of the Vedic times. To this was added the worship of Viṣṇu and/or Nārāyaṇa and later that of Skanda. For as is well known Skanda—Kārttikeya are not even referred to in the early Vedic literature. As far as the archaeological evidence goes, Skanda worship started about the 3rd century B.C.

Surprisingly there is no reference to Śiva in any form, though later—in Uttarakāṇḍa—we are told, in a late interpolation, how Rāma worshipped Śiva at Rāmeśvara. This feature, however, could not have entered in the epic before the 3rd stage.

The astrological-astronomical allusions also belong to this period, whereas the reference to the seven day week, while giving the details about Rāmas birth, which have been deleted by the Critical Edition, could not have found a place, according to this view, before the 5th century A.D., though, as Kane has argued, this could have happened a few centuries earlier. The non-observation of the practice of Satī, and the preservation of Daśaratha's body in oil in a large vessel (probably of iron/bronze or wood) are two very interesting features which taken the beginning of the story to the 5th-6th century B.C., and are a reminder of the practices of this period.

With regard to the polity, the powers and duties of the king as well as. Purohita, and the references to Guha *as sthapati* (local lord) as well as the right of the Paurajānapadas—these well reflect the ideas found in the late Vedic literature, while certain features—the institution of spies and such other details regarding the administration of the kingdom as appear in the series of questions which Rāma asks Bharata-could be found in the *Kautilīya-Arthaśāstra*. This is unfortunately not firmly dated, but after considerable discussion Kangle has gone back to the traditional date, viz., the 4th century B.C. However, Kane has shown that no less than 29 verses of this *sarga* appear in the Sabhāparvan of the *Mahābhārata*, and some of these are inappropriate and irrelevant. This would show that these verses are later interpolated very probably after the Sabhāparvan, and this Parvan was definitely enlarged after the 1st-2nd century A.D., as the reference to Rāmā shows.

Thus though a number of intelligible things, such as the institution of the king, Purohita, mantrins, Sabhā, and Paurajānapada, the invocation of Vedic gods, the absence of the practice of Satī and repeated insistence on the performance of Dharma, show comparatively early features, still the tangible or material things and their description starting with the extent and the layout of the city of Ayodhyā—palaces, furniture, means of transport or conveyance-all these indicate a highly developed state, reminiscent of towns and cities in early historical period between 250 B.C. and 350 A.D. And this is truly the Characteristic of Indian culture. Even now, at the close of the 20th century after Christ, in the midst of the latest scientific and industrial development an early Vedic feature, such as the performance of the *Homa,* will suddenly prop up. But as surely as we cannot date the entire show Vedic, but have to call it ultra-modern, in the same way, while studying our epics and Purāṇas, we have got to use these criteria, supplied by archaeology and history.

Rāhulabhadra is expressly stated to be an adept in the perfection of Guhyasamāja, which he is reported to have propagated in the Draviḍa country. He had also gained *siddhi* in his command over the Nāgas who procured golden dināra for him. Among other disciples of Buddhajnānapāda, we have mentioned the name of Buddhaguhya and discussed the qualifications he possessed. Now, this ācārya had a direct disciple named Vimalamitra. It has been said of him that Buddhaguhya taught the Māyā-cycle to Vimala and the latter to rMa Rin-chen-mchog. The Maya-cycle seems to signify occult practices enabling one to assume various forms. Recorded efforts to gain supernatural power in India go back to the time of the *Atharvaveda.* A representative Atharvavedic text is the Kauśikasūtra, according to which magical rites were performed in almost the same way as in later times. There is hardly any doubt that Buddha also, like his contemporaries, believed in the supernatural powers or *iddhis,* but he considered it to be unworthy of monks to take recourse to these occult powers to exert influence on lay men. In spite of this, even Buddha and saint like Moggallana are found in the Suttas to disappear suddenly from the presence of people or appear suddenly before gods. Numerous miracles are recorded in Buddhist legends and fables, indicating how miraculous and magic powers are guided by meditation. It is interesting to note that one of the legends of the Divyāvadāna, the *Śārdūlakarṇāvadāna,* which was translated into Chinese in 265 A.D., shows how a love-charm was neutralised by Buddha's countermantra. The dimension of the magic increases considerably with the growth of Mahāyāna-Vajrayāna. Indeed, in tāntrik ritual literature, the *sādhanas* or works on magic rituals occupy a significant place. Indeed, to an adept the world is at his command. The preparation of the magic ritual involves the confession of sins, yogic exercises, the use of fingers in a particular way for specific deities, and intense meditation, so that he devotee is totally identified with the deity in mind. The tāntrikś literature was mainly written by the Vajrayānists and Śaiva Tantriks as well as the Siddhas, whose number is reputed traditionally to be 84. The magic powers, as revealed in the Sādhanamālā-literature, of which the bulk was composed between the 8th and the 11th century, were sought to be gained for two purposes, viz. (1) for universal good and (2) for *abhicāra* purposes, i.e. to obtain supernatural power with evil objects in view. The *Sang Hyang Kamahāyanān Mantranaya* is apparently a text of the former category and, in spite of its small size, shows general affinity with the Vajrayāna-system prevalent in eastern India in the early Pāla period.

Geographical Position

Ayodhyā or Ayojjhā or Ayudha is one of the seven holy places of the Hindus. Fā-Hien calls this town as Sha-che and according to Ptolemy it is known as Sogeda. Its capital was Sujanakot or Sancankot,

34 miles north-west of Unao in Oudh on the river Sai in the Unao district. In Brāhmaṇa literature we find that Śunaḥśepa speaks of this town as a village. According to the Vividhatīrthakalpa of the Jains, Ayodhyā is also known as Vinītā, Sāketa, Ikṣvākubhūmi, Rāmapurī and Kośala. It is the birth-place of Ṛṣabha, Ajita, Abhinandana, Sumati, Ananta, and Acala. Seven Jain preceptors were born here. According to this Jain work, Ayodhyā was 12 yojanas long and nine yojanas broad. This town is situated on the banks of the Sarayū river, about 6 miles from the Fyzabad Railway Station. It is also a sacred place of the Vaiṣṇavas. Sarayū or Sarabhū of Pāli literature is the Ghagrā or Gogrā in Oudh. According to the Vividhatīrthakalpa, the river Gharghardaha meets with the Sarayū and is known by the name of Svargadvāra.

This river rises in the mountains of Kumayun and after its junction with the Kālī nadī, it is called the Sarayū, the Ghagrā or the Durā. According to the Mahābhārata, the Sarayū issues from the Mānasasarovara. The Son and the Sarayū joined the Ganges near Singhee, 8 miles east of Chapra in Saran, between Singhee and Harji-chupra, two villages on both sides of the Ganges, about 2 miles to the east of Cherund and 8 miles to the east of Chapra. According to Alberuni, Ayodhyā is situated about 150 miles south-east from Kanauj. In the Buddhist period, Kośala was divided into Uttara-Kośala (northern Kośala) and Dakṣiṇa-Kośala (southern Kośala), the Sarayū. According to the Rāmāyaṇa, the river Syandikā or Sai between the Gumti and the Ganges formed the southern boundary of Kośala.

Rhys Davids points out that Ayodhyā had sunk to the level of an unimportant town in Buddha's time. Some think that Ayodhyā and Sāketa were identical but Rhys Davids says that both the cities existed in Buddha's time. They were possible adjoining cities like London and Westminster. Ayodhyā seems to have been the earliest capital and Sāketa the next. According to the Chinese pilgrim. Yuan Chwang, it was 5,000 li in circuit. The Rāmāyaṇa tells us that Rāmacandra walked south from Ayodhyā to Pancavaṭi. After killing Rāvaṇa, Rāma is said to have proceeded to Kiṣkindhyā and thence to Ayodhyā. Ayodhyā is described in the Rāmāyaṇa as being is situated on the banks of the river Sarayū in the land of Kośala which was a big *janapada* or country and the well-known town of Ayodhyā was included in it. Manu, the progenitor of man, is said to have built Ayodhyā which was 12 yojanas in extent and 3 yojanas in breadth. According to the

Rāmāyaṇa, it took four days and nights to cover the distance between Ayodhyā and Videha at normal speed; swiftly moving envoys could cover the distance in three days. At a distance of one krośa (2 miles) from the capital city of Ayodhyā, was situated Nandigrāma where Bharata ruled over the people of Ayodhyā during Rāma's exile. The Rāmāyaṇa further points out that three days and three nights were generally taken for swiftly flying messengers to reach Mathura from Ayodhyā. Rāma's palace was half a yojana distant from the bank of the Sarayū.

Chinese Pilgrims' Accounts

The Chinese pilgrim, Lā-Hien, who visited Ayodhyā in the 5th century A.D., saw the Buddhists and the Brāhmaṇas not in good terms. He also saw a tope there where the four Buddhas walked and sat. Another Chinese pilgrim, Yuan Chwang, who visited India in the 7th century A.D., after travelling more than 600 li and crossing the Ganges to the south, reached the Ayudha or Ayodhyā country. According to him, Ayodhyā was the temporary residence of Asaṅga and Vasubandhu. He says that Ayudhā is Sāketa, i.e., Ayodhyā. The country yielded good crops, was luxuriant in fruit and flower and had a genial climate. The people had agreeable ways, were fond of good work and devoted to practical learning. There were more than 100 Buddhist monasteries and more than 3000 Brethren who were students of Mahāyāna and Hinayāna. There were 10 deva temples and the non-Buddhists were few in number. Within the capital was the old monastery in which Vasubandhu composed various Śāstras. There was a hall in ruins where Vasubandhu explained Buddhism to princes and monks who used to come from other countries. Close to the Ganges was large Buddhist monastery with an Asoka tope to mark the place where the Buddha preached to Devas and men for 3 months the excellent doctrines of his religion. Four or five li west from this monastery was a Buddha relic, tope and to the north of the tope were the remains of an old monastery where the Sautrāntika-vibhasā-śāstra was composed. In a mango-grove 5 or 6 li to the south-west of the city was the old monastery in which Asaṅga learnt and taught. The three Buddhist treatise referred to by Yuan Chwang were communicated to Asaṅga by Maitreya, viz., Yogācārabhūmiśāstra, Sūtrālaṅkāra-tīkā and Madhyantavibhāga-śāstra. About 100 paces to the north-west of the mango-grove was Buddha relic tope. Asaṅga, according to the pilgrim, began his Buddhist religious career as a

Mahīsāsaka and afterwards became a Mahāyānist. Vasubandhu began his career in the School of the Sarvāstivādins. The Chinese pilgrim also refers to an old monastery 40 li north-west from Asangas chapel. Within this a brick-tope marked the place where the conversion of Vasubandhu to Mahāyānism began. After the death of Asaṅga, Vasubandhu composed several treatises, expounding and defending Mahāyānism. He died at Ayodhyā at the age of 83.

Description in the Epics

According to the Rāmāyaṇa, Ayodhyā was a city full of wealth and paddy. It had spacious streets and roads. Its streets were well-watered and looked gay with flowers. It had lofty gates furnished with doors and bolts amidst the net-work of its streets. Furnished with all kinds of equipments, it looked like a bulwark with its defences. It was the home of a large number of skilful persons trained in arts and carfts. It was full of palatial buildings, green bowers and mango-groves. Around all these, a long row of *śāla* trees looked like a girdle. The city was rendered impregnable being surrounded by a deep ditch filled with water. Animals useful to men like horses and elephants, cows, camels, and asses could all be found there in large number. It had in it merchants from different countries, feudatory chiefs and princes from all quarters. Splendid with its stately mansions, it had a large number of pinnacled houses. The city had lofty seven storied buildings inlaid with gold and precious stones. It was a crowded city and frequently resounded by the drums and the notes of the harp and other musical instruments. It had a galaxy of great men, benevolent sages, and virtuous people. This blissful city had Kamboja horses and mighty elephants. Men of rank could be found in the city moving in chariots, horses and elephants. The parks and pleasure-gardens were resorts of lovers, where merry folks used to gather in the evening. In the Mahābhārata, the city of Ayodhyā is given the epithet of 'puṇyalakṣaṇā, that is, endowed with auspicious signs. It was a delightful spot on earth and its sparkling splendour looked like the shining moon in autumn.

Social History

According to the Rāmāyaṇa, there were four grades of social order, e.g., the Brāhmaṇas, the Kṣatriyas, the Vaiśyas and the Sūdras. They had to fulfil duties and obligations of the respective orders. The Kṣatriyas obeyed the Brāhmaṇas, the Vaiśyas followed the Kṣatriyas, and the Śūdras served the three upper castes. The Kṣatriyas like the

Brāhmaṇas had to perform the triennial worship daily. The Brāhmaṇas occupied the most exalted rank in the social order of the age. Being placed at the highest rung of the ladder, the special privileges that were denied to the Kṣatriyas, were however enjoyed by them. Thus the Brāhmaṇas alone had the right to master the four Vedas and used the sacred sound *Oṅkāra* and *Vaṣaṭkāra*. The Brāhmaṇas had also the right to study not merely the sacred scriptures meant for their own class but also to acquire the sciences and arts intended for the Kṣatriyas.

Ordinarily birth in a family determined once for all the caste of a man. Transgression of this rule was however allowed in special cases. Thus the sage Viśvāmitra, a Kṣatriya by birth, became a Brāhmaṇa by dint of his extraordinary merit and was accepted in the rank of Brāhmaṇa by his great rival Vaśiṣṭha. The instance of Aśmaka, a royal sage, born from the union of sage Vaśiṣṭha with a Kṣatriya queen of the Ikṣvāku ruler of Ayodhyā, as related in the Mahābhārata, shows that offsprings born of such *asavarṇa* union were not unknown. In the code of Manu we find mention of such *asavarṇa* marriages of the *anuloma* and *pratiloma* types.

The Brāhmaṇas were exempted from capital punishment. The robbing of their property was considered to be a heinous act according to the public opinion of the time. They lived on the vegetable diet.

Famine was rare in the city of Ayodhyā. The people were free from diseases. Premature death was unknown. Everyone was charitably disposed and all residents whether male or female used ornaments. Malpractices were unknown and people were faithful in the observance of sacrificial rites. People were faithful, and hospitable to their guests. They used to enjoy a long lease of life with their wives, sons and grandsons. The sick and the destitute were treated to sumptuous dinner. Food and dress were freely given to all during the sacrifice. Walking in circle around a dignified person before parting was the common way of paying homage. In a *śrādh* ceremony a large number of cows, gold and other riches were given to the Brāhmaṇas. Extortion was utterly unknown. During the coronation ceremony, the streets were richly decorated and illuminated, musical instruments were played and the Brāhmaṇas used to chant sweet benedictions. The coronation ceremony was held in an auspicious hour with good stars on a favourable day. Thus Rāma was installed as king by the family priest Vaśiṣṭha and others on a suitable day with the favourable star *Śravaṇā*.

Various evil-killing rites were performed. To follow elder brothers was the golden rule for the younger brothers. Earning money by selling lac, flesh, honey, iron or poison was considered abominable. The offering of oblations in honour of the departed spirit was a common custom, and the offering of watery oblations in honour of the departed ancestors was prevalent. Jealousy among rival brothers was not unknown. It was a commonplace occurrence that a wife should cling to her beloved, a friend should act in a like manner. For a brother to stick to his brother and act in a reciprocal way was something common.

Devotion to husband was considered as the highest virtue for married women. According to the orthodox ideal of the age, the amorous look from other's eyes, the faintest touch from a member of the opposite sex other than her husband would have a sinister influence on the good reputation of a chaste wife.

No act of violence should be committed on the weak and helpless and specially on women. Such unchivalrous conduct looked like an act of cowardice. Stealing others' wives by treachery was an offence. Respectable ladies never exposed themselves to public view. Seclusion of women within the confines of the inner apartment was the usual rule. If necessity arose, they would move in palanquins or some other covered vehicles with adequate veils over their faces and requisite garments over their bodies., On no ordinary account could they come out to public streets by crossing the city-gates on foot or move with an open countenance. The exit of women before the public view was allowed for serving the needs of different kinds of *Vyasanas* like hunting, game of dice, etc. In times of war or public sacrifice, on the occasion of the marriage ceremony or during the work of choosing one's partner from among a large number of suitors in an open assembly (*Svayambara*) or in times of great distress or sorrow women had the right to come out of their harem and expose themselves to public view. The use of deformed men and women for the work of he harem was in vogue at the time of the Rāmāyaṇa. The life of a widow seems to be the worst lot, the highest curse for a woman.

There were expert barbers, as well as good musicians and well trained courtesans, big merchants and traders at Ayodhyā. Disrespect to Brāhmaṇas, parents and priests was considered to be a sacrilege. Preservation of dead bodies in vessels filled with oil was then known.

King Daśaratha's dead body was preserved for some time before its actual cremation by Bharata.

Religious History

At the time of the Rāmāyaṇa, the people and the members of the royal household were on the whole religious. Religious sacrifices were performed and Vedic mantras were chanted. During the horse sacrifice of King Daśaratha twenty-one kinds of sacrificial wood were prepared and set up by expert craftsmen; of these six were made of the timber of the *Bilva* tree, six of *Khadira* wood, six of *Palāsa* plant, one of the *Śleṣmātaka* timber and the remaining two of pine wood. The sacrificial wood was covered with cloth and gold and worshipped with scented flowers. In a sacrifice many cows and a large number of gold and silver bits were given to the priests. On the banks of the Sarajū, Rāma and Lakṣmaṇa offered their morning prayers and repeated the *Sāvitri mantra* at the instance of the sage Viṣvāmitra. In the hermitage of Viśvāmitra, they performed the usual *sandhyā* and morning prayers and offered oblations to the sacrificial fire. As we have already pointed out, offering of oblations in honour of the departed spirit was the common practice. The Kṣatriya kings and princes used to observe ten days of *aśauca* or the observance of impurity caused by the death of relations. Among the Brāhmaṇas, sophists were not unknown and followers of the hedonist school of Cārvāka were also found. Four hundred horse sacrifices four thousand *Vājapeya* and numerous *Gomedha, Agniṣṭoma* and *Atirātra* sacrifices were performed by some eminent king of the Ikṣvāku race. Duly bathed, a Ksatriya king used to offer oblations to fire, and make worship in adoration of his ancestors and Brāhmaṇas and then pray before the images in temples inside his palace. As regards religious rights the Śūdras remained on a low footing of inequality in comparison with the Brāhmaṇas and Kṣatriyas. Śambuka, a Śūdra by birth, was slain by Rāma for making vedic sacrifices.

Jainism

In the history of Jainism, we find that a Jaina tīrthaṅkara named Ajitanātha was born at Ayodhyā. He earned the title of the 'Victorious' for he was so devout an ascetic that he was unrivalled in performing austerities. He soon attained salvation. A Jaina monk named Buddakīrti was well versed in Jaina scriptures. He flourished during the interval between Pārśvanātha and Mahāvīra. Once while performing austerities on the bank of the Sarayū in Palāśanagara he saw a dead fish floating. He carefully watched it and thought that there was no harm in eating the flesh of the dead fish for there was no soul in it.

Lord Ādigurn attained enlightenment on the Āṣṭāvata mountain near Ayodhyā. Twenty-four Jain images were established on this mountain. Dovinda Sūri while wandering at Serisaya took his bath in the Sarayū river according to the Vividhatīrthakalpa. At the instance of the Goddess Padmāvatī a blind artisan was employed to make an image of Pārśvanātha. Three great images were brought from Ayodhyā by air.

Buddhism

Ayodhyā was hallowed by the dust of the feet of Gautama Buddha. He lived there on the banks of the Ganges. While he was there, he pointed out to the bhikkhus the transitoriness of the human body. He told them thus, 'The human body is like a foam, and similarly consciousness, glamour, and human activities, etc. have no essence at all'. The inhabitants of Ayodhyā saw the Buddha entering their town accompanied by a large number of bhikkhus. They built a monastery for him in a dense forest at a curve of the river Ganges and presented it to him. He dwelt there for some time.

Political History

The Rāmāyaṇa refers to the kings of Ayodhyā and the system of administration prevalent there. It is interesting to note here the duties of an Ikṣvāku king. Aroused from his sleep at down by the hymns of prisoners and sūtas, a king was served with water for washing hands and feet. Duly bathed a Kṣatriya king offered oblations to fire and prayed before the images in temples inside his palace. After finishing the morning duties he used to attend to the business of his State and then go to his court where he would meet his ministers. The king with his ministers used to listen personally to the prayers and complaints of his subjects. Worthy treatment was given to State guests including kings and princes. The king used to spend the first half of each day in doing the business of his State and the latter half of his time was spent in enjoying the company of the ladies of his harem.

The chief aim of a righteous monarch was to earn the loyalty and goodwill of his subjects. He used to hear the report of his trusted servants and reliable courtiers in order to ascertain the public opinion about his government. He used to redress the grievances of his subjects as far as possible. Nobody was detained or kept waiting at his door if he came to pray for something before the king. He was assisted in his administration by able ministers, eminent jurists and men well-versed in the sacred lore. Punishment was always in proportion to the nature and gravity of the offence. Life-long exile or transportation was an alternative for death sentence.

The king used to give private interviews to spies and special messengers for confidential talks. Divulging State-secrets or over-hearing such secret talks was highly punishable. The succession to the throne was generally determined according to the law of primogeniture in the Ikṣvāku family.

Rāma's youngest brother Śatrughna ruled Mathurā which he founded. His younger brother, Bharata, with his two sons Takṣa and Puṣkala conquered the Gandhāra country. The cities of Takṣasila and Puṣkalāvati were ruled by the two sons of Bharata. Chandrakānta and Aṅgadīyā were ruled by the two sons of Lakṣaṇa named Candraketu and Aṇgada. Kuśa and Lava were rulers of southern and northern Kośala respectively. Śatrughna, Rāma's younger brother, installed his two sons Suvāhu and Śatrughātī as kings of Mathurā and Vaideśa kingdoms respectively.

In the Mahābhārata, mention is made of sixteen celebrated kings (*ṣoḍaśa-rājikā*) some of whom belonged to Ayodhyā, namely, Mandhātṛ, Sagara, Bhagīratha, Ambarīṣa, Dilīp and Rāma Dāśarathi. The Mahābhārata also refers to Ikṣvāku, Kakutstha, Yuvanāśva, Raghu, Nimi and others. The pious Dīrghayajna was the king of Ayodhyā when Yudhiṣṭhira ruled and performed his Rājasūya sacrifice. Divākara was a king of Ayodhyā who was the contemporary of Senājit, king of Magadha. Both of them were contemporaries of Asīmakṛṣṇa. Ikṣvāku, one of the nine sons of Manu Vaivasvata, reigned at Ayodhyā who had two sons, Vikukṣīśaśāda and Nimi. From the former was descended the great Aikṣvāku dynasty of Ayodhyā generally known as the solar race.

The Ikṣvākus, Aikṣvākus or Aikṣvakas are the titles of the solar race. Ikṣvāku was so called because he was born from the sneeze of Manu. The Purānas give a list of the kings of Ayodhyā.

The Rāmāyaṇa genealogy, according to pargiter, must be treated as erroneous and the Pauranic genealogy is to be accepted. The Purāṇas say that there were two Dilīpas, one father of Bhagīratha and the other father or grandfather of Raghu, but according to the Rāmāyaṇa, there was only one Dilīpa, father of Bhagīratha and great grandfather of Raghu. According to the Rāmāyaṇa, Raghu was the father of Kalmāṣapāda and Aja is placed twelve generations below Raghu but the Purāṇas make Aja was the son of Raghu. The Raghuvaṃśa supports the Purāṇas that Aja was the son of Raghu. The Rāmāyaṇa makes Kakutstha son of Bhagīratha and grandson of Dilīpa but the Purāṇas say that he was the son of Śaśāda. The Mahābhārata supports the Purāṇas. The Raghuvaṃśa also supports the Purāṇas in saying that from his time the kings had borne the title of Kākutstha and that Dilīpa was his descendant.

From Daśaratha to Ahīnagu there is a general agreement. After Ahīnagu, most of the Purāṇas give a list of some twenty kings, Paripātra to Bṛhadbala, agreeing in their names' though some of the lists are incomplete towards the end.

The Aikṣvāku genealogy of Ayodhyā mentions the following kings: (1) Prasenajit who was the contemporary of Matināra; (2) Yuvanāśva II, Māndhātṛ who married Śaśabindu's daughter named Bindumatī Citratathī, (3) Purukutsa, and (4) Trasadasyu, Jahnu of Kānyakubja married the grand-daughter of Yauvanāśva, that is Māndhātṛ.

The Tālajaṇghas attacked Ayodhyā and drove the king Bāhu from the throne, Māndhātṛ of Ayodhyā had a long war with the Druhyu king Aruddha or Aṇgāra and killed him.

Subāhu, son of the Cedi king Vīrabāhu, and Rtuparṇa, king of Ayodhyā, were contemporaries. Jamadagni allied himself with the royal house of Ayodhyā for he married Renukā, daughter of Reṇu.

Sumitrā was the last of the Ikṣvāku kings in the Kali age who was contemporary with the Buddha. The royal house of Ikṣvāku sank into oblivion at the time of this king.

The kings of Ayodhyā were connected with the Vaśiṣṭha family. The Vaśiṣṭhas were their hereditary priests. The earliest Vaśiṣṭha was the famous priest of Ayodhyā in the reigns of Trayyāruṇa, Satyavrata-Triśaṇku and Hariścandra. The next great Vaśiṣṭha was the priest of Ayodhyā in the time of Hariścandra's successor Bāhu who was driven from his throne by the Haihaya-Tālājaṅghas aided by the Śakas,

Kāmbojas, Yavanas, Pāradas and Pahlavas from the north-west but Vaśiṣṭha maintained his position.

Mitrasaha Kalmāṣapada Saudāsa, king of Ayodhyā, had the fourth noted Vaśiṣṭha as his priest. The fifth was priest to Dilīpa II Khatvāṇga and the sixth was priest to Daśaratha and his son Rāma King Kalmāṣapāda Saudāsa beguiled by a Rākṣasa offered Vaśiṣṭha human flesh as food and was cursed by him.

Ikṣvāku obtained Madhyadeśa and was the progenitor of the solar race, with its capital at Ayodhyā.

The kingdom of Ayodhyā rose to very great eminence under Yuvanāśva II and especially his son Māndhātṛ. The latter married Śaśabindu's daughter Bindumatī. He was a very famous king, a Cakravartin and a Samrāj and extended his sway very widely. Māndhātṛ or his sons carried their arms south to the river Narmadā. The supremacy of Ayodhyā waned and the Kānyakubja kingdom rose into prominence under its king Jahnu. The Haihayas overcame Ayodhyā. The foreign tribes settled there after Ayodhyā was conquered.

Ayodhyā rose to prominence again under Aṃśumant's second successor Bhagīratha and Bhagīratha's third successor Ambarīṣa Nābhāgi.

Of the Mānva or solar kingdoms that existed originally three remained, those of Ayodhyā, Videha and Vaiśālī. These three Mānva kingdoms were not dominated by the Aila stock. The earliest Aṅgirasas were connected with Māndhātṛ, king of Ayodhyā, and the earliest Āṅgirasa rishi was connected with Hariścandra, king of Ayodhyā.

Daśaratha called in the help of the rustic Rasyaśṛṅga from Aṅga. The eastern and southern kings and kings of the distant Punjab were invited to Daśaratha's sacrifice at Ayodhyā. Ayodhyā and the Vaśiṣṭhas had no association then with the brahamainically *elite* region as Pargiter points out. The Kathāsaritsāgara refers to the camp of Nanda in Ayodhya.

In Buddhism we find that there was a king of Ayodhyā named Kālasena whose city was surrounded by ten sons of Andhakaveṇhu (Andhakavaṇhudāsputtā dasabhātikā) who uprooted the trees, pulled down the wall, captured the king and brought his kingdom under their sway. The city of Ayujjha was governed by the descendants of king Arindama.

In Jainism we find that Prasannajita, a king of Ayodhyā, gave his daughter named Prabhāvati in marriage to Pārśvanatha.

Ayodhyā seems to have been included within the kingdom of Puṣyamitra Śuṅga. An inscription found at Ayodhyā mentions the fact that Puṣyamitra performed two horse-sacrifices or *aśvamedhas* during his reign. According to a spurious Gayā plate, Ayodhyā was the seat of a Gupta *jayaskandhāvāra* or 'Camp of Victory', as early as the time of Samudīa Gupta. Some coins of Pura Gupta have on the reverse the legend — Śrī Vikramaḥ which may be a shorter form of the full title 'Vikramāditya' Allan identifies him with King Vikramāditya of Ayodhyā, father of Bālāditya, who was a patron of Buddhism, through the influence of Vasuabandhāu. It may be assumed on the basis of this identification that the immediate successors of Skanda Gupta had a capital at Ayodhyā probably till the rise of the Maukharis.

Ayodhyā Coins

A large number of coins were found on the site of Ayodhyā. These coins fall under three classes. The first and the earliest consists of a few rare cast pieces, of which three types are known. The first type is known from one piece only; it has a flower on the obverse and a plain reverse, and may not be a coin at all, but an ornament. Type II is only known from a unique specimen in the Museum; the obverse type is a *svastika* which connects it with type III, and the symbol on the reverse is well known from several series of punch-marked coins. The square coin published by H. Rivett-Carnac (obverse *svastika,* rev. *bull)* is probably also a coin of this series. Type III is the commonest of this class; the obverse, a *svastika* over a fish, is connected by the former symbol with the preceding type; the roughness of the casting makes it difficult to break up the reverse type into its component symbols. These coins probably contain a crescent or a taurine symbol above a steelyard, but might be taurine symbol over on axe. The former is the more probable explanation, and the occurrence of the steelyard suggests that these are local coins of the city, as distinct from the dynastic issues; they may be compared with the Taxila pieces bearing a steelyard. Their date may be conjectured to be the third century B.C.

The remaining coins of Ayodhyā are inscribed with the names of the rulers who issued them, and fall under two very distinct classes; issued by two separate dynasties, one of square cast coins showing no trace of foreign influence in their style and types, and one of round struck pieces which have types rather than symbols. The coins of the rulers of the first dynasty closely resemble one another in style and are connected by their types. The obverse is a bull, or rarely an elephant, before an elaborate symbol not always distinct, which is replaced on the coins of the later dynasty by a ceremonial standard or spear. The reverse type consists of a group of five or six symbols. The characteristic symbols are a small 'Ujjain' symbol, a tree in railing, a group of four *nandipadas* in a square, a *svastika,* a river or snake and another symbol. Two rulers, Viśākhadeva and Śivadaita, have also the type of the *abhiseka* of Lakṣmī. The names of six rulers of this dynasty are known from their coins, which bear simply the Prākrit form of the name in the genitive. They are Mūladeva (Mūladevasa), Vāyudeva (Vāyudevasa), Viśākhadeva (Viśākhadevasa), Dhanadeva (Dhanadevasa), Śivadatta (Śivadatasa) and Naradatta (Naradatasa). At least one other ruler is represented by the uncertain coins on which the name is possible Pathadeva. The type of Viśākhadeva coin first published by Rivett-Carnac and now in the Indian Museum has on the reverse a buckler-like object, a solar symbol with a central boss surrounded by circle of dots within rims. This came from Fyzabad, as did all the coins published by Rivett-Carnac. No attempt to arrange these rulers in chronological order is possible nor have we any literary or inscriptional references to them. They probably cover the second century B.C.

The third class of coins belongs to a later dynasty From Rivett-Carnac and Cunningham we know that these come from the same site. They are round pieces struck from dies leaving the seal-like impression characteristic of early Indian struck coins, and very distinct from the coins of the earlier dynasty. The usual types are obverse: a bull before a standard or spear, which closely resembles the ceremonial spear on the Aśvamedha coins of Samudra Gupta, and reverse a bird, usually called a cock but probably a *haṃsa*, and a palm-tree with a river (or less probably a snake) below. These three elements are to be regarded as separate symbols and not as being combined to form a single type, as their proportions show. Another but rarer reverse type is an elaborate *nandipada* in a framework; the complete form of this type is probably something like the large symbol found on the coins of Almora. This occurs on the coins of Kumudasena, Ajavarman, Saṃghamitra and Vijayamitra, Vijayamitra is the only ruler who coins both types. On the coins of Kumudasena and Ajavarma, the object in front of the bull is probably a form of that on the coins of the earlier dynasty, a kind of triangular standard with cross-bar in railing. Kumudasena is the only member of the dynasty to call himself a rājā; others inscribe their coins with their names only. The rulers represented in the British Museum are Satyamitra (Satyamitasa), Ārayamitra (Ayyamitasa), Saṃgha (Mitra), Vijayamitra (Vijayamitasa), Kumudasena (Rājna Kumudasenasa) to which may be added from the Indian Museum collection the names of Ajavarman (Ajavarmana) and Devamitra (Devamitasa). None of these rulers is otherwise known to history. Their reigns probably covered the first two centuries A.D.

THE HARĀHĀ INSCRIPTION OF ĪŚĀNAVARMAN

The verse 13 of this incription which recounts the conquests of the Maukhari king Īśānavarman contains a reference to Guaḍa which has been differently interpreted by different scholars. There has been, so far, no dispute about the reading of the passage which runs as follows: *'Kṛivā c-āytimocita-sthala-bhuvo Gauḍān samudrāśrayān.'* Pandit Hirananda Sastri, who edited the inscription, translates it as follows: 'After causing the Gauḍas, living on the seashore, in future to remain within their proper realm.' According to Dr. R.G. Basak, the passage means that Īśānavarman made the Gauḍa people take shelter towards the seashore, after causing their land territories to be deprived of their future prospects. Sastri's interpretation gives a better sense but does not satisfactorily bring out the meaning of *'āyatimocita';* while Dr. Basak's rendering of this phrase makes the whole passage somewhat obscure. The real difficulty is caused by the very unusual expression āyatimocita and it appears to me that this reading is faulty. On a close inspection of the facsimile of the record published by Sastri it would appear that the second letter read as *ya* is different from other signs for the same letter, inasmuch as the central vertical stroke, instead of joining the base, is turned to the right and connected with the right hand vertical stroke. It is thus possible to read it as *pra,* though it must be confessed that it is different from other *pra*-s in the same record. But if we read the latter as *pra* the whole passage gives a very good sense and is easily intelligible. It would then read: *'Kṛtvā c-āpratimocita-sthala-bhuvo Gauḍin samudr-āśrayān.* It would mean that the Gauḍas, having failed to redeem or recover their land territory, were forced to remain on the seashore. This interpretation clearly brings out the contrast between *sthala* and *samudra* and would imply that Īśānavarman was partially successful in checking the attempts of the Gauḍas to recover their homeland on the decline of the Gupta Empire. I am unable to explain why this *pra* was written differently, but then the same difficulty encounters us if we read it as *ya*.

2 The Ramayana: *An Immortal Epic*

Among our great festivals, which spread joy and comradeship amongst all our people, there is none which is so popular, more especially in Northern India, than the celebration of the story of Rama and Sita. Valmiki wrote this immortal epic and, in later days, Tulsidas, writing in homely language, made this story a part of the texture of the lives of our people. A story and a book which has had this powerful influence on millions of people, during some millenniums of our changing history, must have peculiar virtue in it.

Ever since my boyhood, I have been fascinated by this India of ours. It has been a mystery often, a revelation some-times, and the more I have sought to understand her the more I have been impressed by her powerful personality which has endured through the ages. In a sense, my life has been a quest, an attempt to understand this great motherland of ours with its infinite variety and its basic unity. No one who sees a part of India only and not the rest, can have a full picture of her. No one who sees the present only and has no realisation of the panorama of her past, can understand her, for our roots go deep down into the past of the history of man. Innumerable weeds have grown up from time to time. But they have never succeeded in uprooting those deep roots which have fashioned our destiny for good or ill. Out of that distant past, which is history, and the present, which is the burden of today, the future of India is gradually taking shape.

We must have an intellectual understanding of these mighty processes of history. We must have even more, an emotional awareness of our past and present, in order to try to give a right direction to the future. I do not think any person can understand India or her people fully without possessing a knowledge of the two magnificent epics that are India's pride and treasure.

Sri Ramachandra

The *Ramayana* is a story of perennial interest. It has swayed the hearts and minds of millions of Hindus for countless ages; it has inspired them to high thinking, noble effort and right conduct. Even today, there is hardly a village in India where the *Ramayana* story is not told and expounded in Sanskrit, or in the vernacular language to hundreds of men, women and children who listen to the discourse with rapt and rapturous attention. Apart from daily or occasional expositions, it is no exaggeration to say that young children are fed by the womenfolk with the main incidents of the story together with their mother's milk.

Romesh Chandra Dutt has rightly observed that "there is not a Hindu woman, whose earliest and tenderest recollections do not cling round the story of Sita's sufferings and Sita's faithfulness told in the nursery, taught in the family circle, remembered and cherished through life. Referring to the two great epics of ancient India, the *Ramayana* and the *Mahabharata,* Jawaharlal Nehru says this in his *Discovery of India*—"I do not know any book anywhere which has exercised such a continuous and pervasive influence on the mass-mind as these two. Dating back to a remote antiquity, they are still a living force in the life of the Indian people."

There are many works in different languages which deal with the lives of Sri Rama and Sita, in prose as well as in poetry. We have the *Raghuvamsha* of Kalidasa in which Rama's life and achievements figure prominently. Sanskrit dramas written by authors of great eminence, like Bhavabhuti and Murari, deal with various episodes in Rama's life. It may perhaps be claimed, however, that the *Ramayana* of Valmiki stands foremost amongst them all. It is one of the greatest epics of the world. It is known as the (*Adi Kavya*) in Sanskrit as it is the first piece of genuine Sanskrit epic poetry. It consists of 24,000 verses in six cantos. The style is simple and mellifluous. There are no harsh words to grate on the ear. The story moves smoothly like the gently flowing water in an expansive river. The lilt of the poetry is lovely.

The work is a supreme example of the definition, वाक्यं रसात्मकं काव्यं All nine *rasas* or sentiments from शृङ्गार (*Shringara*) to शान्त (*Shanta*)are finely portrayed in the course of the work. Valmiki is famous for his similes, and Kalidasa is largely his follower in this respect. Even those who do not know Sanskrit love to hear the original read, as the sounds fall softly on the ear and thrill the heart. Valmiki's *Ramayana* is a masterpiece of literature and attests to the high scale reached by the Hindu civilization in ancient times.

Apart from its excellence as a work of art in poetic composition, it is regarded as a sacred text, as is evident from this *shloka.*

श्रृण्वन्रामायणं भक्त्या यः पादं पदमेव वा।
स यति ब्रह्मणः स्थानं पूज्यते सदा।।

Devout Hindus worship the book. The very name of Rama is the holy of holies. It is the protecting amulet or charm, the तारक मंत्र. The sanctity of the name is thus glorified in the drama called *Hanumannataka.*

कल्याणानां निधानं कलिमलथनं पावनं पावनानाम्
पाथयं यन्मुमुक्षोः सपदि परपदप्राप्तये प्रस्थितस्य ।
विश्रामस्थानमेकं कविवरवचसां जीवनं सज्जनानाम्
बीजं धर्मद्रुमस्य प्रभवतु भक्तां भूतये रामनाम ।।

The *Ramayana* expounds lofty ethics and sublime philosophy in a masterly manner. It indicates and illustrates right conduct, individual and social; and it postulates in many places what is compendiously known as *Sanatana Dharma* or the Eternal Laws. The work is used and read times without number as a prayer-book of devotional poems by aspirants to earthly prosperity and other-worldly happiness. Mainly for two reasons it is called an (*Anugraha-Grantha*). Valmiki, an unlettered sage, wrote the work as a result of Lord Brahma's grace, He conferred on Valmiki supernatural vision which enabled him to see every detail of Rama's life and gave him the ability to express his ideas in choice verse. The Lord pronounced a benediction and said that the *Ramayana* would be in vogue on earth as long as the mountains and rivers last:

यावत्स्थास्यन्ति गिरयः सरितश्च महीले ।
तावद्रमायणकथा लोकेषु प्रचरिष्यति ।।

In his turn, Valmiki states in several places that those who read his *Ramayana* will enjoy in abundant measure the blessing of the Lord:

आयष्यमारोग्यकरं यशस्यं सौभ्रातृकं बुद्धिकरं शुभं च ।
श्रोतव्यमेतन्नियमेन सद्भिराख्यानमोजस्करमृद्धिकामैः ।।

Of late, there has been a rather acute controversy on the question whether Sri Rama was an *avatar* or incarnation of God, or whether he was an ordinary mortal, born as a prince of Ayodhya, who strove to acquire the divine virtues. The orthodox and conventional school of thought adopts the former theory. The modern mind, as typified by the late Rt. Hon. V. S. Srinivasa Sastri, would adopt the latter view. In my humble opinion, however, the dispute is a futile one. It is surely more important to discover what Valmiki had in mind when he wrote the work and how he intended his readers to study and interpret it. From this standpoint, there is hardly any doubt that his intention was to delineate Rama as an *avatar*. At the very commencement of the work, we find reference to the request made to Sri Maha Vishnu by the assembled gods, asking Him to make up his mind to be born on this earth as Dasharatha's son or sons for the destruction of the wicked Ravana. It is not easy to dismiss this chapter as a later interpolation as it forms an integral part of the story relating the *Ashvamedha* sacrifice undertaken by the king. In the famous encounter between Rama and Parashurama, the vanquished Brahmin sage proclaims Rama to be Narayana, the slayer of Madhu.

अक्षयं मधुहन्तारं जानामि त्वां सुरोत्तमम् ।

The Yuddha Kanda makes this very clear. In chapter 35, Malyavan, the maternal grandfather of Ravana, tells him that he thinks Rama was Vishnu.

विष्णुं मन्यामहे रामं मानुषं देहमास्थितम् ।

Ravana himself says in Chapter 72.

तं मन्ये राघवं धीरं नारायणमनामयम् ।

After exhibiting marvellous skill in archery against hordes of Rakshasas, in chapter 94 of the Yuddha kanda, Rama exclaims to the admiring Vanara spectators around him that such prowess is to be seen only in himself or in Shiva.

एतदस्त्रबलं दिव्यं मम वा त्र्यंबकस्य वा ।

Again, in Mandodari's lamentation over her lord's death (Chapter 114 v. 12-13), she refers to Rama in these terms.

तमसः परमो धाता शङ्खचक्रगदाधरः ।।
श्रीवत्सवक्षा नित्यश्रीरजय्यः शाश्वतो ध्रुवः ।।
मानुषं रूपमास्थाय विष्णुः सत्यपराक्रमः ।

After Ravana is killed and the battle won, all the Devas, headed by Brahma, come on to the scene to pronounce their benediction on the conqueror. They expressly say that he is Narayana, who descended into this world to rid it of the atrocious Ravana. It is true that Rama says in reply that he regards himself as a man born as the son of Dasharatha. But this very answer would be inappropriate if a mere man uttered it. Throughout the Aranya Kanda during his visits to several sages, especially Atri and Agastya, the author makes it fairly clear that Rama was regarded as an incarnation and was thus worshipped by the sages.

The incarnation hypothesis derives support from the famous *shlokas* in chapter 4 of the *Bhagavad-Gita,* when we remember the history of Rama's birth.

यदा यदा हि धार्मस्य ग्लानिर्भवति भारत ।
अभ्युत्थानमधर्मस्य तदात्मानं सृजाम्यहम् ।।
परित्राणाय साधूनां विनाशाय चष्कृताम् ।
धार्मसंस्थापनार्थाय संभवामि युगे युगे ।।

It is further reinforced by the verse which is usually recited every day as preliminary to the devotional study of the *Ramayana,* wherein it is stated that when God, who can be known and realised only by the study of the Vedas, was born as the son of Dasharatha, the Vedas themselves took shape as the *Ramayana* of Valmiki.

वेदवेद्ये परे पुंसि जाते दशरथात्मजे ।
वेदः प्राचेतसादासीत् साक्षाद्रामायणात्मना ।।

In his *Gitagovinda,* Jayadeva takes Rama to be an *avatar* of Vishnu in this well-known *shloka* which mentions the ten incarnations.

वेदानुद्धते जगन्निवहते भूगोलमुद्बिभ्रते
दैत्यं दारयते बलिं छलयते क्षात्र क्षयं कुर्वते ।
पौलस्त्यं जयते हलं कलयते कारूण्यमातन्वते
म्लेच्छान् मूर्च्छयते दशाकृतिकृते कृष्णाय तुभ्यं नमः ।।

While it can therefore be maintained with every justification that Valmiki wanted us to take this view of Rama, it is at the same time possible to interpret the *Ramayana* from the angle of approach adopted by modern critics. There is nothing wrong in it. It does not in any way mitigate the reverence due to, or abate our worship of, Sri Rama, if we regard him as an ordinary man elevated to the pedestal of divinity. On the contrary, pursuit along this line of thought enables us to get over and explain some of the alleged defects in the hero's life and conduct. A superman is still a man, though infinitely better than the rest of his kind and he must obviously be subject to some human failings. Under the stress of unbearable misfortune, it is not surprising if Rama wondered at the weakness of his father in yielding to the angry entreaties of the charming Kaikeyi. To become unhinged in mind at the loss of a dear and beloved wife is but natural. To kill Vali from a hidden shelter was justified by force of circumstances as was his alliance with Sugriva. Rama's suspicion that Bharata may like to have the kingdom for himself and not exactly welcome his return to Ayodhya was a thought which would have occurred to most persons placed in a similar situation. One who knew that he was lord Narayana himself, and that Sita was none other than Lakshmi would not have put her to so many ordeals.

Such defects and failings in Rama's life are not, however, really inconsistent with the *avatar* theory. Once God comes down to earth as a man, he must play the role which he has assumed. He covers himself with his own *maya* and is then subject to delusion as much as ordinary human beings are. It is only at the end of the mission that he withdraws himself from his projected activities and becomes Godhead once again. Sometimes, he has to be reminded of the termination of his work, as Rama was, after he had killed Ravana.

The epic *Mahabharata* is known as the fifth Veda and contains the *Bhagavad-Gita* as well as the famous teachings of Bhishma to the Pandava brothers in the Shanti and Aunshasanika *parvas*. Notwithstanding the fact, however, that eminent scholars consider it a veritable treasure-house of wisdom, it does not enjoy the same prestige and popularity as the *Ramayana*. Why is this? What is the secret of the magic spell that the *Ramayana* has over us all? Is it due to the intrinsic worth of the story, the excellence of the poetry, or the wonderful delineation of characters, the faith and devotion of the readers, the enormous spiritual value attached to Rama's name? Or is it in its value as an aid in the matter of plain living, high thinking and spiritual progress? Probably, it is a combination of all these factors, though each by itself is sufficiently potent to explain its hold on our minds. To read the *Ramayana* from the beginning to the end is to succumb to its sweet and pervasive influence.

It is difficult to single out any portion or portions as better than the rest. But if one should be tempted to make a selection, reference might in particular be made to the accounts of the meeting of Rama and Parashurama, the anguish and sorrow of Dasharatha when the two boons are extracted from him by Kalikeyi, Lakshmana's indignation over his father's conduct, the conversation between Sita and Anasuya, the description of the brothers by Hanuman, Tara's lament over Vali's death, Sita's admonition of Ravana, her lonely suffering in the Ashoka garden with the Rakshasi guard round her and Hanuman's message to Ravana. In the Yuddha Kanda, the fights between Lakshmana and Indrajit on the one hand and Rama and Ravana on the other are powerfully vivid and realistic and almost make us feel as spectators of a battle before our eyes.

Valmiki excels in description of forests and the hermitages of sages. Nature, in all its aspects and varieties—trees, mountains, rivers, clouds, dawn, sunset, had a great fascination for him. His sketches of some of the sages have a deft touch and they dwell on the greatness of penance and the sublimity of a spiritual life of self-realisation.

No part of the *Ramayana* can be said to be dull or prosaic; every bit of it is interesting as a story and excellent as poetry. There is a consensus of opinion, however, that the Sundara Kanda covering the exploits, valour and courage of Hanuman, constitutes the best portion. While this may be true, I would venture to give higher praise to the Ayodhya Kanda which delineates and describes human passions and feelings and mental conflicts and emotions in a masterly way. It contains vivid pictures of the nobility of Sri Rama, the weakness of Dasharatha, the craftiness of Kaikeyi, the fulmination of Lakshmana against destiny, the devotion of Sita, the dignity of Kausalya, the wisdom of Sumitra, the friendship of Guha, and the lofty generosity of Bharata. A story told about the late Jagadguru of Sringeri, Sri Narasimha Bharati Swami, is that he devoted the whole of one afternoon to reading this canto from the beginning to end. He was so entranced by its beauty that he became forgetful of the host of admiring devotees who surrounded him and he sat shedding tears of joy and sorrow as the story unfolded itself step by step and stage by stage. When so great a Yogi as he can be thus moved, one wonders to what extent we ordinary mortals can be affected, with no control over our mind or senses and who are a prey to desires and ambitions, hopes and frustrations attachments and hatreds!

The Epic Story

There are two great epics in the Sanskrit language, which are very ancient. Of course, there are hundreds of other epic poems. I am now going to speak to you of the two most ancient epics, called the *Ramayana* and the *Mahabharata*. The oldest of these epics is called the *Ramayana* or "The Life of Rama". The name of the poet, or sage, was Valmiki. And this is how he became a poet.

One day as this sage, Valmiki, was going to bathe in the holy river Ganga, he saw a pair of doves wheeling round and round, and kissing each other. The sage looked up and was pleased at the sight, but in a second an arrow whisked past him and killed the male dove. As the dove fell down on the ground, the female dove went on whirling round and round the dead body of its companion in grief. In a moment the poet became miserable, and looking round, he saw the hunter. "Thou art a wretch," he cried, "without the smallest mercy! They slaying hand would not even stop for love!" What is this? What am I saying?" The poet thought to himself, "I have never spoken in this sort of way before." And then a voice came:

"Be not afraid. This is poetry that is coming out of your mouth. Write the life of Rama in poetic language for the benefit of the world". And that is how the poem first began. The first verse sprang out of pity, from the mouth of Valmiki, the first poet. And it was after that, that he wrote the beautiful *Ramayana*, "The Life of Rama."

There was an ancient Indian town called Ayodhya—and it exists even in modern times. There, in ancient times, reigned a king called Dasharatha. He had three queens, but the king had not any children by them. And like good Hindus, the king and queens all went on pilgrimages fasting and praying, that they might have children; and, in good time, four sons were born. The eldest of them was Rama. As it should be, these four brother were thoroughly educated in all branches of learning.

Now, there was another king, called Janaka, and this king had a beautiful daughter named Sita. Sita was found in a field; she was daughter of the Earth, and was born without parents. All sorts of miraculous births were common in the mythological lore of India. Sita, being the daughter of the Earth, was pure and immaculate. She was brought up by King Janaka. When she was of a marriageable age, the king wanted to find a suitable husband for her.

There were a number of princes who aspired for the hand of Sita; the test demanded on this occasion was the breaking of a huge bow, called *Haradhanu.* All the princes put forth all their strength to accomplish this feat, but failed. Finally, Rama took the mighty bow in his hands and with easy grace broke it in twain. Thus Sita selected Rama, the son of King Dasharatha, for her husband, and they were wedded with great rejoicings. Then, Rama took his bride to his home, and his old father thought that it was now time for him to retire and intstal Rama as Yuvaraja. Everything was accordingly made ready for the ceremony, and the whole country was jubilant over the affair, when the youngest queen, Kaikeyi, was reminded by one of her maidservants of two promises made to her by the king long ago. At one time she had pleased the king very much, and he offered to grant her two boons. "Ask any two things in my power and I will grant them to you", said he, but she made no request then. She had forgotten all about it; but the evil-minded maidservant in her employ began to work upon her jealousy with regard to Rama being installed on the throne, and insinuated to her how nice would it be for her if her own had succeeded the king, until the queen was almost mad with jealousy. Then the servant suggested to her to ask from the king the two promised boons: one would be that her own son Bharata should be placed on the throne, and the others, that Rama should be sent to the forest and be exiled for fourteen years.

Now Rama was the life and soul of the old king, and when this wicked request was make to him, he as a king felt he could not go back on his word. So he did not know what to do. But Rama came to the rescue and willingly offered to give up the throne and go into exile, so that his father might not be guilty of falsehood. So Rama went into exile for fourteen years, accompanied by his loving wife Sita and his devoted brother Lakshmana, who would on no account be parted from him.

The Aryans did not know who were the inhabitants of these wild forests. In those days the forest tribes they called "monkeys," and some of the so-called "monkeys," if unusually strong and powerful, were called "demons".

So, into the forest inhabited by demons and monkeys, Rama, Lakshmana and Sita went. When Sita had offered to accompany Rama, he exclaimed, "How can you, a princess, face hardships and accompany me into a forest full of unknown dangers?" But Sita replied. "Wherever Rama goes, there goes Sita. How can you talk of 'princess' and 'royal birth' to me? I go before you!" So, Sita went. And the younger brother also went with them. They penetrated far into the forest, until they reached the river Godavari. On the banks of the river they built little cottages, and Rama and Lakshmana used to hunt deer and collect fruits. After they had lived thus for some time, one day there came a giantess. She was the sister of the giant king of Lanka (Ceylon). Roaming through the forest at will, she came across Rama, and seeing that he was a very handsome man, she fell in love with him at once. But Rama was the purest of men, and also he was a married man, so of course he could not return her love. In revenge, she went to her brother, the giant king, and told him all about the beautiful Sita, the wife of Rama.

Rama was the most powerful of mortals; there were no giants nor demons, nor anybody else strong enough to conquer him. So, the giant king had to resort to subterfuge. He got hold of another giant who was a magician and changed him into a beautiful, golden deer; and the deer went prancing round about the place where Rama lived, until Sita was fascinated by its beauty and asked Rama to go and capture the deer for her. Rama went into the forest to catch the deer, leaving his brother in charge of Sita. Then Lakshmana laid a circle of fire round the cottage, ad he said to Sita. "To-day I see something may befall you; and, therefore, I tell you not to go outside of this magic circle. Some danger may befall you if you do." In the meanwhile, Rama had pierced the magic deer with his arrow, and immediately the deer changed into the form of a giant and died.

Immediately at the cottage was heard the voice of Rama crying, "Oh, Lakshmana, come to my help!" and Sita said. "Lakshmana, go at once into the forest to help Rama!" "That is not Rama's voice," protested Lakshmana. But at the entreaties of Sita, Lakshmana had to go in search of Rama. As soon as he went away, the giant king who had taken to form of a mendicant monk stood at the gate and asked for alms. "Wait awhile," said Sita, "until my husband comes back and I will give you plentiful alms." "I cannot wait, good lady", said he, "I am very hungry, give me anything you have." At this, Sita who had a few fruits in the cottage, brought them out. But the mendicant monk after many persuasions prevailed upon her to bring the alms to him, assuring her that she need have no fear as he was a holy person. So Sita came out of the magic circle, and immediately the seeming monk assumed his giant body, and grasping Sita in his arms he called his magic chariot, and putting her therein, he fled with the weeping Sita. Poor Sital! She was utterly helpless, nobody was there to come to her aid. As the giant was carrying her away, she took off a few of the ornaments from her arms and at intervals dropped them to the ground.

She was taken by Ravana to his kingdom, Lanka, the island of Ceylon. He made proposals to her to became his queen, and tempted her in many ways to accede to his request. But Sita who was chastity itself, would not even speak to the giant, and he to punish her, made live under a tree, day and night until she should consent to be his wife.

When Rama and Lakshmana returned to the cottage and found that Sita was not there, their grief knew no bounds.

They could not imagine what had become of her. The two brothers went on, seeking everywhere for Sita, but could find no trace of her. After long searching, they came across a group of "monkeys," and in the midst of them was Hanuman, the "divine monkey".

Rama, at last, fell in with these monkeys. They told him that they had seen flying through the sky a chariot, in which was seated a demon who was carrying away a most beautiful lady, and that she was weeping bitterly and as the chariot passed over their heads she dropped one of her ornaments to attract their attention. Then showed Rama the ornament and he recognised it at once, saying, "Yes, it is Sita's." Then, the monkeys told Rama who this demon king was and where he lived, and then they all went to seek for him.

Now, the monkey-king Vali and his younger brother Sugriva were then fighting among themselves for the kingdom. The younger brother was helped by Rama, and he regained the kingdom from Vali, who had driven him away: and he, in return, promised to help Rama. They searched the country all round, but could not find Sita. At last, Hanuman leaped by one bound from the coast of India to the island of Ceylon, and there went looking all over Lanka for Sita, but nowhere could he find her.

You see, this giant king had conquered the gods, the men, in fact, the whole world; and he had collected all the beautiful women and made them his concubines. So Hanuman thought to himself, "Sita cannot be with them in the palace. She would rather die than be in such a place." So Hanuman went to seek for her elsewhere. At last, he found Sita under a tree, pale and thin, like the new moon that lies low in the horizon. Now Hanuman took the form of a little monkey, and settled on the tree, and there he witnessed how giantesses sent by Ravana came and tried to frighten Sita into submission, but she would not even listen to the name of the giant king.

Then, Hanuman came nearer to Sita and told her how he became the messenger of Rama, who had sent him to find out where Sita was; and Hanuman showed to Sita the signet ring which Rama had given as a token for establishing his identity. He also informed her that as soon as Rama would know her whereabouts, he would come with an army and conquer the giant and recover her. However, he suggested to Sita that if she wished it, he would take her on his shoulders and could with one leap clear the ocean and get back to Rama. But Sita could not bear the idea, as she was chastity itself, and could not touch the body of any man except her husband. So, Sita remained where she was. But she gave him a jewel from her hair to carry to Rama; and with that Hanuman returned.

Learning everything about Sita from Hanuman, Rama collected an army, and with it marched towards the southernmost point of India. There Rama's monkeys built a huge bridge, called Setu-Bandha, connecting India with Ceylon. In very low water even now it is possible to cross from India to Ceylon over the sand-banks there.

Now Rama was God incarnate, otherwise how could he have done all these things? He was an Incarnation of God, according to the Hindus. They in India believe him to be the seventh Incarnation of God.

The monkeys removed whole hills, placed them in the sea and covered them with stones and trees, thus making a huge embankment. A Little squirrel, so it is said, was there rolling himself in the sand and running backwards and forwards on to the bridge and shaking himself. Thus in his small way he was working for the bridge of Rama by putting in sand. The monkeys laughed, for they were bringing whole mountains, whole forests, huge loads of sand for the bridge—so they laughed at the little squirrel rolling in the sand and then shaking himself. But Rama saw it and remarked. "Blessed be the little squirrel; he is doing his work to the best of his ability, and he is therefore quite as good as the greatest of you." Then he gently stroked the squirrel on the back, and the marks of Rama's fingers running lengthways, are seen on the squirrel's back to this day.

Now, when the bridge was finished, the whole army of monkeys, led by Rama and his brother, entered Ceylon. For several months afterwards tremendous war and bloodshed followed. At last, this demon king Ravana was conquered and killed, and his capital, with all the palaces and everything, which were entirely of solid gold, was taken. Rama gave them over to Vibhishana, the younger brother of Ravana, and seated him on the throne in the place of his brother, as a return for the valuable services rendered by him to Rama during the war.

Then Rama with Sita and his followers left Lanka. But there ran a murmur among the followers. "The test! The test" they cried, "Sita has not given the test that she was perfectly pure in Ravana's household." "Pure! She is chastity itself!" exclaimed Rama. "Never mind! We want the test," persisted the people. Subsequently a huge sacrificial fire was made ready, into which Sita had to plunge herself. Rama was in agony, thinking that Sita was lost; but in a moment the god of fire himself appeared with a throne upon his head, and upon the throne was Sita. Then, there was universal rejoicing, and everybody was satisfied.

Early during the period of exile, Bharata, the younger brother had come and informed Rama, of the death of the old king and vehemently insisted on his occupying the throne. During Rama's exile Bharata would on no account ascend the throne, and out of respect placed a pair of Rama's wooden shoes on it as a substitute for his brother. Then Rama returned to his capital, and by the common consent of his people he became the king of Ayodhya.

After Rama regained his kingdom, he took the necessary vows which in olden times the king had to take for the benefit of his people. The king was the slave of his people, and had to bow to public opinion, as we shall see later on. Rama passed a few years in happiness with Sita, when the people again began to murmur that Sita had been stolen by a demon, and carried across the ocean. They were not satisfied with the former test and clamoured for another test, otherwise she must be banished.

In order to satisfy the demands of the people, Sita was banished, and left to live in the forest, where was the hermitage of the sage and poet Valmiki. The sage found poor Sita weeping and forlorn, and hearing her sad story he sheltered her in his Ashrama. Sita was expecting soon to become a mother, and she gave birth to twin boys. The poet never told the children who they were. He brought them up together in the Brahmacharian life. He then composed the poem known as *Ramayana*, set it to music, and dramatised it, and taught Rama's two children how to recite and sing it.

There came a time when Rama was going to perform a huge Sacrifice, or *Yajna*, such as the old kings used to celebrate. But no ceremony in India can be performed by a married man without his wife: he must have the wife with him, the *Sahadharmini,* the "co-religionist"—that is the expression for a wife. The Hindu householder has to perform hundreds of ceremonies, but not one can be duly performed according to the Shastras, if he has not a wife to complement it with her part in it.

Now Rama's wife was not with him then, as she had been banished. So, the people asked him to marry again. But at this request Rama for the first time in his life stood against the people. He said: "This cannot be. My life is Sita's ". So, as a substitute, a golden statue of Sita was made, in order that the ceremony could be accomplished. They arranged even a dramatic entertainment, to enhance the religious feeling in this great festival. Valmiki, the great sate-poet, came with his pupils, Lava and Kusha, the unknown sons of Rama. A stage had been erected and everything was ready for the performance. Rama and his brothers attended with all his nobles and his people, a vast audience. Under the direction of Valmiki, the life of Rama was sung by Lava and Kusha, who fascinated the whole assembly by their charming voice and appearance. Poor Rama was nearly maddened, and when in the drama, the scene of Sita's exile came about, he did not know what to do. Then the sage said to him. "Do not be grieved, for I will show you Sita." Then Sita was brought upon the stage and Rama was delighted to see his wife. All of a sudden, the old murmur arose: "The test! The test!" Poor Sita was so terribly overcome by the repeated cruel slight on her reputation that it was more than she could bear. She appealed to the gods to testify to her innocence, when the Earth opened and Sita exclaimed, "Here is the test," and vanished into the bosom of the Earth. The people were taken aback at this tragic end. And Rama was overwhelmed with grief.

A few days after Sita's disappearance, a messenger came to Rama from the gods, who intimated to him that his mission on earth was finished and he was to return to heaven. These tidings brought to him the recognition of his own real Self. He plunged into the waters of Sarayu, the mighty river that laved his capital, and joined Sita in the other world.

This is the great, ancient epic of India. When you study these characters, you can at once find out how different is the ideal in India from that of the West. For the race, Sita stands as the ideal of suffering. The West says, "Do! Show your power by doing." India says, "Show your power by suffering." The West has solved the problem of how much a man can have: India has solved the problem of how little a man can have. The two extremes, you see. Sita is typical of India—the idealised India. The question is not whether she ever lived, whether the story is history or not, we know that the ideal is there. There is no other Pauranika story that has so permeated the whole nation, so entered into its very life, and has so mingled in every drop of blood of the race, as this ideal of Sita. Sita is the name in India for everything that is good, pure and holy; everything that in woman we call womanly. Through all the suffering she experiences, there is not one harsh word against Rama. She takes it as her own duty, and performs her own part in it. Think of the terrible injustice of her being exiled to the forest! But Sita knows no bitterness. That is, again, the Indian ideal. Says the ancient Buddha. "When a man hurts you, and you turn back to hurt him, that would not cure the first injury; it would only create in the world one more wickedness." Sita was a true Indian by nature; she never returned injury.

3 Rāmāyaṇa in Kūṭiyāṭṭam, Kūttu and Pāṭhakam

The present-day Hindu culture is directly traceable to the two great Itihāsas, the *Rāmāyaṇa* and the *Mahābhārata* and the one great Purāṇa, *Śrimadbhāgavata*. Our ancestors in Kerala had made effective institutional arrangements for the popularisation of these classics among the masses. In their original form they were read, recited and expounded regularly in temples. We have evidence of a functionary known as '*Bhārata-Bhaṭṭa*' in our temples, who was paid out of temple funds and whose duty was to expound *Mahābhārata* daily in the temple premises. Reading and expounding *Śrimadbhāgavata* in the course of seven days, known as *Saptāha Pārāyaṇa,* in temples as well as in homes, is still practised. Devout Hindus still read during the month of Karkaṭaka (July-August) the Malayalam rendering of *Adhyātma Rāmāyaṇa* by Ezhuttacchan, at their homes.

Representational and performing arts were made use of for presenting the incidents vividly before the people to drive home effectively the eternal truths and the ethical teachings portrayed in these Classics. This was done at several levels. There were theatres attached to temples, known as *kūttampalams,* where plays in Sanskrit based on these three great works were performed in a rigidly traditionalised manner. This was known as *Kūṭiyāṭṭam* and *Kūttu*. My attempt in this short paper is to give some idea of this. The *Kṛṣṇanāṭṭam* performance based on the *Kṛṣṇagiti kāvya* by a Zamorin at the temple of Guruvāyūr, which covers the story of Kṛṣṇa in eight nights, and the performance of Āṭṭakkathas based on incidents from these classics, though interesting in themselves, are excluded from the scope of this paper. I have also to exclude the performance of *Tolpāvakkūttu* attached to Kāli temples in Central Kerala where the Tamil version of *Rāmāyaṇa* by Kampan is expounded in Malayalam.

Kūṭiyāṭṭam and Kūttu are usually performed in Kūttampalams, which are majestic permanent structures constructed to specific patterns within some of the bigger temples. Where there are no Kūttampalams, these may be performed in temporary structures or in the surrounding halls of the temple. Kūṭiyāṭṭam, like Utsava, is an important annual festival of several temples, and has been liberally endowed by donation of landed property. It is also believed that performance of Kūṭiyāṭṭam confers great merit on the donor. Yet this traditional theatre art is fast disappearing from the temples owing to various reasons.

The right to perform Kūṭiyāṭṭam and Kūttu is vested in two communities, viz., Cākyārs and Nampyārs. All the male roles are taken by Cākyārs and the female roles are played by Naṅgyārs, viz., the women of Nampyār community. Instrumental support to the performer is provided by a Nampyār who plays on Mizhāvu, a huge copper pot covered on the mouth by a piece of calf-hide, and a Naṅgyār who wields a pair of small cymbals.

The Abhinaya in Kūṭiyāṭṭam is highly traditionalised. Based on Bharata's *Nāṭyaśāstra,* the Kūṭiyāṭṭam performance makes liberal use of dances and gestures as in Kathakali. But Kūṭiyāṭṭam is more elaborate and the actors also speak, unlike in Kathakali, where the Vācika Abhinaya is provided only by the musicians. The Vācika Abhinaya of the main characters in Kūṭiyāṭṭam is confined to the recital of texts in Sanskrit or Prakrit. The Vidūṣaka speaks in Malayalam and has become almost the fulcrum of Kūṭiyāṭṭam performance. He not only does recite his set speeches, but interprets what others speak, and incidentally brings in a lot of humorous and serious stories and incidents. In fact the Vidūṣaka dominates the Kūṭiyāṭṭam stage.

The repertoire of Kūṭiyāṭṭam is limited to portions of ten Sanskrit plays, viz., *Svapnavāsavadatta, Abhiṣeka, Pratimā, Bālacarita* and *Pratijñāyaugandharāyaṇa* by Bhāsa, *Mattavilāsa* by Mahendravarman, *Nāgānanda* by Harṣa, *Āścaryacūḍāmaṇi* by Śaktibhadra and *Tapatisaṃvaraṇa* and *Subhadrādhanañjaya* by Kulaśekhara. Of these ten plays *Abhiṣeka, Pratimā* and *Cūḍāmaṇi* are based on the story of Rāma. In *Pratijñā,* where the story is connected by Udayana's love for Vāsavadattā, the whole of Rāmāyaṇa is expounded by the Vidūṣaka during the course of one full month. the performance of Kūṭiyāṭṭam takes liberties with the original plays to introduce stories from the epics and the purāṇas. When Udayana is put in jail by King Mahāsena, the Vidūṣaka is made to approach the mother of Udayana and to console her, narrating the story of Rāma, who had to put up with greater difficulties and indignities than those suffered by her son. Needless to say, this is an invention of the performers of Kūṭiyāṭṭam and is intended to create an opportunity or expounding the whole of *Rāmāyaṇa* during the performance of the play.

To expound the story a text was required, and formerly the need for a text was met by culling verses from Vālmīki's *Rāmāyaṇa* until the present text was compiled by the famous Nārāyana Bhaṭṭa of Melputtūr in the early decades of the 17th century. In this text, known as *Rāmāyaṇa* Prabandha, consisting of both prose and verse, we find verses quoted from Bhoja's *Rāmāyaṇa Campū* and works like *Hanumannāṭaka*. *Niranunāsika,* which consists of six ślokas and a long piece of prose spoken by *Śūrpaṇakhā* after her mutilation by Lakṣmaṇa, and consequently composed without using any of the nasal sounds, is from the gifted pen of Nārāyaṇa Bhaṭṭa.

Expounding of Prabandha without connecting it with any nāṭaka is termed as Kūttu. This is also performed by Cākyārs dressing up as Viduṣaka. Expounding of the same Prabandhas are used for Kūttu by members of other communities is known as Pāṭhakam. There is evidence to believe that to begin with Campūkāvyas in Malayalam were made use of for Pāṭhakam, which were later supplanted by compositions in Sanskrit.

Kūṭyiāṭṭam, Kūttu and Pāṭhakam are not only excercises at popularising the stories of Itihāsas and Purāṇas and expounding the religious teachings contained in them. These art-forms are also the best means of spreading knowledge of Sanskrit language among the people without any special effort on the part of the learners. Besides making the audience familiar with Sanskrit language, these performances also introduced them to the subtle beauties of suggestive poetry and gradually made them cultivated Sahṛdayas.

As stated earlier, these art forms are now on the decline. The number of gifted performers is decreasing year by year. Consequent upon the land reforms, the endowments have become defunct, and the temples are unable to support the performances. There is a general decline of Sanskrit scholarship in the country. The night-long performances are also out of tune with modern life rhythms.

It will however be a great pity if these forms of art disappear completely from our midst. Something will have to be done to keep them alive, and that something will have to be done without any further delay.

—*N.V. Krishna Warrior*

4 Economic Data in the Mahābhārata

Epic literature emerges out of 'heroic ages' and often retains the flavour of such an age in spite of repeated redactions of the text and the interpolation of later ages. This lends to the text elements of internal contradictions as well as a compendium-like quality. The *Mahābhārata* is no exception. The range of time over which the interpolations have been added reduces the flavour of the original. nevertheless one method of attempting to do the virtually impossible in trying to reach out to the original is to examine the text from the perspective of one theme and ascertain the dominant form. An attempt is being made in this paper to try and locate the predominant economic structure which forms a background to the events described in the early sections of the story. Some distinction between early and late may perhaps be allowed in terms of the context of the evidence quoted. If an action is part of the intrinsic narrative of the epic, it may be taken as belonging to an earlier stratum that a situation which is being described at an abstract level in the many didactic portions of the text. There is a greater probability of the latter being interpolations.

A study has already been made of the geographical and economic data available in at least four sections of the text—the Ādiparvan, Sabhāparvan, Araṇyaparvan, and Bhīṣmaparvan. The intention of this paper is to examine the data and compare it with other parts of the text and to suggest that the predominant economy of the epic is a mixture of pastroalism and agriculture with an earlier emphasis on the former (as evidenced in the narrative sections) gradually changing to the latter which is more apparent in the didactic sections. The epic in origin relates to clan-based tribal society with effective power invested in tribal chiefships and where the term tribal does not precluded social stratification: a society which gradually gave way to monarchies of the more conventional type based on developed agriculture.

Among the more interesting and perhaps lesser known studies of the *Mahābhārata* are two which have for many years been neglected by Indologists but which are now coming into notice again. Marcel. Mauss in his study of gift-giving and gift-exchange devotes a substantial part of the book to a discussion of *dāna* in the Anuśāsanaparvan. G.J. Held took as his cue a statement from this book in which Mauss asserts that, 'Le *Mahābhārata* est I' historie d'un gigantesque potlatch'. Held has argued that the Kauravas and the Pāṇḍavas were two phratries involved in a potlatch competition; the latter being symbolised in the two major events of the epicthe game of dice and the war.

Both potlatch and gift-exchange as economic systems generally relate to tribal chiefships. Traces of the system very often continue into later times when chiefships have given way to kingdoms and the traces are particularly evident in ritual situations. But their economic function begins to decline when the economy of the society changes. The potlatch is a ceremony in which property is lavishly given away or even destroyed in order to acquire or to maintain social status, the distribution of wealth being symbolic of status. The Wealth is often a ceremonial gift/gifts given by a tribal chief acting as the host to other chiefs and their kinsmen: the gathering of chiefs thus becoming a kind of council of both appeal and approval. The potlatch is also often the occasion when an event of importance is announced such as a birth or a marriage or the acquisition of office or of territory and sanction is given to the event by those present. The giving of gifts on such occasions is strictly in order of precedence and priority as is also the seating arrangement of those present which in turn reinforces social rank and social solidarity. Gift-giving is not a one-way process since it is assumed that at some later date the invitees will also have a potlatch, and this keeps goods in circulation. A rival potlatch can be held if there is an alternate claimant to the title. This results in competition with even more wealth being distributed or, if need be, destroyed. A further form is what has been called 'a face-saving potlatch', where if an indignity has occurred, the potlatch is the means of wiping it off. (Here perhaps, the closest Indian equivalent would be the *Prāyaścitta*).

Gift-exchange is characteristic of societies which have passed the stage of clans and families making exchanges but have not arrived at the stage of the money and market economy. It involves individual gift-making at two levels: one is largely to ensure the circulation of goods and the other is where the gift is substantial enough to serve the purpose of acting as a symbol of status and recognition. Gift-giving revolves around the notions of obligation, of purchase and of sacrifice. The spirit of the person is attached to the gift and a return gift of equal value becomes obligatory. In the form of sacrifice, the secular notion underlying a gift is the need to circulate and distribute wealth which is emphasised by the belief that if wealth is distributed it returns in a larger amount. Gift-giving has many dimensions. There is the ceremonial exchange among kinsmen on ritual occasions, particularly birth and marriage. There are payments in the form of gifts for services where the actual transaction is disguised as a gift. There are exchanges of material goods against privileges and non-material possessions. There may be the exchange of material goods of little value merely to assert a social and ritual relationship. The most directly functional form of gift-exchange is, of course, barter.

In the Mahābhārata the first big occasion for gift-giving is the *rājasūya* sacrifice to be performed by Yudhiṣṭhira and the details of which are described in the Sabhāparvan. The *rājasūya* is in some ways a combination of potlatch and gift-exchange. On the announcement of the *rājasūya,* various tribes and peoples bring their gifts, the nature of the gift indicating a status of equality or subordination. Another method of ranking the gift-bearers is whether or not they are admitted to the ceremony in the first round, some having to enhance their gifts before admission. The ranking showed whether the gift was to be treated as political tribute, although the nature of the *rājasūya* being what it was, the assumption was that all gifts were tribute and are therefore referred to as *bali*. The elaborate ceremonies required of the *rājasūya* ritual were a means of distributing the accumulated wealth. After Yudhiṣṭhira had successfully completed the *rājasūya* in spite of the crisis over the status of Kṛṣṇa, Duryodhana as a matter of rivalry wished also to perform a *rājasūya,* However, he was discouraged from doing so and it was suggested that he substituted a Vaiṣṇava sacrifice for the *rājasūya*. Was this perhaps to avoid a rival potlatch which would have meant a rapid consumption of wealth quite apart from the sharp and immediate tension among the kinsmen and the tribal chiefs? The Vaiṣṇava was clearly a lesser known rite and consequently its rewards were not widely publicised. To give it status it was said that it had previously only been performed by Viṣṇu himself.

Held has pointed out that there is a link between the *rājasūya* ritual and the game of dice since the latter is one of the ceremonies in the sacrifice. The importance which the game of dice takes on in the epic makes it a substitute for the rival *rākjasūua* as potlatch: the end result of which is to divest the Pāṇḍavas of their wealth and that too at their own volition. Dicing certainly carries non-heroic undertones for the kingdoms of heroes should be lost in battle and combat and not at the throw of dice. Yet neither with the Pāṇḍavas nor with the story of Nala is any condemnation attached to the losing of wealth, territory and family in gambling. Perhaps the cosmological parallels of dicing with ritual and fate (as for example in the names used for the game and the throws) exonerated the heroes. A more immediate association could be with the distribution of grazing land which often required the drawing of lots or the throwing of dice. Thus the throwing of dice could have symbolised the distribution of wealth. Curiously, winning at dice would have made the Kauravas the legitimate heirs and the epic could well have terminated at this point. But the interposing of other claims, some even negative such as the blindness of Dhṛtarāṣṭra disqualifying him from succession, introduces new concerns of legitimacy and the story continues.

If potlatch and gift-exchange involve concepts of wealth it would be worth examining the tangibles which are included in the definition of wealth. In the geographical sections of the Bhīṣmaparvan where Bhāratavarṣa is being described, the trich areas are said to possess gems, metals and fruit-bearing trees. More specific description of wealth are available elsewhere, as for example in the details of the items brought by various people as tribute to Yudhiṣṭhira. These may be tabulated as follows.

And also a long list of other people who brought unspecified wealth.

From the list it would seem that the major items of wealth were gold, horses, elephants, slaves and textiles. The first three items could come from relatively less complex societies such as livestock breeders and trappers, unless as in the case of the Sūdras of Bharukaccha the items were imported from elsewhere. Slaves could indicate societies with some stratification unless they were mainly captives as in the case of the mountain tribes. In any case the numbers of slaves may well have been exaggerated. From societies with a greater specialisation

Source	*Items*
Kāmboja	Fleeces of sheep, gold-embroidered fur, deer-skin jackets, 300 horses, camels, varieties of nuts
Govāsena Dāsamiya	Golden jars
Bharukaccha	100,000 slave-girls from Kārpāsika, deer hides, horses
Vairāma Pārada Kitava	Goats, sheep, cows, donkeys, camels, gems, gold, blankets
Bhāgadatta	Horses, jade vases, swords with ivory carved hilts, gold
Barbarians	Silver, horses
Chinese	Textiles, wool, deer-hides, silk,
Hūṇas Śakas Odas, etc.	Cotton, skins, thousands of asses swords, spears, lances, battle-axes, gems perfumes and wine.
Tukhāra Kaṅka Romaśas Sṛngiṇo narāḥ Khaśas	Many thousand horses, gold, palaquins, beds and chariots, gems, javelins, iron arrows and shafts
Ekāśanas Jyohas Pradaras Dīrrghavenu Paśupas Kuṇindas Taṅgana	Gold produced by Pipīlaka ants, yak tail plumes, honey and herbs
Mountain tribes Vāriṣena	Sandalwood, aloeswood, hides, gems, gold, perfumes, rare birds and slave-girls
Lohitya Vaṅga Kaliṅga Tāmralipta Puṇḍraka	Dukūla cloth, silk, cloaks and elephants
Gandharva	500 Horses and gold harness
Śūkara	hundreds of elephants
Virāṭa	2000 elephants
Pāṃśu	26 elephants and 2000 horses in gold trappings
Yajnasena	14,000 slave-girls, 10,000 slaves with their wives, 26 elephants
Siṁhalas	Elephant trappings, pearls, beryls and conches.

of labour and craft production the expectation would be the inclusion of more items as finished products showing the expertise in the craft: thus, varieties of woollen material rather than fleeces of sheep, finely worked objects of gold rather than mere gold, jewellery rather than gems. The list of tributes is more suggestive of tribal chieftainships rather than areas of commodity production. The variety of the textiles and weaponry coming from central Asia however indicates something of the latter. There is a surprising absence of any reference to high-quality grain which in small quantities would not have been difficult to transport. Possibly the notion of tribute was more attuned to raw materials than to finished products.

Another definition of what constituted wealth can be culled from the sequences in the game of dice in which Yudhiṣṭhira stakes his wealth. This consists of pearls set in gold, a hundred jars each full of a hundred gold pieces, a special chariot and eight steeds, a thousand elephants with eight cow-elephants each, a hundred-thousand slave girls and hundred-thousand men slaves who fed and entertained the guests, a hundred-thousand chariots and warriors, Gandharva horses, sixty-thousand broad-chested men selected from each *varṇa* and fed on rice and grain and milk, four hundred coffers of gold, cattle, horses, cows, sheep and goats. When he has lost all this wealth he then stakes his city (*pura*), territory (*janapada*) and the wealth of all his people barring the brāhmaṇas and ultimately himself and the family. Here again the emphasis is on gold, animals and slaves. Those clearly mentioned as slaves are domestic slaves working in the household and are not slaves used in herding or agricultural activities. This is an important distinction. The sixty thousand broad-chested men are puzzling. They are associated with rice and grain and draught animals so they could be cultivators. If so, why would they be specially selected from each varṇa? Had they been slaves working in the fields or with the herds they would have been described as such by the use of the word *dāsa* or *bhṛtya*. They are not described as soldiers nor as warriors. They appear to be a specially selected body of retainers. In the computing of his wealth Yudhiṣtira makes no mention of any private land owned by him or his family. His staking of the wealth of his people is in a sense a rhetorical way of staking his right to rule.

The importance of livestock to the concept of wealth is further demonstrated in the description of the city of Girivraja which is said to be rich in cattle, always flowing with water and with fine houses.

It is almost as if livestock had become synonymous of wealth. In the alternative sacrifice of the Vaiṣṇava which Duryodhana is encouraged to perform, the main rituals consist of a large feast (which is characteristic of a potlatch) subsequent to the central rite of ploughing the land with a golden plough, the latter being made out of the tribute brought by various peoples to the ceremony. There is no mistaking the agricultural emphasis of this ceremony, yet it is regarded at best as a substitute for the better known *rājasūya*.

The objects brought are seen either as gifts or as tribute and not as taxes, whether they come from close neighbours or distant people. The term used in most cases is *bali,* even for the gifts from the central Asians. *Bali,* therefore, did not imply any regular tax as in later periods. The gifts were occasional and symbols of goodwill and were eventually to be distributed as part of the largesse associated with the ritual. Even the listing of these gifts as tribute was the moentary vision of the heroes and their bards. The bringing in of gift does not appear to take the form of any regular trade, else mention would have been made of traders accompanying the gifts. There is also a noticeable absence of reference to coins in the listing of wealth. An itinerant or peddling trade must certainly have been a common feature with probably a series of sporadic markets dependent on availability of produce.

Passages containing lists of tribute-bearers would be among those to which in epic style additions could be made quite easily. Thus as the geographical and economic reach widened fresh names and items could be added on. It has been argued that the inclusion of the central Asians in this list would date this passage to the second century B.C. The names and the items may well have been added at this period or possibly even somewhat later, but the structure of the relationships implied belongs to an earlier period. The items listed as coming from these areas may well have been the cargo of the regular trade between north India and central Asia in the post-Mauryan period. What is significant is that they are not mentioned as trading cargo but as tribute for a specific occasion. Poetic fancy apart, many of the items listed as tribute were probably familiar to the trading network of the late first millennium B.C. and the early centuries A.D. yet the trading network is kept out of this section of the text. During the Mauryan and post-Mauryan period there were exchanges of royal envoys bearing gifts between Indian rulers and those of west Asia and the

Mediterranean. The items included as gifts—rare species of fauna, special varieties of food or fruit, objects of craft specialisation—are very different from the items listed in the epic.

Some of the items from the latter are the natural produce of the forests such as fragrant wood, honey, herbs, furs, and deer-skins. These are valued both in themselves and because forest produce was appreciated by the host society. Association with the forest is indicated by other features as well. Although life in the forest is contrasted with that of the court, the physical entity of the forest was not clearly demarcated or segregated. It was land beyond the village and evidently not much acreage had been cleared for fields since forests seem to have been easily accessible to village dwellers. Forests were often regarded as sacred groves and said to be protected by supernatural beings both kindly and malevolent. The Saugandhika-vana was protected by Kubera, the king of the Yaksas, and the Hidimba-vana was the haunt of *rākṣasa* Hiḍimba. These were substantial forests and not just a small clump of trees. The heroes could walk for some distance before meeting the protector and the uprooting of trees was common during the conflicts which sometimes occurred within the forest. The association of deities or demons with the forest was an archaic practice which survived into the ritual of the sacred grove.

The Khāndava-vana was protected by Indra, and Agni had to appeal to *Kṛṣṇa* and *Arjuna* for assistance before the forest could be destroyed. The burning of the Khāṇḍava-vana is a vast conflagration involving a large area. It has been suggested that this event refers to the burning of forests to clear land for agriculture. The burning of a forest is indicative of the early stages of an agrarian economy when population groups are relatively small and can survive on this low yielding method of cultivation. In the case of the Khāṇḍava-vana it may be argued that, although there was a familiarity with the more advanced plough agriculture, a primitive method of clearing land was used because of the extent of the area which had to be cleared, an area large enough for the Pāṇḍavas and their followers to establish a *janapada*.

In Vedic literature the *araṇya* often symbolises that which is alien as compared to the *grāma*. In the *Mahābhārata* however the purity and the sanctity of the forest receives greater emphasis. The theme of exile in the forest is also a theme of penance and purification for ultimately the forest is not only the sacred grove but also the natural habitat of the ascetic and the location of the hermitage. The forest is not an alien place. The gathering economy imposed by life in the forest was regarded as an almost ideal way of living in its self-sufficiency. Even if the forest was introduced as a deliberate literary device in order to contrast it with life at the court, the idealisation of the forest reflects a relatively familiar way of life. It could be argued that the mere fact of idealisation indicates a totally changed environment in which the forest is an archaic symbol. However, the inter-linking of the forest with pasture lands would suggest the continuing economic function of the forest.

The pastoral economy finds repeated reference both directly and indirectly. Some pasture lands are included in forest areas such as the Dvaita-vana, and the Kauravas organise a *ghoṣayātra,* a cattle expedition to this area. Karṇa suggests that he and Duryodhana should take permission from Dhṛtarāṣṭra and go on an expedition to visit the cowherding stations in Dvaita-vana. Karṇa, spoiling for a fight, knew that the Pāṇḍavas were in the vicinity and therefore trouble might ensue. The cattle expedition was obviously a recognised procedure since the *ghoṣayātra* is the time for counting the cows and branding the calves and incidentally the forest also provides the occasion for hunting. A vast expedition sets out consisting of the princes and their friends and retainers, an army of eight thousand chariots, thirty thousand elephants, one thousand soldiers and nine thousand horses, together with many hundreds of hunters and womenfolk. It is specifically mentioned that traders also follows in their wake suggesting the organisation of temporary cattle fairs. That the permission of the king had to be obtained and that the princes were personally involved in supervising the expedition indicates that it had an important function in the economy and also suggests that the princes were more in the nature of tribal chiefs rather than well-entrenched monarchs. That the *ghoṣayātra* also carries an element of the potlatch is evident from the distribution of presents and gifts to the cattle-herders by the princes. The battle between the Kauravas and the Gandharvas on this occasion is doubtless a reference to the cattle raids which must have occurred as a part of these expeditions. Rights over grazing lands and hunting lands would be territorial rights the infringement of which would be opposed as strongly as the infringement of cultivated fields in later stages. What mattered in the former situation was the prohibition on trespass rather than on the fear of being dislodged from the land. It was the trespass on the part of the Kauravas which the Gandharvas were opposing.

Meat-eating as a regular part of the diet would reinforce the dependence on hunting and pastoralism. Thus the Pāṇḍavas hunt deer to feed themselves and the *brāhmaṇas* who had followed them into the Kāmyaka forest. Draupadī offers a meal of fifty deer together with rabbit, boar and buffalo meat to the kings of Sindhu and Suvīra. It was not only in the privation of forest life that meat was eaten. Even in the didactic sections the practice cannot be condemned out of hand. It is said that under the constellation of Rohini one should gift meat, rice, *ghi,* milk, etc., to brāhmaṇas. Although there is a plea in support of *ahiṃsā* and therefore an attack on the eating of animal flesh, nevertheless it is said that meat if sanctified in accordance with the Vedas can be eaten since animals were created for sacrifice. A list of food items for *srāddha* is given arranged in increasing proportions of gratification to the *pitṛs* as follows: sesame, fish, mutton, hare's flesh, goat, pork, fowl, venison, buffalo, cow, *pāyasa,* the meat of *vadhrināsa* (?), and rhinoceros meat. The rewards for performing the *śrāddhas* are also listed and among these are the obtaining of beautiful wives and children, horses, cattle and other animals, silver and gold, profits in trade, splendour and fame. Curiously land does not figure in the list of wealth and rewards.

In another part of the epic there is a discussion of the places to which pilgrimages should be made. There follows a list of rewards which a person acquires on making such pilgrimages. Most of the rewards are, not surprisingly, intangible, such as going to the worlds of various deities—Soma, Sūrya, Mitra, Viṣṇu, Manu Prajāpati, Varuṇa, Brahma, Śakra, etc. Others are equivalence rewards, where a particular pilgrimage has the same merit as the performance of a sacrifice such as the Agniṣṭoma, *Aśvamedha,* Rājasūya, etc. Such equivalences were perhaps necessary when geographical mobility improved and cult deities had to be accommodated into religious ritual. As far as the more tangible, rewards are concenred they relate mainly to the acquisition of cows and gold and to longevity.

References to agriculture and agricultural processes are relatively infrequent in the narrative sections of the text. In one passage we are told that the peasant ploughs, sows and then waits for the rain to fall. Should the rain fail there is nothing that the peasant can do. The lack of mention of any methods of irrigation connected with agriculture is surprising. Elsewhere there is a specific mention of the need for keeping a sufficient number of tanks full of water in case of drought affecting the harvest, and in times of scarcity providing the farmer with a loan. This latter passage is from a section in which Nārada is defining a well-run state and it would appear to be a didactic section on statecraft. A well-established agrarian economy would compute wealth in terms of fields and grain apart from other items such as animal livestock and gold. There would be references to methods of irrigation to supplement years of poor rainfall. It would also reflect some differentiation in land ownership and among those working on the land. The *Rāmāyaṇa* has many passages referring to the agricultural wealth of Ayodhyā, Kośala and Mithilā, and where the definition of wealth itself refers to grain, orchards and ponds full of water. The early Buddhist literature also includes cultivated fields and grain as wealth and describes methods of irrigation. It also draws a distinction between the owners of land and the cultivators of land where the latter include independent cultivators, hired labourers and slaves. The category of *dāsabhṛtaka* is mentioned both in the context of the household as well as in agricultural work.

Slaves referred to in the *Mahābhārata* are generallys said to have been those captured in war or those reduced to slavery as a result of loss in gambling or those born as such from slave mothers. The overwhelming number appear to have been domestic slaves used for running the household or more often entertaining guests. These are the slaves mentioned in large numbers without name or identification. Those reduced to slavery through gambling or loss of a bet are mentioned by name, as in the story of Kadrū and Vinatā or Devayānī and Śarmiṣṭha. Some seem to serve joint masters such as the couple Gaṇḍā and Paśusakha serving the seven *ṛṣis*. Slaves given as part of a gift or tribute on special occasions are often described in exaggerated figures. Thus Yudhiṣṭhira boasts of a hundred thousand slave girls and the same number of slave men, all employed in entertaining his guests. It is unlikely that he would have had resources sufficient to maintain them. Slaves as tribute are only listed a couple of times and the fact that there were more slave girls than men would emphasise the use of slaves in domestic functions rather than slavery for production whether in agriculture or in mines. The slaves given with their wives may have been used to clear land and bring it under cultivation.

However the use of slaves in this capacity is not alluded to. Even Yudhiṣṭhira when staking his wealth, item by item, does not mention any slaves used on the land. Cultivation was probably still within the confines of the clan and the internal stratification within the clan would demarcate the categories. One of the occasions when a distinction is made between the *dāsa* and the *rājanya* is at the *rājasūya* of Yudhiṣṭhira when the Cedi king accuses *Kṛṣṇa* of being the former and not the latter. But the identification of *Kṛṣṇa* with his clan is not in doubt. The incidence of debt bondage involving land seems rare, the main forms of recruitment to slavery being by capture or by birth. The intensification of agriculture with the use of slaves from outside the clan appears to have been absent. The terms *dāsa, karmakāra* and *bhṛtya* are used as a phrase in one part of the text but in a general sense without specifying the functions of these categories. The context suggests 'dependants' rather than any specific function.

By and large the general hesitancy to store wealth and the constant urging that it be distributed would result in an absence of the kind of surplus associated with intensive agriculture, long-established monarchical systems and professional priests entirely dependent on the community for a living. But this picture begins to give way to a changed economic situation. The gradual change from a pastoral-cum-agricultural economy to one more intensively dependent on land is perhaps most clearly seen in the pattern of gift-giving classified as *dāna*. The pattern is recognisable from a wider range of sources and has been analysed elsewhere, but it becomes apparent ever within the confines of a single text. Two features are particularly noticeable. One is that the material content of *dānas* changes from livestock wealth and gold to land. The second is that the emphasis shifts from widescale distribution of wealth to the bestowal of wealth on deserving brāhmaṇas alone. This may be linked with the growth of professional priests, a body of people exclusively concerned with religion and religious ritual who have little means of support other than *dāna*. Even their professional fees are preferentially described as a form of gift-giving than as wages.

The distribution of wealth during the *rājasūya* of Yudhiṣṭira took the form of feeding the many millions present at the ceremony, of a generous giving of alms, the supporting of eighty-eight thousand *snātakas* each with thirty maidservants and the feeding off gold plate of ten thousand ascetics. In contrast to this, in another part of the epic, the distribution of wealth is strictly limited to deserving brāhmaṇas. The duty of the king is to recite the Vedas, acquire wealth and with this wealth perform sacrifices, since wealth is created for the performance of sacrifices and must be given only to those who are deserving of it. This is a modification on the emphasis on the act of giving with a stress on the legitimacy of the person to whom the gift is made.

Not only is the deserving brahmana now the sole recipient of *dāna* but the amount of *dāna* to be given to him also increases enormously. At the inauguration of the *sabhā* of the Asura Maya, Yudhiṣṭhira gave to each of the ten thousand brāhmaṇas present a sumptuous meal, a new set of clothes and a thousand cows. The Pāṇḍavas performed the sacred rites at the *tīrtha* on the Gomati and gave cows and wealth to the brāhmaṇas. For the attainment of various heavens the gift of a cow or an ox was necessary. But in the Śāntiparvan and the Anuśāsanaparvan various kings are eulogised for their generosity and the figures mentioned are quite staggering. Thus, Bhāgīrathi gave a million women covered with gold ornaments, the same number of chariots each with four horses, a hundred elephants, a thousand horses, a thousand head of cattle and a thousand goats and sheep. Śaśabindu bestowed on the brāhmaṇas at his *Aśvamedha,* a hundred elephants, ten thousand chariots, one million horses, a hundred million cattle and ten billion sheep and goats. Gaya performed the *Aśvamedha* and donated a hundred thousand cattle, many hundreds of mules and covered an area of a hundred cubits by fifty cubits with gold which gold was then given in *dāna*. Sagara gave mansions with golden columns and golden beds and beautiful women. *Dāna* was efficacious not only in ensuring heaven but also in cleansing one of sins. Thus a hundred thousand cows compensated for a *brahmahatyā* and twenty-five thousand Kapilā cows in calf or a hundred Kāmboja horses would cleanse one of all sins. The excessively large figures need not be taken literally. They appear to be stereotypes in the definition of great wealth. What is significant is the increase in the numbers and the constant listing of animal wealth, female slaves and gold. There was also the added emphasis on the appropriateness of the occasion—*śrāddhas* or *yajnas*-when the gift was to be made.

The gradual but growing importance of agriculture becomes more apparent from one part of the text where a new type of *dana* is mentioned, that of donating a tank. It is stated that such a gift merits respect in all three worlds and pleases the gods. The construction of tanks containing water at different times of the year is said to be as meritorious as the performing of sacrifices such as the *agnihotra, agniṣṭoma, atirātra,* and *aśvamedha,* and some are also equivalent to a *dāna* of kine or gold. Associated with the gifting of tanks and water is the merit of planning trees, indicating an increase of agriculture on cleared land with a concern for the availability of water for irrigating during the different seasons. The ideal tank is one in which the water fills during the rains and remains available throughout the year. The intrusion of this type of *dāna* may well be a later interpolation in the text. If this is so then it is more likely to have been an interpolation from areas requiring the use of tanks. It is curious that the building of wells or of *bunds,* both common sources of water supply, are not listed in this important category of donation.

Ultimately there is a section eulogising the gifting of land in which *pṛthvidāna* is described as the best form of *dāna*. It is equivalent to all other gifts of tanks, trees and sacrifices. The rewards are multiple: a heaven full of *apsaras,* rebirth as king and the transcending of all sins. Further, there is an explanation for why land is so superior as a gift. Land is immovable and indestructible, its value is enhanced each time there is a crop (therefore cultivable land is preferable) and it can yield other kinds of wealth such as grain, the nurturing of animals and possibly mineral wealth. It is repeatedly said that only the *kṣatriya* can gift land.

Significantly the gifting of land is included in the didactic section of the text suggestive of the custom being relatively recent and requiring strong moral and religious sanction. That the *kṣatriya* alone could donate land might indicate that the period was one when the *kṣatriya* were land-owners by virtue of being members of land-owning clans. The donation of land by the individual king points to the emergence of the king's rights over land although there is scant evidence of land having become a saleable commodity. Even in the gifting of land the element of potlatch is by no means absent as is clear from the following verse:

māmevādatta māṁ datta māṁ dattvā māṁ avāpsyatha/
asmiṅl loke pare caiva tataś cājanane punaḥ//

5 The Heroic Ideal

> What is action and what inaction?—as to this even the wise are bewildered. I will declare to thee what action is, knowing which thou shall be delivered from evil.—Bhagavad Gita

The Disinterested Act

The values and goals of a society tell us much about its institutions and the ways in which men relate to one another. In this study we are primarily concerned with three goals of ancient Indian society that provide a useful frame of reference for the analysis of Indian social thought and political philosophy. These are religious salvation (which may be achieved in a variety of ways), material gain, and the heroic act. Scientific, aesthetic, and humanistic considerations are relatively less important in shaping Hindu theory, and the ideal of knightly valour, although it was of major significance in the early phases of Indian history and shaped the norm of conduct for the kshatriya class, was to prove incapable of surviving the decline of the tribal policy.

Ancient India had no "citizen" ideal as such, but, as we have seen, one class in Aryan society, the kshatriyas, did have a tradition of political experience. The kshatradharma was basically a martial ideal, from which the concept of the rajanya as protector of the people developed. We turn now to the question of what happened to the old aristocratic values, which appear to be moribund by the beginning of the Christian era. There is no *Heldendāmmerung,* only a paling and dwindling into irrelevance.

In his study of the *Mahabharata,* E.W. Hopkins comments:

> One is too apt to dispose of the general Hindu as Max Müller does with the words: "To the Greek, existence is full of life and reality; to

> the Hindu, it is a dream and a delusion." ..... If we study the coarse, sensual, brutal, strife-loving, blood-hungry Hindu warrior; if we revert to the Vedic ancestor of this ferocious creature, and see what joy in life as life is portrayed in battle-hymn and cattle-hymn, we shall be ready to admit, I think, that through the whole history of the Hindu, from the early Vedic until the pseudo-Epic period, there reigned the feeling, in the larger class of the native inhabitants, that existence is full of life and reality.

Our problem is that this lustier view of life can only be inferred from such sources as the epics, since the brahman editors and compilers were intent on shaping the narrative to their own purposes. The stark anatomy of the hero is discreetly clothed with moralisms; the crude ethos is tempered and muted.

It is sometimes argued that the victory of the Pandavas over the Kauravas in the great battle in the *Mahabharata* is to be interpreted as a pragmatic justification for employing methods of warfare (frequently with divine blessing) that had not yet been reconcil with the traditional code. For at the time of the composition of the epic the political struggle was entering a new phase, and in the work itself the ideals of the military aristocracy are contrasted with the new requirements of Realpolitik. Hopkins holds, and his argument is more convincing, that the moral and spiritual elements are, for the most part, an overlay, and that the bulk of later interpolations in the *Mahabharata*—the *Bhagavad Gita* among them—were intended to excuse the transgressions of ancient heroes who had become models of knightly honour and thus to bring them into conformity with brahman teachings regarding kshatriya duty and the proper behaviour of a king. Later religious feeling, he contends, "was less simple and less pure than the earlier, but the later morality was higher and stricter than that of a former age."

This subsequent ethical concern pervades the epic and is often strikingly at variance with the robust amorality of an earlier and less civilized culture. We are reminded of a similar development in ancient Greece—the transition from the heroic ideal of the Homeric nobility, when the esteem of one's peers was highly valued and honour was the major regulating principle, to the later classical period with its sense of man's impotence and its preoccupation with the dire consequences of hubris. The Aryan invaders were a vigorous, beef-eating, liquor-drinking lot—Indra of the tawny beard and powerful arm, cattle-raider and stormer of citadels, reduced to human proportions. The verses of the *Rigveda* are the hymns of these victorious warriors. But the boasting, life-affirming hero of the Vedic and Homeric ages was to succumb to the god-fearing penitent. In the struggle for power among the gods themselves, the justice-dispensing Varuna and the awesome Rudra are clearly gaining ascendancy.

The persistence of tribal elements in the Indian myth makes the interpretation of legend and symbol difficult. The battle itself, by the time of the epic, must probably be seen as having ritualistic implications. Conflict is in the order of things—or at least is essential to the preservation of that order. This is as true of the sacred world of the gods and the ritual (which perhaps is better understood as a form of combat) as it is of the world of men. It is for this reason that fighting comes to be considered the mission of one segment of the population. This conflict, which may have had early expression in phratry antagonism, assumes an increasingly elaborate symbolic form. Krishna, for example, and his brother Balarāma represent contrary characteristics. Krishna, the trickster, is black; Balarama, the benefactor, is while. But Krishna also embodies both qualities in himself. This ambitendency would seem to be partially explained by the position Krishna occupies, intermediate between the gods and men.[1] He is at once the terrifying demon of the initiation and the initiate.

The eponymous hero, Cornford remarks, "owes his position not merely to his really exceptional character and powers, but to the fact that there already exists a representation, personalized and daemonic, of that super-human *mana* which is recognized as embodied in his individuality......His actual achievements blend with the other glorious acts of tribal history in a composite memory that defies analysis." According to Cornford, this charismatic figure is essentially a *persona,* a representation of the collective genius. He establishes his own norm. For all his later sanctity, Krishna initially appears in legend as such as *ubermensch.* He is often represented as advocating action that would be hard to conceive as virtuous in any sense.

In the earlier portions of the *Mahabharata,* which reflect the Vedic aristocratic mores, the brave knight Arjuna, whose character is taken to represent the kshatriya ideal, slays the warrior Karna, who has been rendered helpless. In the hands of the priests, however,

Indrāvaraja is made the true instigator of the act. Thus the hero is relieved of responsibility and the god is credited with occult reasons for his order. Here, then, was an attempt to explain away the reprehensible.[2] The priests could not call men to a life of virtue and at the same time eulogize those for whom rules meant nothing. The actions of the warriors and princes were governed by a norm, the "Aryan way," which knew no ethical injunction.[3]

No greater shame could befall the warrior than to take flight in the face of the enemy.[4] But he who dies in the field may anticipate heaven: "the path to heaven lies in fighting." The story of Vidulā, in which a cowardly son is reproved by his mother for not discharging his duties as a kshatriya, glorifies the heroic act and the "Aryan way." We are reminded at once of Krishna's famous counsel to Arjuna in the *Bhagavad Gita,* but it is possible and even likely that remarkable and sweeping changes had occurred in the Indian belief system between the two stories.

In the Vedic period man could look forward to a happy postmortal existence in heaven if he lived an acceptable life. Such a prospect had ceased to exist for the ordinary Indian by the seventh and sixth centuries B.C. With the development of the doctrine of the soul's passage to another body at death (samsara), salvation came to be rooted in esoteric knowledge—a gnosis which made possible a kind of magical power over the ends sought by man. Eventually this magical element lost much of its former import, but knowledge remained the basis of control. Knoweledge might be acquired in ways that eliminated even the activity of thought. And where philosophy took as its premise the contrariety of two principles, spirit and matter, the devaluation of the latter would devalue action, the traditional justification of the kshatriya. The heroic ideal yielded to the ideal of the wandering ascetic and the bodhisattva.[5] The term for hero (*vīra*) now comes to be applied to the saint rather than to the man of action.

Responsibility for the change does not lie solely with Buddhism,[6] though this is an explanation popular among historians. The depreciation of the assertive and heroic is symptomatic of a general religiosity that pervaded Indian society—a phenomenon that was very probably related to the erosion of older communal ties. Now, in the society reconstituted along functional lines taken to represent degrees of purity, when Krishna advises the reluctant Arjuna to join his fellow warriors in battle he is justifying the tasks necessary for the preservation of the social order, although they may be morally tainted.

The hero of the epic is already a different person from the warrior of the *Ṛigveda*. The proud knight is not afraid to contend with the gods themselves; "to him they are unreal; to him even the new god is but a myth of fancy... The knight's acts are his own; his reward is his own making; his sin is self-punished. Fate, or the embrace of Death; Duty, or to follow the paths of custom—these are his only moral obligation. His supernatural is understood too little to be true; or it is debased to incantation and witchcraft. The knight of our present poem stands on the borderline between two faiths." In the *Mahabharata* the impersonal force, *daivam,* had begun to replace the old Vedic deities in importance: "Fate I deem the highest thing; manliness is no avail." This theme punctuates the epic, suggesting the new influences at work. However, the older, more positive approach to the world did not yield without a struggle, as the following lines from the *Shantiparva* indicate: "Do not fear the results of karma, rely on your strength... all things belong to the man who is strong." Words like these are taken to anticipate the power philosophy of the *Arthashastra*. It would be as accurate to say that they look back to the "Aryan way."

The emphasis on punishment (danda) as that which ensures the constancy of the universe presupposes the projection into the supernatural realm of man's demand for justice. The gods had originally been viewed as jealous of their honour, resentful of any slight (as was the Vedic hero himself), but not preoccupied with considerations of justice. The emergent sense of justice, with its political manifestation in the concept of danda—which supported the social order as the sacrifice ensured the cosmic order—culminated in the idea of inherited guilt. The sins of this life are punished in the next. The sinful might prosper, but the reckoning would come. This doctrine serves the purposes of the eschatological aspects of the Semitic theologies. The beginnings of a sense of sin, with the concomitant heightening of sensations of guilt, may be observed in the increasing prominence of the mysterious Varuna, guardian of Rita and the major ethical deity in the Vedic pantheon. The conception of Varuna is essentially theistic. Nothing could be concealed from him, and he could not be bribed by the sacrifice. He inspired dread and awe, which distinguished his power from that of other early Vedic gods.[7] He could even inflict punishment for the sins of the father. But though merciless in his loathing of sin, he was on occasion moved to compassion.

This developing awareness of human helplessness and utter dependence on an arbitrary power is noticeable also in the growing significance of the later Vedic god Rudra, who has much in common with Indra but lacks his more appealing qualities. The great wielder of the thunderbolt, who had been the example for the Aryan warrior, had never inspired the fear that Rudra was able to evoke. Rudra, like his early counterpart, was beyond good and evil. But whereas Indra shared many human weaknesses, Rudra was a distant figure never entirely comprehensible to men. In the twilight of the vedic age the gods had lost their humanity, and not until devotional religion introduced a more positive element into the mainstream of Indian belief did the divinities take on an attractiveness comparable to that of the early Vedic gods. Unlike the gods of the Greek epic, those of the *Mahabharata* do not comfort and assist the epic warrior. They are active in man's behalf only in the stories of the Vedic past that have been incorporated into the narrative. Krishna's intervention (in the *Gita*) is evidence of the impact of later devotional and theistic religious thought.[8]

Implicit in the epic is a debate over the ability of personal valour and prowess, the heroic quality (*vīrya*), to combat the force of destiny (*kāla*). Those who take the determinist position hold that the hero is made by the age. If the times are not with him, the man of courage and virtue will be swept away. Man is impotent against fate. In discussing a problem of this kind it is always difficult to be sure that one is not reading too much of the modern world into the remote past. The ancient Indian, like the Greek knight of the Homeric age, may have distinguished action of a volitional nature from actions subject to a power beyond the actor—such as a divine agency or even the restraints of family and class relationships. In the Greek epic the hero experiences a strange infusion of energy (*menos*), fortifying his spirit and increasing his strength. This energy appears to be of a somewhat vagrant nature, but to the ancients—the Aryan aristocracy as well as the Homeric heroes—it is the gift of the gods.[9] This intervention of the gods had diminished to relative insignificance by the time the main body of the *Mahabharata* was composed. But theistic developments and the eventual humanizing of the gods were to encourage a return to the concept of divine intervention. Although the god is generally regarded as aloof, avatars (extensions of the divine essence) appear on earth from time to time in moments of crisis. Krishna bestowed the superhuman power on the kshatriya Arjuna, just as the spirit of the Lord came to Samson in his hour of need. Thus does fatalism come to be modified. The Krishna story may well be an attempt to locate the source of kshatriya strength in moral and supernatural agencies, but religion had at this time evolved beyond the more primitive device of ritualistic control of the supernatural as exercised by the brahmans.

In India access to this mysterious potency had once been the province of the priests, who acted as link between the gods and man. But fate itself (daivam) seems to have been immune to prayer and spell, a force superior to the gods and one that defied personification. Attempts to circumvent the priestly power had to transcend the Vedic pantheon, which was so intimately connected with the sacrifice and the magical formulas of the brahmans. The impersonal daivam—Zimmer's "godly essence"—is encountered when the "comforting illusion of the magical tradition" has been thrown off. Man apparently had no choice but to seek the transformation of the mundane self, neutralizing the power of destiny by becoming as one with the universe, the essence of which is daivam. The *Gita* and the doctrine of the personal god offer an alternative to this philosophy or resignation and renunciation.[10]

The *Bhagvad Gita,* which is generally held to have attained its final form in the first or second century before Chist, is considered the first major attempt to bring together heterodox doctrine (based on the dichotomy of matter and spirit and the exalting of spirit through discipline) and the later Vedic concept of the transcendent eternal One.[11] Certain religious innovators of the time had begun to regard sin as a condition of will, challenging the older idea of inherited guilt, which was closely linked to brahman ritual purification. Motive and conscience take on new importance as the moral element threatens to replace the supernatural, and fear of magical pollution gives way to a sense of individual responsibility. This development, however, is not enough in itself to explain the poem, which has become the very cornerstone of Hinduism. Krishna calls for action prescribed by one's "calling," but unhampered by the sense of personal accountability. hishma's counsel to Yudhishthira is recalled in the words of the divine charioteer: "Verily the renunciation of any duty that ought to be done is not right." Warfare, for Arjuna and the kshatriya caste he represents, is a sacred charge sanctioned by the other of things. Society functions properly only when each group fulfils its obligations. Those who allow themselves to be controlled by lust and hatred become the victims of their own action. "He who is free from self-sense, whose understanding is not sullied, through he slay these people, he slays not nor, is he bound (by his actions)." Action is called for, even though it brings death and destruction, and fatalistic withdrawal is rejected.[12] The spirit is not slain when the body dies.

This famous poem of the sixth book of the *Mahabharata* was perhaps originally intended as the exhortation to the common soldier who lacked kshatriya motivation. The hesitation of the knight Arjuna, who has never before in the epic given any hint of such sensitivity, provides the occasion for a sermon on duty. Death, he is told, is preferable to defeat—or, put more strongly, the highest duty of the warrior is death in battle. This device was used by later philosophers to popularize Hindu theistic doctrine, and it was evidently acceptable to the brahmans because it provided a further justification of class differentiation and harnessed kshatriya dharma to religious conceptions. Such theistic sects as the Bhāgavatas, which directly influenced the *Gita*, did not break completely with orthodoxy, and it was not difficult to conceive of their deity as an emanation of the supreme principle of Brahmanism.

The *Gita* directs mystical experience away from contemplation and towards action, from esoteric knowledge to exoteric activity. And yet it is an exhortation against egoism, ambition, and greed, calling for the rejection of individuality as a value in itself and of the world as possession. Krishna asks that everything a man does be done as an offering to him. The fruits of action are dedicated to God; they must therefore not be cherished by man. The philosophic poem thus offers an alternative to the world-renouncing ascetic ideal of the monks who severs his ties with everything that might distract him from his true ends. Worldly activity is valued in the *Gita* as long as it is not motivated by selfish desire. Motive was emphasized: man could find his salvation through disinterested action. It was not necessary to forsake the world in order to attain moksha. The *Bhagavad Gita* contends that man is in the world, though not of it.[13] "Out of attachment comes desire; from desire, fury and violent passion" and ultimately the ruin of man. Living life in a mood of devotion to God, accepting but not attaching oneself to action leads finally to escape from karma. And so man is to accept and fulfil his duty without ever desiring that which does not have enduring worth. "Think of nothing but the act, never its fruits, and do not be seduced by inaction"—this is the message of Krishna. In this anti-materialism the physical body itself, the very instrument of action, is discounted and devalued.

Caste gains in religious significance in such a philosophy, while, at the same time, the promise of salvation is offered to every man who leads a life of detachment, pursuit of caste obligation, and devotion to God. Krishna holds out the hope of salvation even to the shudra who turns to him. There is, however, some confusion in the poem as to whether deliverance can be attained in this life or only after death, and, if the latter, whether the soul must ascend the ladder of varna as the condition of salvation. Nor is it entirely clear whether man is sometimes or always the instrument of divine will, whether he is determined in his actions by his character, or free to choose the path of righteousness. Radhakrishnan interprets verse XVIII, 63 ("Thus has wisdom more secret than all secrets, been declared to thee by Me. Reflect on it fully and do as thou choosest") as meaning that Krishna is concerned that each man come to God by his own choice. Radhakrishnan compares this emphasis on man's freedom to decide for himself with the position of Duns Scotus: "since freedom of will is God's command, even God has no direct influence on mans decision. man can cooperage with God's grace but he can also refrain from it."

The attitude of enlightenment that marks the highest stage of self-realization may well reflect a doctrine older than the more "democratic" concept of devotion (bhakti), the love of the redeemer. Both knowledge and devotion are accepted means to salvation. Knowledge (jñāna) represents what Professor Sircar refers to as the Absolutist view, and has as its goal absorption in the Absolute. Bhakti, the service of God and communion with him, is the Theist view. The appeal of the poem is both intellectual and emotional. But the combination makes for certain difficulties. The Supreme Being in the *Gita* is aloof and unconcerned (here the Absolutist view would seem to dominate the conception of God). Nevertheless Krishna describes himself as constantly active—and his action must inspire a similar activity in man ("there is nothing which I must get, and yet I labour forever"). The Lord does not demand the immediate allegiance of all men, and he is tolerant of many ways of expressing worship. Each persons, in fulfilling the prescribed social obligations of his varna in a spirit of equanimity, worships God. Thus we find in the *Gita* an effective middle way between the passive, detached life (*nivṛtti*) and the energetic, worldly existence (*pravṛtti*).

The ideal of conduct recommended by Krishna could be described as asceticism of this world, and is comparable in some respects to the Calvinist ethic. Karma-Yoga, the ethical principle at the root of the *Gita,* demands that the individual pursue his "calling,"[14] the vocation that has come to be understood as a kind of commission from God: "Be thou nought but my tool." As in Calvinism, man's actions serve to glorify God. The *Gita* counsels man to act without becoming personally involved in the action; Calvinism, without consuming wealth in self-indulgence. Sensualism is condemned in both theologies, but the *Gita* goes beyond this to discourage any accumulation of wealth or power that would lead man away from his true interest. Man is to act without seeking success. Calvin says simply that "we will only follow such fortune as we may enjoy with innocence." The cumulative effect of the Protestant doctrine and its theory of predestination as worked out by Calvin was to lead its adherents to find in worldly success the sign of salvation. This is a major distinction between the two systems of religious thought. In the doctrine of Krishna we do not find the uncertainty of salvation that contributed to the psychological consequences of Calvinism which so interested Weber. In fact, it is the *certitudo salutis* that makes salvation possible. And, too, work has less value in and of itself in the *Gita:* Calvinism emphasizes the moral value of work, whereas in the Hindu poem it is work of moral value that is stressed. Like Calvinism, the teaching of the *Gita* —though influenced by the kshatriya ethos—is a rejection of much that we associate with the aristocratic way of life, such as indulgence, leisure, and the cultivation of mind for its own sake. But action is not to be directed towards specific goals in which the individual has a personal interest; it is anything but the expedient rationality of the bourgeois.

The Rationalized Act

Although the territorial state represented a revolutionary departure from the tribal polity, the organizational model employed by the theorists of the new state (the authors of the Arthashastra literature) borrowed images associated with the Aryan tribe—particularly the kshatriya ideal of the active man. But the kshatriya was always more the hero than the achiever, and in this sense the ideal of the selfless man depicted in the Gita is not a radical departure from the traditional figure of the knight. He is more political man than economic man. The Vedic hero, the man of action for its own sake, could never satisfy the requirements of the state, which, in this interlude between the simple and direct relationship of family, clan, and tribal leaders and the frozen pluralism of caste regulation, depended on a corps of administrative officials whose dominant loyalty would be to the state, but whose values would be more appropriate to its material interests. It may be said that the *Gita* and the philosophical currents it contains are an attempt to civilize the knight and turn his energies to the larger goals of the community. But it remained for such theories as Kautalya to emphasize achievement and to declare that artha (material gain) was the fundamental principle of society.

in Vedic times warfare had been the sport of kings, the means of fulfilling the kshatriya duty and attaining glory and honour. The traditional literature on caste function continued to view war as its own justification, a positive good in itself and intrinsic to kshatriya dharma. by the age of empire (and implicit in the *Arthashastra* of Kautalya), war had ceased to be regarded as an aristocratic pastime having as its main objective military flory, and had come to be conceived as an instrument for strengthening the state and enriching its treasury. War is now serious business, not to be undertaken lightly and without weighing carefully the probabilities of success and defeat. The kshatriya ideal of honour in battle and the discounting (and even disparaging) of material profit were undoubtedly hindrances to empire-building. Traditionally the annexation of territory had not been approved, and conquest was not generally regarded as a means to power and wealth. The chakravartin (*cakravartin*) was regarded as the greatest of kings, the overlord, and not as the head of a comprehensive state controlled directly from the capital. This ancient ideal of *dharmavijaya,* "righteous conquest" or war motivated by considerations of glory rather than by material gain, is as old as the Vedas and has an important place in the *Mahabharata.* But this ideal was little esteemed by the ambitious architects and rulers of Magadha, the Gangetic state that was to become the core of the great Mauryan empire. Nor could the antimaterialism of heterodoxy and those sects whose beliefs eventually found expression in the *Gita* have been of political value to these statesmen except insofar as it represented a challenge to brahman power and encouraged a tractable population.

Kautalya retained the kshatriya ideal of action, but opposed the disinterested action idealized in religious theories that consider desire and acquisition responsible for the evils of the world.[15] Kautilya must be understood as attempting to liberate the heroic ideal from the debilitating influences of religion and from the older noble preoccupation with honour as the goal of action (which threatened to degenerate into idleness and superficiality as the knight's role became that of courtier). Although his image of man appears often to be close to the vaishya, Kautalya was not a champion of the lower orders of society. The *Arthashastra* quotes (for purposes of refutation) a statement to the effect that if one must choose between losing noble men or losing vulgar men, the latter is more serious in that it causes obstruction to work. No, Kautalya answers, "it is possible to recruit vulgar men since they form the majority of the people; for the sake of vulgar men nobles should not be allowed to perish; one in a thousand may or may not be a noble man; he it is who is possessed of excessive courage and wisdom and is the refuge of vulgar people." Nobility, it would seem from this, is a quality of character rather than of birth, but the brahman minister was too committed to class ideology to have been convinced that noble virtues would often appear among the lower classes. If he was in truth Chandragupta's minister, the possibility of the low birth of his master may account for the manner of expression. A number of passges from the *Mahabharata* state explicitly that the hero is made by the occasion and not simply born to the role. He who offers protection is king.

Kautalya, like Machiavelli (with whom he is frequently compared), combined a pessimistic view of man's nature with a belief that man can shape his own destiny if he is able to develop heroic stature and place the common good above private interest. In *The Prince,* Machiavelli speaks of a strange force, which he calls *fortuna.* He does not permit this force to justify pessimism and inaction. *Virtu* is, for him, the supreme value, and virtue—the ability to translate plans and ideas into practice—is man's response to fortuna. This courage and energy necessary for effective action are the essence of Kshatra, the distinguishing trait of the warrior and ruling caste in India. It is this quality that Kautalya saw as the antidote to the fatalism, passivity, and renunciation of the belief systems of his day. He, too, sees nature as fortuna (*śrī*) and life as the interplay between virtu and contingency. The rules of the battle (the image is extended to life itself) are those which the occasion dictates to the shrewd. Instead of action without regard for its results, we have action without regard for fate. Fatalism persists in Kautalya's world-view, but it is not resignation. This attitude is reflected in his somewhat cavalier regard for transcendent values. Man must supplement virtue with organization in order to preserve and extend the victories over fortuna and thus secure the social framework that moral virtues presuppose. In this Kautalya seems to agree that "the king is the maker of his age." The *Mahabharata* is often even more candid than Kautalya: "Right proceeds from might. . . . Right is itself devoid of command."

The *Gita* admits that although man may act with detachment, without self-interest, and in faithful pursuance of duty, he can never be certain of the consequences of his actions nor even of the meaning of the act. He can never know what chain of action and reaction has been set in motion. (Hence philosophy throughout the ages has warned of the dangers of entanglement and advised man to be wary of the illusion of freedom.) Krishna, knowing that "all undertakings are enveloped by evil, as is fire by smoke," asks only that every act be of the nature of worship. Kautalya is no less aware of the moral ambiguity of action. This ambiguity is especially apparent in the problem that the collectivity faces when it insists on its sovereignty yet judges the actions of the state by standards which exist for individual citizens who, by nature of their membership in the community, cannot claim such independence. Preoccupied as he was with a grand design for creating the basis of imperial power, Kautalya, the brahman counsellor, could have no sympathy for a metaphysics such as Buddhism, which was interpreted as advocating nonaction and withdrawal as the condition for preserving the true freedom of man. (Ashoka, master of India, could afford to renounce war—but even so, we have no record of Ashoka's disbanding his army.[16] And later kings who embraced Buddhism or Jainism did not reject war as an instrument of policy as Ashoka had done.)

Kautalya understood that distinterested action, such as that represented by the chivalric or Krishnaite ideal, could not build strong organisations, and that to renounce action altogether was to renounce the real world. His systematic theory in effect brings together the idealization of action, the concept of self-discipline (which had reached its fullest development in heterodoxy), the rajadharma tradition a strong statement of the artha position ("on material gain depends the realization of dharma and desire"), and the matsyanyaya[17] view of nature. What is new is the shaping of these concepts to the needs of the territorial state; the relating of economic, military, and religious models to the requirements of political institutions and political conduct; and the pervasive worldiness that tends to exalt the vaishya material function—merging the aristocratic ideal of action with the virtue of production, and even applying the fabrication image to political activity, as Plato and Machiavelli do.

Kautalya must have disregarded his fellow brahmans as those who must implement ideas and proceed by a "sense of the situation" reject those who remain in the pure world of images that need never entirely conform to reality. In Greek philosophy, however, contemplation and fabrication appear to have had an affinity that may be illustrated by Plato's craftsman who is guided by the "idea" of the object he creates—an idea that he imitates in the process of fabrication. Contemplation is thus tied to the creative experience and the transformation of external reality; when applied to the political realm the image serves to justify the authority of the expert and to locate the source of authority in the supernatural. We might speculate that the great brahman, inspired with the idea of empire, ultimately reconciled his own traditional function with the requirements of state-building in a similar fashion. As Plato sought to preserve philosophy, so Kautalya knew that the brahmans, if they were to survive, must relate their roles more realistically to the complexities of political life.

It is worth recalling Professor Voegelin's suggestion that the abstract cosmic principle of China and the less complex symbolism it in fact made possible contributed to a conception of social order dependent not on the emperor alone (as Son of Heaven), but on councillors and bureaucrats as well. Instead of being projected into the cosmic order, political events were confined to the area of human activity—which was conceived in terms of power and conflict, a model inappropriate to the impassive transcendent realm. If this hypothesis is valid, we might ask whether the triumph of the Mauryan secular administration in the later fourth and third centuries B.C. may not have had some philosophical relation to the emergence in Indian culture of a comparable cosmic principle several hundred years earlier. The conception of a soul or "self" seeking identification with the cosmic force left the ritualistic sacrifice far behind.

But the bureaucrat acquired a charismatic quality only toward the end of the Mauryan epoch, and then it was hardly comparable to that of the Confucian scholar. In India, it was rather a case of justifying material and secular ends as important in their own right, legitimate human pursuits that the increasing differentiation of the cosmic and human realms may have indirectly encouraged. And when salvation had become more distinctly a private affair, the state was allowed a freer scope for its activities that could have been the case in the age of brahman supremacy.

A clearly perceived tension between sacred and profane could produce either the spirit of world-renunciation and asceticism or the frank acceptance of the contrary demands of the two levels of existence. Other ancient Oriental empires were established before such a differentiation took place, and in India a vestige of the older amalgamation of the religious and the political survived in the concept of the chakravartin or *sarvābhauma,* the world emperor, whose role was analogous to that of the ruler of the cosmic order.[18] In the Christian era new invasions from the Northwest tended to restore the older cosmological analogy—with new implications for the theory of the king's divinity.[19]

As organisation (in the sense of arrangements entered into by men for the accomplishment of specific purposes) spreads into more and more areas of social life, we might expect that the "historical imagination" would begin to capture the minds of men. The sociological and philosophical are linked in the awareness of man's new capacity for controlling forces external to himself and achieving definite objectives through a hierarchical system of command and co-ordination—as compared to his former dependence on the magically induced correspondence of the political order with the natural order. The belief in the efficacy of united effort encouraged man to see new possibilities in his environment: the world need not be the same tomorrow as it is today. The cyclical view of time is thus tempered. Once the nobles became involved in actual state-making, moulding a portion of the world to their purposes, the universe began to lend itself to human comprehension in ways that would not have appeared possible in the age when the power to transform was attributed to the gods alone. Thought loses its esoteric character and becomes instrumental to action.

The theory is complicated by the fact that there are two basic types of organisation reflecting two goals that are present in varying degrees in every ordered collectivity. Where the attainment of a particular objective (the winning of a battle, the making of a decision, the production of a commodity, and so forth) is of major importance, a sense of the future emerges, a feeling of expectation and, commonly, of optimism. These are responses not generally associated with the cyclical view of time, based as it is on the concept of the eternal return. But where the organisation is more concerned with its own survival and the maintenance of its equilibrium—goals which eclipse the express purposes that were its original justification, or which persist after those purposes have been achieved—we are confronted with a different situation.[20] This is the problem that Michels, believing such a transformation of means into ends to be the inevitable fate of all social organisation, termed in its political aspect the "iron law of oligarchy."

During the change from "instrumental" organisation to that type in which integrative needs and mechanisms are given a higher priority than the mobilization of facilities to accomplish a specific purpose,[21] we may observe important modifications in the structure of authority. Authority is less likely to be based on rational knowledge, expert skill, or extraordinary power of some kind, than on the fact of incumbence in office. And as *dux* becomes *rex,* as the "representative" tribal organisation gives way to the "punishment-centered" state, the purposes of the ruling elite diverge from those of the other members of the collectivity. With this dissensus in ends, obedience comes to be stressed for its own sake. Formerly, values and shared purposes made possible noncoercive types of socialization and social control. In the later development, the integrative requirement of organisation can no longer be ignored. There are now different purposes or claims to be related and reconciled. This amounts to saying that dharma must be supplemented with danda; punishment is necessary to bring the purposes of one part of the community into line with the purposes of the other.

The empires of ancient Persia that may have inspired Kautalya were often extensively bureaucratized (as in the case of the Achaemenid state), but they functioned less as agencies for the realization of the collective purposes of the people than as "punishment-centered" bureaucracies intent largely on their own perpetuation and aggrandizement. In such a structure the empire comes to be seen as universal in the scope of its authority, and the king seeks to derive (tautologically) his authority from his own exalted position in society and its correspondence with that of the chief of the gods.[22] The cosmological style of symbolization finds its fullest expression. The conservative ideological implications of the cosmological-correspondence symbolization are generally congenial with the interests of the ruling groups.

This type of organisation, which stresses the integrative elements necessary to the survival of the collectivity, is personified in the brahman, whose function is largely equilibrating and whose concern is the preservation of order. But the brahmans could offer little in the way of organizational concepts, and the priests did not represent a positive affirmation of worldly existence. Ironically it was a kshatriya who figured as the most influential force in the triumph of the spirit of quiescence and the sacralizing of experience, and who stood in a relationship to the brahmans as did the world-decrying prophet to the magisterial technician-priests. When a disciple of the Buddha, the emperor Ashoka, adopted the new religion as an appropriate basis for the organismic state, the importance of organisation must have become apparent to the brahmans. And now as different religious ideals began to compete with the traditional ideology for the king's favour, the brahmans were forced into closer collaboration with the ruling clique—in what amounted to a return to the ancient partnership in the sacrifice of officiating brahman and sponsoring king.

The role of the brahman had become that of legitimating the royal power and harmonizing the diverse interests of social groups. Whereas the function of the sacrifice had been to ensure victory, the later collaboration of *regnum* and *sacerdotium* in Hindu culture guaranteed the caste division of rights and duties. Caste ultimately replaced the system of ministers, officials, and superintendents as the major regulating mechanism. This was the concluding phase of the evolution of control from the tribal struggles for hegemony and the competitive operations of incipient capitalism, later rationalized in the imperial bureaucracy and state controls over the economy, to a system that distributed social functions on the basis of birth into certain social stations. The state had become the punishment-wielding power, ensuring that the order remained "self-regulating". By the beginning of the Christian era, the shoots of capitalist enterprise had withered and all but died.

What remained of the more virile culture of the Vedic age was the idea of the exceptional man who is able to remake the world—the "historical man" who emerges to save the dharmic order from whatever decay may be at work in the structure. This is the avatar or chakravartin, who retires into legend once the cosmic order is re-established. Never was the point reached where a whole people came to be regarded as having a historical mission, as happened in ancient Israel.

Archaic man, as Eliade remarks, when "placed between accepting the historical condition on the one hand, and his reidentification with modes of nature on the other . . . . would choose such a reidentification." In the transition from the archaic to the cosmological, the modes of nature had perhaps become less "natural", a society regulated mainly by kinship and tribal norms and the ideals of the heroic culture was eventually replaced, not by a rational administration designed to develop and co-ordinate the resources of society for the realization of collective goals, but by what we might call the "integrative" organisation, which saw itself, if not as a replica of the cosmos as such, as least as the embodiment of the moral principle embedded in the cosmic order. It was the complete triumph of the organisational concept over the political. The state itself had paled into relative insignificance by the later Gupta period. The oligarchic tribal polity, that still flourished at the time of the Buddha, was a political structure in which a representative segment of the community participated in making decisions, and an appreciable number were treated as the social equals of those in positions of power. The new forms of integration, the territorial state and caste stratification, were hierarchical; no longer was there a place for the older political arrangements. Kautalya sought a centralized government by experrts; caste represented a return to a traditionalist type of legitimation.[23]

All of this is relevant because of the central importance for our study of the centuries from the close of the Vedic period to the establishment of Magadha as the most powerful state in India. In this period the rudimentary forms and processes of capitalism made their appearance and there was a systematic attempt to build a rational bureaucracy for the purpose of unifying the Gangetic plain and, ultimately, all of Aryan India. The development of the organisational apparatus by the Mauryans and their ministers made possible a centralization of control that had never been known before. And the organisation, when it succeeded in eliminating the contingencies of the world, left the hero without his stage[24] Virtu is dependent on fortuna.

History also becomes irrelevant as men approach the organisational utopia. There remains only a need for the administration of things (as Lenin put it). In the process men themselves tend to become things. Their actions are less the expression of their personality than the necessary responses to the requirements of the system. Achievement and performance have taken the place of the expressive symbolism of the act. Man stands apart from his own action—as though he had acquired the psychological consequences of the message of the *Gita* without the ethical content that justifies such alienation.

In India the heroic ideal revived from time to time, particularly under the Rajputs, who typified kshatriya values, and, in the seventeenth century, with the martial programmes of the Marathas and Sikhs. But soteriology, class solidification, and the imperatives of polity had crippled the ancient ideal irreparably. In the imperial state, which we turn to now, there was no longer a place for the old heroic ideal apart from the purposes of the state.

REFERENCES

1. "It is exactly this indeterminateness in his dealings with gods and men which constitutes one of the outstanding features of the culture-hero." (Josselin de Jong, "The Origin of the Divine Trickster." cited in Held (171), p. 175).

2. Cf. *Apastamba Dharmasutra* II. 6.13. 8-10, where we find the passage: "Transgression of the law and violence are found amongst the ancient (sages). They committed no sin on account of the greatness of their lustre. A man of later times who seeing their (deeds) follows them, falls." Buhler (*Sacred Books of the East,* II. xvii) comments that "these utterances prove that Apastamba considered himself a child of the Kali Yuga, the age of sin, during which, according to Hindu notions, no rishis can be born."

3. Of the Bantus of Kavirondo, an African tribe dependent, as were the Aryans, on cattle-raiding, it has been remarked that "the fact that the

two ultimate motives in warfare were the raiding of cattle and the conquest of territory has a definite bearing upon the conduct of warfare, as it involves conflicting aims. While it lies in the interest of expansion to carry on aggression in a ruthless manner which drives the enemy away as far as possible, the aim of raiding cattle clearly requires the presence of enemy groups in the neighbourhood. Owing to the necessity of balancing these two aims, warfare tended to be conducted with certain restrictions, above all with provisions for terminating a period of hostilities and with generally observed rules regarding the treatment of slain warriors and of women and children. Such 'rules of warfare' were more pronounced in the conduct of hostilities between the various Bantu groups than between Bantu and non-Bantu." (Fortes and Evans-Pritchard (125), p. 228.). Possibly it was to the economic advantage of the Aryan clans to impose similar limitations on the conduct of hostilities.

4. We may surmise that, for all the talk about honour and duty, courage may also have been nourished by the fear of the consequences that awaited the deserter, who might even be put to the flame. (*Vide Shantiparva 97* 22). In such a culture public humiliation can be a very dreadful thing.

5. A sociologist would describe this as the shift from performance to learning. In the former, the change in the situation exceeds that in the individual, whereas the learning experience can be said to produce a greater change in the individual than in the situation in which he operates.

6. Professor Kosambi, for example, refuses to hold Buddhism responsible for the relative lack of what he calls the "poetry of prowess" in later Indian literature. Many Buddhist kings pursued militant policies. We might question whether Buddhism led to an externalization of inner conflict, as Kosambi suggests, and whether, if it did, it should have "made intercourse within a society smoother." ([220], p. xiv n.)

7. *Vide Rigveda* VII, 89. Basham has compared the sense of humility and guilt that Varuna inspired with the sentiments expressed in the penitential psalms of the Old Testament. ([24], p. 237.)

8. Although often considered an Upanishad, the *Gita* differs from the Upanishads in that it is a revelation of a system of ethics by a god— rather than a mystery that the teacher transmits and comments upon.

9. Theognis, Dorian elegist and champion of courage and discipline, bemoaned the fact that more depended on a man's daemon than on his character. Fortitude availed little if the daemon was inferior.

10. Of the Hindu literature available to us, the *Bhagavad Gita* is without doubt the best known work. The title of the poem comes from Krishna's designation in the Bhagavata religion as Sri Bhagavan. Krishna's

message incorporates much of the Bhagavata creed. The name of the author of the work is lost to us, but many commentators believe that the *Gita* is an elaboration of the advice of an actual Krishna, as the similarity to the teaching of Ghora Angirasa, the teacher of Krishna, in the *Chandogya Upanishad,* suggests.

Readers of the poem are sometimes confused by Krishna's attempt to incite the warrior Arjuna to violent action. But Krishna is not defending war as such, and Arjuna is advised to fight always without passion or meanness. Life in this world must be accepted, but man must try to improve the world where possible—and he must understand that the concerns of this world are never more than a means to a higher end. It may be helpful to recall the story of Brahma's grandsons in the *Vishnu Bhagavata* (VI. 5). The youths were instructed by their father, Daksha, in the life of action. But Narada taught the young men (15,000) in number) the path of renunciation as the preferable way of life. Daksha argued that the pursuit of earthly things must precede the life of the spirit. Men have obligations to the community and the race that must be fulfilled—the ashrama of the householder must come before that of the recluse. Sensory phenomena cannot be rejected as being of trivial importance until they are first discovered and understood. Dharma is of prime significance, but artha and kama must not be ignored.

11. Cf. Zimmer (441), pp. 378ff.; scholars do not agree on whether the Sankya system or Vedantic monism is the dominant influence in the Bhagavata creed and in the *Gita*. Radhakrishnan describes the work as both metaphysics and ethics: "*brahmavidya* and *yogashastra,* the science of reality and the art of union with reality." (Radhakrishnan [327], p. 12.) It may be said that it provides a bridge between Hindu metaphysics and our study of political thought—which is, in the final analysis, concerned with the problem of action.

12. Much of that attitude of mind that Max Weber considered the psychological (rather than logical) consequence of Calvinism is more or less explicit in the *Gita*. Although fundamentally a fatalist, Kautalya, the designer of the bureaucratic state, warns against defeatism and what we might call the psychology of determination.

13. Hannah Arendt's discussion of Plato is of interest here because the predicament she claims existed for Plato is parallel in many respects to that of the *Gita*. "It is essential to remember that the element of rule, as reflected in our present concept of authority so tremendously influenced by Platonic thinking, can be traced to a conflict between philosophy and politics, but not to specifically political experiences. That is, experiences immediately derived from the realm of human affairs. one cannot understand Plato without bearing in mind both his repeated emphatic insistence on the philosophic irrelevance of this realm, which

he always warned should not be taken too seriously, and the fact that he himself, in distinction to nearly all philosophers who came after him, still took human affairs so seriously that he changed the very centre of his thought to make it applicable to politics. But the rule of the philosopher-king and the domination of human affairs by something outside its own realm are demanded precisely because, from the standpoint of philosophy as well as the philosopher, under no circumstances must they acquire a dignity of their own." ("What Was Authority?" in Friedrich [133], pp. 93i.)

14. "It is well known that the Middle Ages conceived of society as an order fashioned by God in which every form of life, every estate, every profession, had its own ethico-religious ideal to which the individual had to adapt himself if he wished to be obedient to God. But it is only after Protestantism unequivocally condemned monasticism that this ideal passed into the foreground as a norm of life subordinate to none other." (Carlo Antoni, *From History to Sociology,* transl. Hayden White [Detroit, 1959], pp. 154f.) The condemnation of monasticism had its counterpart in the *Gita's* reaction to world-renouncing asceticism. A difference exists, of course, in that the calling is prescribed by the class into which one is born. Weber, in his study of Indian religion, does not attempt a comparison of the *Gita* with the Calvinist ethic, but inasmuch as he considers such religious movements as Buddhism to represent a variety of asceticism diametrically opposed to that of calvinism, it is instructive to examine the teaching of the *Bhagavad Gita* (critical as it is of many fundamentals of Buddhist doctrine) in terms of the analysis Weber [424] employed in his discussion of the Calvinist mentality. The following comments differ from Weber's treatment of Calvinism in that they are necessarily confined to the content of the poem itself rather than to the effect of the doctrine on those who responded to its inspiration. Weber's analysis dealt not with Calvin's theology but with the mentality it helped to form.

15. R.E. Hume ([187], p. 59 n. 1) holds that the *Katha Upanishad* II, 20 and 23f. (cf. *Muṇḍaka Upanishad* III, 2.3). and the *Svetāśvatara Upanishad* represent a foreshadowing of the strict Calvinist doctrine of election—a reaction to the typical Upanishadic doctrine of salvation through knowledge. Verse 20 (second valli) of the *Kaṭha Upanishad* is one of the first expressions of the idea of grace (*prasāda*), though the conception appears in *Rigveda* X, 125.5. It might be mentioned that the *Kaṭha* verse follows two which are identical with *Bhagavad Gita* II, 19f.

16. *Arthashastra* I. 19 (p. 41): "Prosperity depends on effort. . . . readiness is the king's vow." (The page references are to the second edition of the Shama Sastri translation [Mysore, 1923]) *Vide* pp. 196f. below.

17. *Vide*, pp. 369f. below.

18. The Great Rock Edict no. 10 is evidence of the emperor's attempt to replace the ideal of valour with that of piety, which was considered to be attainable by all but was thought to be more difficult for those of high status to attain.

19. The world belongs to the strong—literally, the law (*nyāya*) of the fishes (*mātsya*).

20. Even here Achaemenid influence may have been more important than Indian tradition.

"After the Mauryan state collapsed, a hierarchical quasi-feudal structure took its place. Though we must exercise a certain caution in using the term "feudal," the titles of Kushan chieftains imply a relationship of lord and feudatory, and the existence of a collection of tributary political units.

22. "Whatever the plans of their creators, organisations, say the natural-system theorists, become ends in themselves and possess their own distinctive needs which have to be satisfied. Once established, organisations tend to generate new needs which constrain subsequent decision and limit the manner in which the nominal group goals can be pursued." (Alvin Gouldner, "Organisational Analysis," in Merton [267], p. 405.

23. It should be noted that some organisations have as their purpose the gratification that membership itself provides. Our concern here is not with associations of this type but with those organisations which, as Parsons expresses it, "produce an identifiable something which can be utilized in some way by another system." (*Vide* "A Sociological Approach to the Theory of Organisations," in [317]).

24. In the post-Mauryan period of Indian history we actually find several instances of states in which the king functioned as the vicegerent of a god—who was conceived to be the true ruler.

25. Unlike the Greeks, the Indians had difficult seeing the state as a natural product, and so were also less likely to see it as an ideal. It is the system of social roles (the Purusha analogy, etc.) that was considered the reflection or worldly symbolization of the principle of order that governed the universe; the state was viewed primarily as an instrument of that transcendent principle of order and justice. Punishment is the very essence of the political function. We might surmise that the priests, who wished to prevent too close an identification of the political and the cosmic, encouraged such a conception of the province of government.

26. Cf. Wolin [434], p. 423: "The special irony of the modern hero is that he struggles in a world where contingency has been routed by bureaucratized procedures and nothing remains for the hero to contend against."

6 The Epics and Law

The period most fertile in the formulation of political ideas was the age, asceticism and the mystical gnosis, metempsychosis, and the belief into the early centuries of the Christian epoch. By the beginning of this age, asceticism and the mystical gnosis, metempsychosis, and the belief in avatars of the gods had been incorporated into Indian religion. The Upanishads were instrumental in guiding Hinduism away from dualism and giving it a primarily monistic theological form. In addition to the great philosophical systems of the age, there developed a new and in some instances almost secular, literature, which included the two great heroic epics—the *Rāmāyana* and *Mahābhārata,* the *Arthaśāstra* of Kautalya, and the law books of Manu, Yājñavalkya, Nārada, and Brihaspati. Some of these works—especially the *Mahabharata*—reflect institutions and ideal of earlier periods of Indian history as well as conditions of the time in which they were written, compiled, or revised. In the centuries encompassed by this literature, political units had grown to a considerable size, and their earlier tribal character had all but disappeared. The Aryans had settled as far east as modern Bengal, and as far south as the Andhra country.

The epics are, in part, attempts to popularize Vedic religion and metaphysics. However, it is clear that significant portions of the *Mahabharata* were influenced by Sankhya doctrine—perhaps the most important philosophical influence on the development of early Hinduism—before the epic was revised to conform with Vedānta. but the Sankhya of the *Mahabharata* may never have been entirely that of the philosophers. In its classical form the system was atheistic and rationalist, but it was very closely associated with theistic Yoga in many respects, including basic technique. Yoga incorporates a God far superior in power to the purusha (pure spirit) of Sankhya. Though contradictory to the central philosophical conceptions of Sankhya, the concept of God appeared in the course of the development of the system. This God figured as but one of the purushas, and was therefore not conceived as designer of the universe. It might be said that God represented the highest excellence—and example for man and an object for his devotion. And he was seen as sympathetic to men: if they would place their trust in him, he could be relief upon to help them attain spiritual release.

In Sankhya, man himself is responsible for the working out of his destiny. But God's ways are sometimes mysterious, and social actions have no particular relation to salvation. Weber has remarked that, in its religious theory, the *Mahabharata* leaves us with the question of Job:

> King Yudhisthira of the Epic in his blameless misfortune discusses with his spouse the reign of God. The woman comes to the conclusion that the great God only plays with men according to his whims. A genuine solution is as little found here as in Job: one should not say such things, for by the grace of God the good receive immortality and, above all, without this belief the people would not practice virtue. This has quite a different ring from the philosophy of the Upanishads which knows nothing of such a world regime by a personal God.

This new concept of faith, the need for devotion to a redemptive agent, figures prominently in the *Bhagavad Gītā*. Right action pertains to caste obligation. Action must be performed without thought of gain; the actor who remains detached is freed from the guilt that might accrue from his actions. The poem is primarily concerned with the swadharma of the warrior noble, whose role could not be reconciled with ascetic withdrawal. It is probably valid to say that Sankhya did not encourage an ethic for the conduct of worldly affairs. From a social point of view it was necessary that its gnostic mysticism be modified by caste considerations. Conduct was regulated by caste prescriptions and prohibitions, detailed and particularistic regulations sanctified by the older religion.

Nevertheless, in the epic, the discipline of concentration and meditation has begun to replace the earlier emphasis on sacrifice, though clearly it is understood that not all men are qualified to pursue this technique. The relationship of myth and ritual was no longer as direct as it had once been; liturgical attempts at "correspondence" had declined in significance. Caste distinctions were fully admitted, and the worst of crimes was to challenge the caste order. Some new gods appear, among them Kama, god of love, and Kubera, god of riches. However, although the popularisation of brahmanism and the influence of new religious and philosophical systems did appreciably change the nature of belief and worship, the debt of Hinduism to non-Aryan spiritual elements should not be taken to imply a break with the older hieratic religion.

Sankhya doctrine and the emphasis on yogic practice in effect replaced the professional gnosis of Brahmanism; instead of the comprehension of the holy, the goal becomes the attainment of a miraculous ability. There was never a complete departure from the older brahman conception of the magical quality of gnosis. Yogic technique could not be judged heterodox. The position of the brahman was not questioned, nor were ritual duties as such disparaged. but in fact, salvation conceived in Sankhya or Yoga terms constituted a serious threat to the authority of the sacred writings and allowed no substantial role for ritual—except as a preparation for gnostic knowledge. The brahmans could not condone such devaluation of Vedic rite. It was the Vedanta system, with its stress cn the value of social and ritual duties in the attainment of the higher wisdom, and its relation (as the name suggests) to the Vedic samhitas, that was to prove more congenial to the priestly group. The impersonal principle of Brahman which had come to take the place of the older Prajapati in esoteric thought, made too many demands on the imagination to permit any wide appeal. Brahma at length emerged as a personal deity not appreciably different from Prajapati who, in the Vedic age, stood supreme over the frequently capricious gods of the pantheon.

The bulk of the *Mahabharata*, the "fifth Veda," is a collection of legends of the northwest, and especially the Punjab—India's holy land. The *Ramayana* contains the stories of the northeastern kingdoms. But here the legends were rewritten by one man, the poet Vālmīki, who played a role analogous to that of Homer. The *Ramayana* contributes little to political theory, though it does dwell on the need for government and the misery and misfortune that result from its absence.[2] The work recounts the exploits of one of the incarnations of Vishnu, the indefatigable hero Rama, who is depicted as bringing civilization to the benighted aborigines.[3] Macdonell believed that

Ramayana II-IV antedate the *Mahabharata* in its epic form. And there is little doubt that the first and last of the seven books of the narrative are later in composition than the others. But because the Rama legend presumably relates to the Aryan invasion of South India, we are probably not justified in concluding that it is an earlier work than the *Mahabharata* on the grounds that the setting of the latter seems to indicate that Aryan civilization had extended over a broader area and the culture had become less homogenous than that described in the *Ramayana*. It can be said, however, that in their final form the *Mahabharata* and the *Ramayana* were approximately contemporaneous.

Such incarnations as Rama and Krishna provide a means for relating the worship of specific and manifold forms with monotheism—a monotheism that in itself eludes precise definition. It is the function of the avatar to rescue dharma in times of stress and disorder. The concept of the avatar introduces into Indian thought a type of leadership that deviates from traditional authority based on ascription and committed to the established institutions and values of the community. When the basis of the social order is threatened, the hero emerges to restore authority through his charismatic power.

The *Mahabharata*[4] is frequently more secular than religious in tone; the work had its origin in lays composed to commemorate the deeds of a great warrior and may have been connected in some way with the royal sacrifice. Many of the incidents go far back into the remote Vedic period. Transition from one story to another is often confused and awkward. These lays were later worked over by the priests, who expanded the meaning of the ballads, linked them together with prose narration, and interpolated treatises on ethical and theological problems. The major brahman modifications and additions probably date from about the second and first centuries B.C. A considerable part of the rajadharma portion of the *Shantiparva,* which shares so much with the dharmashastra texts, belongs to the first centuries A.D. Many of the peoples mentioned could not have been known to the Indians before this time. And some of the practices referred to in the epic suggest certain quasi-feudal institutions of Gupta times. But a large portion of the epic predates the apotheosis of the knight Arjuna, which would make it earlier than the time of the grammarian Pāṇini, who lived in the fourth century B.C. The mythology of the *Mahabharata* may in some respects be more ancient than the *Rigveda* itself.[5]

The great conflict at the heart of the epic, arising from a dynastic controversy in the Kuru tribe and involving Pāṇḍava and Kaurava cousins, probably took place in the tenth or ninth centuries B.C. although popular tradition has located it as early as 3102, the beginning of the Kali-yuga. All India supposedly participated in the battle, which stormed for eighteen days on the plain of Kurukṣetra, in the vicinity of modern Delhi. Bhīṣma the senior statesman of the Kurus, destined to die within half a year from wounds acquired in battle, grants the combatants his parting words of wisdom on law and policy and the more abstract problems of philosophy and ethics. These words, and those recounting the rivalries of the two noble houses and the adventures of Yudhishthira (*Yudhiṣṭira*), add up to a narrative bulk eight times the size of the *Iliad* and *Odyssey* combined. In the *Bhagavad Gita,* Krishna, avatar of Vishnu and charioteer of the warrior-prince Arjuna seeks to convince the kshatriya of the need to fulfil his caste duty. Arjuna, who had lost conviction in his motives for fighting, returns to the battle confident of the importance of upholding dharma. This rationale has sometimes been interpreted as a criticism of Buddhist pacifism. Its significance is still debated.

Hopkins many years ago concluded that the original narrative core of the epic is impossible to isolate from the later mythical and moralistic accretions, and few present-day students of the *Mahabharata* would question this judgement. Several years before Hopkins' commentary on the epic, Dahlmann argued that the work must be analysed in terms of both narrative and didactic components, but he concluded that the story of the great battle had been made the vehicle of a moral lesson by a diaskeuast sometime in the later Brahmanic period—and went so far as to suggest that the engagement between the Kauravas and Pandavas may never have taken place. Fifty years earlier, Holtzmann had advanced, the theory that at first the Kauravas were the representation of virtue, and that traces of this earlier moral superiority remain[7], giving the epic a tone of moral ambiguity. It is not only this ambivalence that has confused scholars—the very figure of Krishna alternates between saintliness and deception. Held rejects the solution, popular among students of the *Mahabharata*, that evidences of Krishna worship are later interpolations, and insists that the dual character of Krishna must provide the point of departure for a proper interpretation of the work. This ambiguity is most evident in the relationship of the two combatants. Employing the analogy of the phratry relationship (but without equating the two peoples with the tribal moieties). Held claims that the Pandavas and Kauravas exist in a state of "hostile friendship"[8]—an association that creates the tension on which the ritual life of the tribe depends.

Held would have it that the Kauravas and Pandavas are specialists in the ritual functions of the potlatch and of the initiation, respectively. The primary instance of the potlatch and the gaming competition often associated with it is to be found in the second book of the *Mahabharata*, in which the splendor of the Pandava's sabha and the magnificence of the food and gifts are described. After the festivities, Duryodhana, the son of the Kuru king and cousin of the Pandavas, experiences a series of humiliations and swears vengeance. The Kauravas counter with a sabha of their own and build a pavilion that glows with countless precious stones. Here was an opulence and extravagance that had never before been known. At the potlatch Yudhishthira was challenged to a game of dice. Gambling was Yudhishthira's fatal flaw, and his ruin was rapid and complete. Stripped of their wealth and their realm, he and his brothers and their common wife, Draupadī, were banished for thirteen years—after which time they were to receive back their kingdom.

For the initiatory rite, the ritual that reveals the sacred to men, we must turn to the *Bhagavad Gita*. On the eve of the great battle between the Pandavas and the forces of Duryodhana, which followed the refusal of Duryodhana to honour the settlement whereby Yudhishthira and his brothers would recover their rights, Krishna instructs the initiate Arjuna in the ways of knowing God and the obligations of the varnashramadharma. We shall turn presently to this divine counsel.

Several scholars have attempted to solve a problem that has long fascinated Indologists. The five Pandava brothers share a wife—and yet we know that among the Aryans polyandrous relationship were rare. Wikander has reached the conclusion that the five sons of Pāṇḍu[9] were actually not his sons, but children of the gods. Three of them, Yudhishthira, Bhima, and Arjuna, were sired by Dharma (a later name for Mitra), Vayu, and Indras, respectively. Their mother was Pandu's wife Kuntī. Pandhu's other wife, Madrī, conceived the twins Nakula and Sahadeva by the Vedic twin deities known as the Aśvins. Nakula and Yudhishthira, therefore, have no blood relationship. According to this thesis, Yudhishthira represents the sovereign authority of Mitra, and Bhima and Arjuna are the great warriors who symbolize the two types of kshatriya character. Although Indra is depicted as intemperate and boastful, he is mildness itself when compared with the vigorous Vayu. The hero who represents the latter type is, in Dumezil's words, "a human beast," a lusty adventurer, a trifle stupid but free of malice. His fellow warrior, Arjuna, the son of Indra, stands for the true chivalric spirit; he is civilized and ordered in his ways, knowledgeable in the use of arms, and sociable. The twins, like the helpful Aśvins, exist to serve their "brothers"[10] they personify the vaishya virtures.

Their wife, Draupadi, appears to be the human counterpart of the Vedic goddess Sarasvatī (or Vāc), who serves to synthesize the three functions. This, then, could explain a marriage arrangement that was surely atypical. Though we know that at one time Mitra was associated with the Brahma and Varuna with the Kshatra principle, the equating of Yudishthira with the brahman ideal poses difficulties, since so much of the epic is devoted to teaching him the proper conduct of a *king* and since Draupadi herself is critical of him for his anti-kshatriya attitudes. It is of course impossible to construct a consistent theory on the basis of a text that has been reworked time and again and that in its extant form reveals a heavy brahman influence. The brahmans, intent on making the world safe for orthodoxy, must describe the kind of rule most compatible with sacred law and most congenial to their interests. In certain of the episodes in the great epic, Krishna appears to have been appropriated by the priests and made the vehicle of their arguments. But he also represents values that had begun to threaten the integrity of Vedic culture. The revised document may be understood as an attempt to buttress brahman authority against the threat of alien beliefs. We may assume that secular ideals were still fairly uniform throughout society and that, as in the last years of the eleventh century when the clergy of Europe began to adapt the *chanson de geste* to its own ends, the heroic epic was a means of influencing the humbler strata of society.

Insofar as Yudhiṣhthira would make political and military considerations secondary to the ethical and religious, he may be viewed as the embodiment of the spiritual principle—which, according to the brahmans, must be the true sovereign power. The mythology probably goes back to the time of the original atharvan priests, an age before the brahmans had achieved an authoritative position in the social hierarchy. We might even surmise that the two kshatriya types (Vayu and Indra) were the most vivid expression of the distinction that became the symbolic basis of the later Brahma-Kshatra duality. Possibly the original Mitra-Varuna dichotomy was restated to preserve the early kshatriya dual character (which may have symbolized the two main Aryan groups), and Mitra appropriated by the rising brahman class. Eventually the twofold principle of sovereignty would be restored.

More revealing for the study of political thought is the dual character of Lord Krishna himself. Krishna, who appears in the epic as a tribal god, was probably an actual person. In the stones that surround him (which may well represent different traditions) he is portrayed as the divine herdsman and great lover and as the clever consultant to his cousin warriors in their campaigns. Krishna was closely associated with the kshatriya nobility, and his role as avatar, protector of the dharma, would necessarily involve him in kshatriya functions. We should expect Krishna, as an expression of divinity, to personify righteousness as well as honour. We are not prepared, therefore, to find him described as a trickster, a master at deception, a wily fox. The explanation goes beyond Huizinga's contention that in archaic culture, departures from the rules of the game were not regarded in the same way that we would regard them today.

In ancient civilizations order and tradition were sanctified. Mitra, as we have seen, represents stability and symmetry. But Mitra, though supreme, is dependent on Varuna, and Varuna stands for the active, assertive quality that we have contrasted with the cohesive. Here is the essence of the ambiguity: the sacred is clearly distinguished from the lower political order, and yet the indispensable role of protection and regulation, and even of violence, in preserving dharma is recognized. We might speak of the kshatriya or political function as a "sanctioned sin." Arjuna sees clearly (in the *Gita*) the evils of war; it is the divine Krishna who reminds him of the kshatriya obligation to fight. The kshatradharma maintains the order of things, just as the avatar comes forth to restore the sacred order when dharma is threatened. This "sinfulness" inherent in the kshatriya duty (because order demands its very opposite, violence) makes the warrior dependent on the brahman for absolution. This is not a grudging admission of the political function. The brahmans are themselves too convinced of the tendency to anarchy that results when the governing power is weakened.

The idea of the of the political as sinful (albeit a necessary evil) is not unique to India. It can be seen in the warning of the high priest Samuel; in the moral ambiguity surrounding David, who went so far as to disregard the very ritual taboos by which the warrior role was purified—but who succeeded in reconciling the covenant between God and Israel with the authority of his own house. In Platonic theory it can be seen in the qualitative difference between change *per se* and the "change" that establishes an order based on the Good (an idea that may have its source in the ancient Greek concept of the Great Legislator[11]). And Plato hoped to eliminate most of what we would consider the political, once this order was established.

Public policy may have to deviate at times from accepted values and standards of conduct. It is not simply that expedience serves the private purposes of those in power. Far more important is the need to reconcile conflicting claims with one another and with social norms. The Romans sought to meet this difficulty by rooting authority in the act of foundation itself—the charismatic and peculiarly political act that creates community. With Christianity the concept of revealed Truth reappears, but the Roman emphasis on tradition shaped the Christian theory of temporal authority. In medieval philosophy, before the Aristotelianism of St. Thomas, government was closely linked to man's capacity for sin: political institutions were at once the punishment and remedy for sin, and the consequence of man's imperfection. And finally, at the beginning of the modern era, we find Machiavelli insisting that morality can exist only in a context that is itself not created by morality, and counselling the leader to learn "how not to be good" if he would know the ultimate secret of political life. The violent act of Romulus is justified by its results, and the Roman myth of foundation receives a new significance in Machiavelli's argument that society is ever being founded anew. Authority struggles to free itself from tradition.

Krishna and the kshatriya noble represent the inevitable tension between the action that social justice and social order require and the very principles upon which this order is structured. The dilemma, which haunts the political and gives it the semblance of amorality, is first expressed in the figure of Indra, the boisterous god of the Aryans, whose sins are carefully chronicled in the brahman texts. In this chapter and the next, we shall deal with the attempt to tame Indira and the heroic ideal of action he represents, the recognition of the reality and necessity of power, and the search for a principle of legitimacy that could provide the basis for distinguishing force from authority.

The *Shantiparva* is the major source of political commentary in the *Mahabharata*. The subject of this didactic collection of folk-wisdom, the twelfth book of the epic, is *nīti*—the science of worldly pursuit. In it the king's responsibilities are enumerated and the broader questions of caste obligations, right conduct, and ethics of government are discussed. We are told repeatedly that in the state which has no king, the natural order of the universe is disrupted and destroyed. Therefore, when kshatriya power declines and the social order is threatened, members of any class may take action to prevent lawlessness, for anarchy is to be avoided at any cost.

The state of nature, as Bhishma describes it to Yudhishthira, was first a condition of righteousness and bliss. Dharma kept everything in its proper place and there was no need of danda.[12] Decadence, taking the form of anti-social personality traits that developed gradually in man, at last made necessary the restraining power of the king. The shadow of greed and lust fell over the peaceful scene and a disorder, comparable to Hobbes' state of nature, resulted. This condition of anarchy is *mātsya-nyāna,* the "law of the fishes" (i.e., no law). It is a metaphorical description of lawlessness employed frequently in the literature of Hindu polity. In these verses it is the gods—not the people—who appeal to Brahma in the time of chaos. The dandaniti[13] composed by Brahma was ineffective without an executive power to enforce the sacred laws. Vishnu was therefore appointed to this office by the gods and, entering the body of Prithu, who had made a compact with the people and sworn to uphold brahman immunities, he became king.[14] Hence the king was seen as the heir of Vishnu, a product of the divine energy, and his legitimacy was derived from his divine ordination.

It appears that we are really more justified in considering this a contract between the king and the brahmans, and a unilateral contract at that: the king promises to protect and respect the brahmans and to grant them privileges. This view of the origin of kingship is almost certainly a later addition to the *Shantiparva,* and it has been contrasted with the ideas that appear in chapters 67 and 68 of the *Shantiparva.*

The intent of both portions is to exalt the authority of the ruler. Very little is said of restrictions on this authority. The crucial importance of danda in combating the evils of anarchy is stressed. Without the king, who wields the rod of punishment, "men cannot enjoy their wealth and wives." And for this reason, "an intelligent man should protect as his own what belongs to the king . . . . The king is the heart of his people; he is their great refuge; he is their glory; and he is their greatest happiness. Those men, O king, who are attached to the king, can conquer both this and the next world." Here the state of nature seems to be from the beginning a state of anarchy, a situation radically different from the golden age of Buddhist theory. "if there were no king on Earth for holding the rod of punishment, the strong would then have oppressed the weak after the manner of fishes in the water. We have heard that men, is days of yore, in consequence of anarchy, were ruined, devouring one another like stronger fishes devouring the weaker ones in the water." In these passages kinship is not the result of a bilateral agreement between the people and one of their own; it is the creation of divine will, and in the agreement, if we may call it such, the people make extravagant promises to the (reluctant) king designated by Brahma. One verse does refer to the "election" of the king, but in no modern sense of the world does election play a part in the theory of the origin of the coercive authority of the state.

According to the *Shantiparva* ("The Book of Peace"), what men want most—or at least what is most necessary—is order; and "when the science of politics (chastisement) is neglected, the Vedas and all virtues decline." The king who possesses the rod of chastisement, says Arjuna, "sways all subjects and protects them. The rod of chastisement is awake when all else is under sleep. For this, the wise have designated the rod of punishment as righteousness itself. . . . . If punishment were done away within this world, creatures would soon be destroyed." The theory is postulated on the same assumption of man's natural wickedness that we find in earlier writings. Danda is that which sustains righteousness. We are provided with a vivid image of the "god" chastisement. "In form he looks like a blazing fire. His complexion is dark like that of the petals of the blue lotus. He is equipped with four teeth, has four arms and eight legs and many eyes. His ears are pointed like shafts and his hair stands erect. He has matted locks and two tongues. His face has the hue of copper and he is clad in a lion's skin."

The ruler who fails to protect his subjects is compared in the *Shantiparva* to the barren wife, the dry cow, and the bull that bears no burden. A king was theoretically unable to take refuge in the particular nature of the age in which he lived as an excuse for failure to fulfil his duty as protector and upholder of dharma.[15] The *Mahabharata* declares, on the contrary, that the king is the maker of his age. Dandaniti was conceived as the guarantor of the proper functioning of the universe. This concept, expressed more positively as rajadharma,[16] the royal duty, is the keystone of the arch of duties, the duty upon which all others depend, the securer, of property and the guardian of the family.

But in times of emergency it may be necessary to depart from the customary precepts of dharma. We read that duties may be based on truth (*satya*), on reasoning (*upapatti*), on good custom (*sādhrācāra* or *saddācāra*), and on expediency (*upāya*). The recommendations of the sage Bharadvāja, who expounds a programme of expediency, are meant to apply only in crisis situations when dharma can be preserved only by extreme measures. If possible, the king must avoid using the "wily wisdom." Although the ruthless techniques employed at critical times were not to govern the conduct of the state in normal times, we must remember that the "normal" situation for this society was a condition approaching what we would today call cold war. Stability depended on diplomatic arrangements that shifted as the loci of power shifted, and that were based on the calculation of advantage, the wily wisdom.

As Bhishma explains it, the kshatriya dharma is beyond good and evil. Rama declares at one point that he is renouncing the kshatradharma, which masks sin as righteousness and invites hypocrisy. The "sinfulness of Indra" is the theme of *Shantiparva* 97: Yudhishthira expounds on the iniquity inherent in the king's duty. But the guru Bhishma answers that the stain of sins incurred in battle leaves the hero with his very blood. It is the kshatriya duty to die in battle. In the faithful and selfless accomplishment of the rajadharma, sin is unavoidable. (It is the premise of Buddhism, without the conclusion.) "I do not see any creature in this world," announces Arjuna, "that supports life without doing any active injury to others. Animals live upon animals, the stronger upon the weaker. . . . . There is no act that is entirely pure."

In *Shantiparva 64-66* we find a great paean to the kshatriya dharma—that upon which all else depends. But several chapters earlier the dying Bhishma conceded (if the commentator Nilakaṇṭha is correct) that the kshatriya role must always be understood as inferior to the duties of the brahman—inasmuch as the principle of action in subordinate to that of renunciation. If renunciation is the essence of the Brahma, then it would not do to have the knights coveting for themselves that which was the *raison d'etre* of the priests. "Wise men, therefore, do not praise Renunciation as the duty of a Kshatriya. On the other hand, the clear-sighted think that the adoption of such a life (by a kshatriya) involves even the loss of virtue." Bhishma rebukes Yudhishthira for wishing to turn to the forest in order to find spiritual merit and avoid the performance of the morally ambiguous duties prescribed by his noble status. Yudhishthira's brothers and his wife condemn renunciation as dereliction of kshatriya duty, and the theme of devotion to one's dharma reverberates throughout the books of the massive work.

The Principles of Sound Polity

The admonition to avoid war when possible, and to engage in hostilities only when attempts at peaceful settlement have failed, may tell us more about the ideals of those responsible for the later recession than about the kshatriya nobles apotheosized in combat. When war was inevitable, the kshatriya had no choice but to dedicate himself to the preservation of the state and the dharma, and to fight in accordance with the code governing hostilities. The moral law forbade the use of weapons against those not actively engaged in battle (such as peasants and craftsmen), or those who retire from the fray, who are unarmed or disabled, or who plead for mercy. Camp-followers and sleeping soldiers are also protected. A warrior could contend only with another who was similarly armed (e.g., charioteer against charioteer), and he must not use poisoned weapons. He must always give due notice of his intention to strike. The narrative itself provides a lively picture of the Hindu warrior in battle. At the height of the conflict he seems to have used anything he could get his hands on: iron clubs, spits, swords, knives, darts, arrows, wheels, axes, iron balls, staves, cow-horns, moratars, lances, and even uprooted trees. Anything from molasses and snakes to plowshares and chariot planks might be employed. And when such ammunition was exhausted, there were always dirt, stones, fists, and teeth.

The constant warfare of the centuries preceding the consolidation of the great empires severely modified the ethics of diplomacy and made survival justification in itself for all manner of actions. However, the epics advice against a militaristic and garrison state, and indicate that the Hindu monarchy was essentially civil. Yet the ritual-sacrifice itself, the *brahmaṇah parimara* (the "dying around the magic power") and the ashvamedha (a virtual invitation to hostilities) produced what Zimmer has called a "magic arthaśastra" which makes futile the attempt to disentangle political expedience and religious practices. These practices contributed to an age of internecine war to terrible that the nobler kshatriya was sorely tempted to renounce the world and find peace and fulfilment in the forests. The soul-searching of Yudhishthira and Arjuna culminates in the teachings of Buddha and Ashoka. The unhappy turn in the fortunes of the brahmans during the regime of the emperor Ashoka may provide a clue to the insistence by later redactors on the faithful performance of traditional duties and the importance of the sacrifice—on which brahman supremacy traditionally depended.

The ancient canon of morality could be laid aside on the theory that without the state to ensure its existence the code would be meaningless. This dilemma produces moral flexibility as well as cynicism: "There is no act that is wholly meritorious, nor any that is wholly wicked." "Sin, O king, sometimes assumes the form of virtue, and virtue sometimes assumes the form of sin." Bhishma, in the *Shantiparva,* enunciates the doctrine that might makes right; elsewhere right is defined as "that which a strong man understands to be right."

When the king is counselled to eschew war if at all possible, the intent of such advice is not necessarily that the king should avoid conquering, but that he should acquire "victories" without battles. The king is urged to tempt his enemy into ways of self-indulgence, to encourage him to deplete his resources in expensive sacrifices and to rely on religion and fate rather than on his own efforts. The formula for diplomacy involves deception, appeasement of the powerful and suppression of the weak, hypocrisy, bribery, economic exhaustion, soothing reassurance and lightning onslaught, ruthlessness, vigilance and secrecy, and readiness to risk and to sacrifice. But, if feasible, victory should be gained without hostilities.

The king must be always alert to detect the peculiar vulnerabilities of his foes. In order to discern these weaknesses, he should employ spies, In times of peace the spy served to detect conspiracies and antisocial actions. In no corner of the kingdom could the king be completely certain of the loyalty of his subjects. Virtue is the cornerstone of the king's legitimacy, but vigilance guards his authority. And shrewdness supplements caution: "Carry your enemy on your shoulder," the king is advised, "until you have got from him what you want, then throw him off, shattering him like an earthen jar against a rock." To fail to do so is to run the risk of the mother crab who is consumed by her offspring. It is always dangerous to conclude peace with an enemy. The king is advised to fear that which merits fear. Uncritical trust is an invitation to disaster. The king must be sweet in speech, yet always on guard.

As we have seen, the *Shantiparva* is one long argument for the vested interest of the community in the welfare of the king. This is surely the reason for the lurid picture of the state of nature presented in chapter 67. But the king should merit loyalty; he must have conquered pride, lust, and weakness—replacing them with righteousness, vigour, and wisdom, "The king should first conquer himself and then try to subdue his enemies. How can a king who has not been able to conquer his own self be able to conquer his enemies?" Birth, military skill, and courage are mentioned as the chief attributes of royal office. Bhishma exhorts the king to be both mild and strict (without becoming oppressive) in order to preserve respect. It will be to his advantage to assume a variety of forms, as the occasion demands. Yet the king must be man enough to endure unpopularity in the greater interest of the state. "He is the best of kings who is wise, who is liberal, who is ready to take advantage of the short-comings of foes, who has an agreeable countenance, who is conversant with what is good and what is bad for each of the four orders of his subjects, who is prompt in action, who has anger under control, who is not vindictive, who is high-minded."

The coronation oath of the Kurus limited royal authority to the protection of the people, the maintenance of custom, and punishment, and made the king subject to the laws of the realm. Failure to carry out responsibilities was as grave a misuse of authority as the unlawful use of power. The absence of the superstitious and the mystical in the Hindu coronation oath has often been remarked upon. Prithu is addressed directly and asked to swear to

> accomplish all those tasks in which righteousness ever resides! Disregarding what is dear and what not so, look upon all creatures with

> an equal eye. Cast off at a distance lust and wrath and covetousness and honour, and, always observing the dictates of righteousness, do thou punish with thy own hands the man, whoever he may be, that deviates from the path of duty! Do thou also swear that thou wouldst, in thought word, and deed, always maintain the religion inculcated on earth by the Vedas! Do thou further swear that thou wouldst fearlessly maintain the duties laid down in the Vedas with the aid of chastisement, and that thou wouldst never act with caprice!

And then we come to what is perhaps the root of the matter: "O powerful one, know that Brahmanas are exempt from punishment, and promise further that you would protect the world from an intermixture of castes."

The *Shantiparva*, if conceiving the king as at all divine, locates divinity in the office rather than in the personality of the king. Heredity and primogeniture determined royal succession in epic polity, though the formality of nomination was preserved. Some scholars interpret the succession of Rama's younger brother Bharata, to the throne as the result not of a promise of King Daśarathsa to his wife (as is sometimes argued) but of Rama's willing resignation. It is an instance of self-sacrifice to save his father's honour rather than of injustice to Rama. The king could not legally contradict the custom of regal succession. Rama had no disabilities that could disqualify him from office, as Dhritarashtra and Devapi had.

A kind of contract relationship existed, in theory, between the ruler and the governed. Taxes were considered the king's remuneration for protecting and furthering the interests of his people. In taxing his people the king must be like the subtle leech and the gentle cowherd, extracting the necessary revenue with mildness and care, and without destroying initiative.

> That avaricious king, who foolishly oppresses his subjects by levying taxes not sanctioned by scriptures, is said to wrong his own self. As a person wanting milk never gets any by cutting off the udders of a cow, similarly a kingdom, assailed by improper taxes, never gives any profit to the king. He who treats a milch cow with kindness, always obtains milk from it. Likewise the king, who rules his kingdom by proper means, gets much fruits from it.

Therefore, the king should try to convince his subjects of the need for the tax: "Pointing out to them the necessity of repairing his forts and of meeting the expense of his establishment and other heads, striking them with the fear of foreign invasion, and pointing to them the necessity that exists for protecting them and enabling them to ensure the means of living in peace, the king should impose taxes upon the Vaishyas of his kingdom."

The king was advised to consider the selling price of a merchant's goods and the distance these goods travelled before taxing them. The customary tax on the produce of the land was one-sixth (though it often varied considerably), and the king is occasionally referred to as *shadbhagin,* "he who gets one-sixth."

Despite the liberality recommended in the tax policy, the king is told to keep his treasury full. Wealth is a necessity, and the king need only take his cue from the people, who "make as much as they can."[18]

The state may take the property of the wicked, for ownership is ultimately based on virtue. But maintaining the security of property remains one of the fundamental duties of the state. In case of loss of property, such as that resulting from theft, the king is called on to make good the amount taken from his subjects. "That king, who, realizing his tribute of sixth, does not protect his kingdom, shares a fourth part of the sins of the kingdom." The very fact of thievery indicates that the rajadharma is imperfectly realized. It is unlikely that the ruler took such extreme responsibility seriously. The concept is linked to the broad theory that all virtue and stability ultimately rest on political foundations.[19] Commandments of the early heterodox religions not to steal or trespass on the possessions of other suggest the importance private property had begun to assume. In the *Mahabharata* property is conceived as the creation of the state. The argument is that with the emergence of civil society, property—in the sense of title—comes into existence. A distinction is made between *bhoga* (possession) and *mamatva* (ownership).

Certain circumstances justified the subjects in deposing and killing the *king*. The people, according to the *Anuśasanaparva,* should take up arms and slay the king who fails to protect them or who attempts to take their wealth or to level class distinctions. Force is prescribed to oppose the unlawful use of force. And the king who failed to protect his people should be abandoned—like those other undesirables, the vixen wife, the leaky boat, the barber desiring the forest and the cowherd the village, the teacher who does not instruct, and the priest who is ignorant of scripture.

The king is not to destroy the special customs of families, corporations, and defeated nations, unless the welfare of the state makes it imperative to do so. On the contrary, he is obligated to preserve the traditional order of things, for custom is regarded as sacred. A passage in the epic that describes a prince, defeated in battle, worrying about what he will say to the priests and the heads of the corporations suggests that the ruler had to maintain the favour of influential members of society.

The *Shantiparva* describes the creation of the castes from the mouth, arms, thighs, and feet of Brahma. The *Gita* also attempts to justify the varna structure, but its theory is more sophisticated. God, it is argued in the *Gita*, assigned duties to men according to their inherent abilities. If man would but carry out the functions proper to his social position, he would ensure his salvation. All this is by now familiar and will be considered again in the following chapter. But there appears at this time the idea that different social functions are equally valuable in the attainment of individual salvation. The theory undoubtedly represents the influence of other religious systems, such as Buddhism, which had a notable impact on the society of the time. Although the epic in its present form is a brahmanic work, it is sometimes critical of the excesses of Brahmanism; Krishnaite influences are in evidence from time to time. The priest, despite the brahman manipulation of the text, is still clearly far from the king's master.

The later readactors leave no doubt in our minds as to what they thought the priest's power should be. Just as fire has no effect on water, so the kshatriya can have no power over the brahman. The ruler without his brahman adviser is like an elephant without its driver. The kshatriyas are exhorted to work in close co-operation with the brahmans, but it is evident that the priests exercise little direct political power. The arguments and tales worked into the older narrative are frequently in dramatic contradiction to the main story. However, the influence of the brahmans is clearly increasing.[20] The epic reveals a general willingness to allow tribal units to preserve the integrity of their cultures, yet it was thought essential to work out some *modus operandi* between these groups and Brahmanism: the priests were expected to guide the major ceremonies, administer the necessary sacraments, and modify those beliefs which were flagrantly in opposition to brahman theory.

In the *Shantiparva* we find mention of legislative council in which, according to Hopkins, the commercial class enjoys almost twice the representation of the two upper classes.[21] But the passage Hopkins relied upon is not in the critical edition of the *Shantiparva*. It does not appear, however, that all the castes were represented and though the shudras had only a negligible position in the higher councils, their presence points to a recognition of the need for their loyalty and their opinion on matters of policy. Nine members of the council were to be chosen to confer with the king, and, of these, four were to be selected for his immediate circle of advisers. There of four councilors were considered the ideal number, since fewer might lead to a combination of ministers contrary to the interests of the country, and more would tend to diminish efficiency. Only the man who has sublimated his senses is fit for such offices.

> Such persons as are endued with modesty, self-control, truth, sincerity, and courage to say the proper thing, should be your law-makers. . . . Those who are of good birth and good behaviour, who can interpret all signs and gestures, who are shorn of cruelty, who know the requirements of place and time, who always seek the well-being of their master in all works, should be appointed as ministers by the king in all his affairs.

It appears that members of the mantri-parishad (the large council) were consulted individually on urgent matters. The inner council was, however, regularly consulted on general affairs. The king is advised to respect his ministers, for it was unlikely that he would be wise enough to be able to forgo counsel on complex issues. The first indication of complete secrecy in the councils dates from this time. In the *Ramayana*, the king's ministers are referred to as *amātyas;* they are usually eight in number, and are possibly a hereditary class. The position of the brahman is generally more secure in the *Ramayana*. Hopkins held that the *Mahabharata* reflected three stages in conciliar development. In the older legends there is still evidence of the power of the people, but it is limited to civil affairs. The popular assembly gave way to that of the nobility—which probably originated in the war council and continued to be more concerned with military matters. Finally, in the late didactic parts of the epic (not part of the story itself), the priests assume the prerogative, insisting on their right to advice the king on all questions in counsel protected by absolute secrecy.

Sabha, by this time, referred to the king's court, or to any judicial, political, or festive gathering. Jayaswal makes a case for an administrative body, the *paura,* which was charged with the conduct of municipal affairs in the capital and consisted of an advisory council of leading citizens—apparently representing all social classes. The *janapada* served as a constitutional assembly for the rest of the state. But paura probably refers to a resident of the city and not, as Jayaswal infers, to an assembly member. His interpretation of the janapada as an institutional form rests on the thinnest evidence, and though the king may have taken pains to determine the will of the people, it is doubtful that a formal constitutional check governed the king's activities. If the paura-janapada assemblies actually existed, there would certainly be more evidence in the records that have come down to us than the occasional references Jayaswal cites (e.g., the *Ramayana*), which are decidedly ambiguous.[23] Popular expression of opinion, in the *Mahabharata*, is extraconstitutional. The emphasis is less on assemblies and village elders than on royal courts and dancing girls. Everywhere but in the easternmost regions, public opinion continued as a force to be reckoned with, although there was a tendency, as government became more complex in its authority and function, for popular participation to become formalistic. There is still the suggestion that many monarchs felt compelled to strengthen their claim to the throne by eliciting the approval of their subjects, or at least the support of the more influential segment of the populace.

As for the administration of the realm, we are told that the king should think of his subjects as his own children. But he should show no mercy in the settlement of disputes. Charges and defences in judicial suits must be heard by men distinguished for their wisdom and experience in the ways of the world. Honest and reliable men are to be appointed to supervise the mines, the ferries, the elephant corps, and the warehouses. A headman must be selected for each village, a superintendent for each ten villages, and so forth.

The *Mahabharata* indicates the existence of a number of states in the north and west where sovereignty seems to have rested with the people and monarchy was more form than fact (e.g., the Kurus of what is modern Sirhind).[24] Though concerned chiefly with the monarchical form of government, the epic does comment on republics (or clan-republics), and specifically on the need for unity and co-operation among them. Their main vulnerability is their tendency towards internal dissension, Bhishma's critique amounts to a commentary on the divisive effects of the combination of political equality and economic inequality.[25] Each man comes to covet the wealth of others. Another problem is the frequent need for secrecy—which the councils of these ganas cannot by their very nature maintain. The remedy is to concentrate power in the natural nobility of talent and character.

The *Mahabharata* is a manifesto in behalf of the strong monarch. But the monarch does not rule arbitrarily: he must govern in accordance with the sacred authority represented by the brahmans, and he knows that "the eternal duties of kings are to make their subjects happy, to observe truth and to act sincerely."

REFERENCES

1. The *Mahabharata* reaches its philosophical culmination in the *Bhagavad Gitā,* which appears in Section VI of the sixth book (*Bhiṣmaparva*).
2. The anarchic state of nature is described in detail in *Ramayana* II, 69, but the discussion differs little from that in *Mahabharata* XII, 67.
3. For a brief account of the Rama myth, *vide* W. Norman Brown (49), pp. 291 ff.
4. The Great Poem (or War) of the Descendants of Bharata. The work exists in two recessions, known as the "Northern" and the "Southern" versions, the latter of which is the longer. A critical edition is being prepared by the Bhandarkar Oriental Research Institute in Poona. It will be based on all the extact manuscripts of the work.
5. For a guide to the elaborate and confusing array of epic deities and mythologies, *vide* Hopkins [181[.
6. It is worth nothing that the word for foe (*bhrātṛvya*) menas, etymologically, cousin, son of the father's brother.
7. The Kauravas, for example, can be conquered only by means of fraud.
8. "From whatever angle we may view the relation between the two parties, it is ever that selfsame wavering between the extremes of friendship and enmity which we perceive." (Held [171[, p. 298.).
9. The young brother of the blind Kuru king Dhṛtarāṣtra.
10. It is significant that the lower orders of society are not considered blood brothers of the ruling classes, and that even the three who represent the brahman and kshatriya groups are only stepbrothers.
11. From the great deeds attributed to a Draco, Solon, Lycurgus, and Cleisthenes, there was drawn the towering figure of the law-giver, suddenly intruding to save the disintegrating life of the *polis* and to

re-establish it on a fresh foundation." (Wolin [434], p. 53.) The statement could as accurately describe Krishna—except that the avatar gives new inspiration to old forms.

12. Jayaswal held that this condition once the ideal—that men believed that dharma could and should rule without danda. The term for this positive state of nature he took to be *arājaka*. And he went so far as to claim that such a political experiment may have taken place, though it must have been confined to small political units. (1199), pp. 86f.) This idea has been criticized by Ghoshall (146); [144]; p. 213, n. 3), who goes back to the texts themselves to prove that ***arājaka*,** the rulerless state, was far from a Tolstoyan ideal. Jayaswal admits the cynical view of the *Mahabharata* which makes arājaka synonymous with matsyanyaya (survival of the strong). Part of the difficulty is that Jayaswal draws attention to *Shantiparva* 59. 14 ("All men used to protect one another piously") without noting that the spirit of this verse is quite distinct from the tenor of *Shantiparva* 67, 17f. In view of clan and family regulation (what we might call "traditional" authority), a political unit without a central government is not an impossibility. But Ghoshal is right in stating that Jayaswal's theory of early Indian idealism does not do justice to the facts.

13. The *Mahabharata* uses the term dandaniti to designate the science of constraint or, more broadly, of government.

14. The first mention of Prithu (*Pṛthu*) as the original anointed king appears in the *Shatapatha Brahmana*. Prithu was not the first king, but seventh in line. Experience under his predecessors had been so unfortuante that he was constrained to take a coronation oath before ascending to his office.

15. Hinduism divides time into *kalpas*, which are further divided into *mahāyugas*, which, in turn, consist of four ages. According to the *Mahabharata* (III, 12, 826) and *Manu* (1, 69) a mahayuga lasts 12,000 years. A thousand mahayugas make a kalpa, which is equal to one day in the life of Brahma it is our bad fortune to be living in an age of evil which follows an idyllic period that existed some five thousand years ago.

16. The study of polity was first designated *rajadharma* and, as the word suggests, referred more specifically to principles of royal conduct.

17. Note especially the remarks of Nakula: "O king, the person who in sacrifices gives away his fairly acquired wealth to those Brahmanas who are well conversant with the Vedas, and contracts his soul, is, O monarch, regarded as the true renouncer. . . . . A person becomes a true renoucner by casting off internal and external attachments, and not simply by leaving home for the forest." (*Shantiparva* 12, 7f. and 12.35.)

18. On the importance of wealth, *vide Shantiparva* 8.16f.

19. Heinrich Zimmer [439] retelis a popular Indian tale known as "The Twentyfive Stories of the Specter in the Corpse. There are five Sanskrit versions of this story of king Vikramāditya, who is believed to have lived around the first century B.C. It involves a series of enigmatic situations, one of which concerns a prince and his friend, the son of the chancellor of the prince's father, who one day discover a beautiful girl bathing with her companions in a lake situated in another kingdom. A liaison is arranged between the prince and the girl through signals interpreted by the chancellor's son. The girl, later fearing that her amounts will be betrayed, determines to poison the prince's friend. But he, anticipating such a plan, disguises himself as an ascetic and, to teach her a lesson, causes the girl to be condemned as a witch responsible for the death of the infant prince of the kingdom in which she lives. The girl is left to die in the jungle outside the town, and as soon as she is abandoned, the two young men carry her off to their kingdom and she of course marries the prince. But grief-stricken and disgraced, her own elderly parents soon die. Who, asks the spirit in the corpse was guilty of these deaths? The answer-which is considered to be correct—is that love excuses all as far as maid and prince are concerned. The chancellor's son is cleared because be was always acting in the service of his master and, presumably, any act is justified it is in line with duty. But the king of the girl's country is responsible for allowing such things to happen in his realm; he should he able to detect trickery and penetrate disguise. "Therefore, he is to be judged guilty of failure in his kingly duty, which was to be the all-seeing eye of his kingdom, the all-knowing protector and governor of his folk."

20. Hopkins ([184], p. 162) believed that the brahman's power originated in the secret council, where his rhetorical and logical skill outshone that of the nobles and he awed the king with his religious authority.

21. Hopkins [184] refers to twenty-one vaishyas on a council of thirty-six; cf. *Shantiparva* 85.6ff.

22. Paura-janapada is used in the plural in the *Ramayana* (II, 14, 40 and 14, 54) to refer to the citizens as such. The term is employed in *Manu* (VIII, 40), to refer to men of all castes.

23. Professor Altekar (6), p. 108f., points out that the paura-janapada assemblies—if such existed—are not mentioned on a single one of the thousands of copper plate grants (going back to A.D. 500) which have been discovered, even though every possible authority is cited. No inscription or work on polity refers to such a popular assembly.

24. The Pandava princes are reported to have been restored through popular pressure. It is worth remarking that the world *gana* (cf. *Shantiparva*

107. 6) seems to refer to self-governing communities rather than to guilds or coronations—or to an elite, as it is sometimes translated.

25. Bhishma's caveat has been compared with Aristotle's warning regarding the "stasis" of Hellenic city-states.

7 The Epic Ideals of Human Relations

Early Lays and Legends

As the Indo-Aryans crossed mountains and river valleys in the long march from their homeland into the valley of the Sarasvati and the Drushadvati, their mind was full of memories of heroic episodes and great happenings. These included not merely bitter and long continued wars between the Aryans and the non-Aryans, described as the Devas and the Asuras, in which warriors, sages and ascetics all participated but also feuds and conflicts between groups among the Indo-Aryans themselves. Gradually tales of war and victory, courage and loyalty, tragedy and grief crystallised themselves into epic song verses (*gathas*), hero lauds (*narasamsis*) and clan histories, (*akhyanas* and *itihasas*). These came to be embodied later on in the Brahmanas and recited by the bards at intervals during the great Asvamedha and other sacrifices that took several months at a stretch. Princes of the Kuru and Kosala kingdoms were among the celebrated sacrificers, and it is no wonder that legends of Ikshvaku and Harishchandra and of Arjuna, Pariksit and Janamejaya, the first two of whom appear as gods in later Vedic literature, were sung from mouth to mouth in accompaniment with the lute or the seven-stringed lyre. The *Satapatha Brahmana* makes mention of the hostility between the Kurus and the Srinjayas, which in the Mahabharata often looms as the battle of Kurukshetra, while a gatha in the Chhandogya Upanishad (IV,17, 9-10), according to Hopkins, alluded to the disaster of the Kurus. Valmiki and Vyasa, the celebrated authors of the Ramayana and the Mahabharata respectively, are mentioned in the later Vedic texts. Asvalayana and Panini (5th century BC) refer to such lays and legends.

The latter refers to the Mahabharata and mentions the name of Yudhisthira. Certain bas-relifs of the second century BC illustrate the date of Dasaratha and Rama. The Ramayana is certainly older than the Mahabharata which mentions Valmiki as well as the epic itself, while the tale of the Pandu king of the Mahabharata seems to be indicated by Greek writers of the fourth century BC who refer to the Indian Heracles (Krsna) and to Pandia (the Pandus). Kautilya's *Arthashastra* also refers to the stories of misdeeds of both Ravana and Duryodhana of the Ramayana and Mahabharata respectively. Jacobi points out that the Ramayana must have been generally familiar as an ancient work before the Mahabharata reached its final form. Sukthankar suggests that the Ramayana was composed in the interval which separated the Bharata from the Mahabharata, the Chaturvimshasri and the Satashasri. Most scholars consider that the Mahabharata arose between the second and fifth centuries AD. Sylvain Levi observes in this connection that the *Mahabharata, Satasahasri Samhita* and *corpus absolutissimum* of the Brahmanical Smrti, pertains to the series of those great corpora which flourished even in the first centuries of Christian era, that is of the Satasahasrika Prajnaparamita and of the Vinaya of the Mulasarvastivads movements of Buddhism and of the Brhatkatha by Gunadhya, a monument in profane literature.

Dharma in the Ramayana

The heroes and heroines, the fighting men and sages of both the Ramayana and the Mahabharata, have moulded the character of the people through the ages. The unswerving obedience of Rama to truth and righteousness, to parents and the people, the supreme loyalty and attachment of brother Lakshmana, the fidelity and tenderness of Sita "following her husband like a shadow," her heroism and serenity when she is under Ravana's grip and her fortitude and dignity as she faced the worst humiliation from Rama, or the self-effacing devotion of Hanuman, all these repeated in magnificent poem (*kavya*) and poignant drama, thrilling song and sweet cradle-tale in all the languages of India, have been the perennial springs of goodness, justice, love and sacrifice of the Indian people through the generations.

Indian personality and virtues are writ large in the gods, heroes and heroines of the epics. National morality is embodied in the colourful drama as it moves on from one end of each epic to the other. And what better clue to Indian character and civilisation can there be than the story the composition of the first rhythmn and *sloka* in Indian literature out of Valmiki's over-flowing compassion at the sight of the blood-stained bird *krauncha*, killed mercilessly by the hunter and bewailed bitterly by its mate? The compassionate poet's admonition of the hunter marks the creation of the first rhyme in India. In this new inspired metre born of tenderness, pity and indignation, the whole of the Ramayana was composed by Valmiki.

Like its sitter epic, the Ramayana is a veritable encyclopaedia of archetypal myths, tales and legends in which we find at once the combination of the din and roar of battles of titans and gods with the serenity of the forest hermitages of sages and ascetics of the pomp and magnificence of stately capitals with the beauty and enchantment of rain, autumn and spring, of the cunning, treachery and inhumanity of vicious men and rakshasas small and great, with the glorious human attributes of friendship, loyalty, sweetness and infinite tenderness towards man and beast. Over the kaleidoscopic succession of great episodes of war and peace and chequered human relations broods the spirit of righteousness (*dharma*) grounded in the truth that ensures the victory of mortal man over destiny and death. The Ramayana is a humane though heroic national epic, full to the brim of the milk of human kindness that is spilled on all sides over human and every sentient creature, and saturated with a profound love of nature and sense of the unity and continuity of life. It is the perennial mainspring in India of boundless love, compassion and self-effacement, of divine courage, fortitude and serenity in the face of human failings, conflicts and defeats. Every autumn the main episodes such as the meeting between the exiled Rama and Bharata in the forest, the return of Rama to Ayodhya, the defeat of Ravana and the banishment of Sita are acted as plays and pageants, while the worship of Devi by Rama on the eve of the Battle of Lsnka is commemorated by the autumnal festival of the Goddess throughout India.

The Myth of Agricultural Colonisation of the South

The story of the abduction of Sita and her recovery by Rama embodies a myth of agriculture and colonisation of the migrating Aryan people as they marched to fresh fields and pastures new. Sita is not born of human parents but sprung from the furrow as Janaka, king of Mithila, ploughed the field and hallowed it. She is a daughter of the earth-goddess and literally means furrow. Ramachandra is the moon-god, who rules the world of vegetation, and wins Sita by his exhibition of strength in bending the marvellous heavy bow given by the gods. The bow is the implement of the hunting stage of civilisation; and Rama as he strung, bent and broke the blow that neither gods, nor Asuras nor men could wield, ushered in the richer agricultural civilisation, under the inspiration of the Kshatriya sage, Visvamitra, now a Brahmarshi. The Ramayana hides the story of Aryan advance to the South, with the aid of various indigenous peoples with monkey, bird and other animal totems. Such myths that have already become obsolete in a sophisticated. civilised age of magnificent cities with their high walls and deep moats indicate vestiges of distant social history.

The Rakshasa and Vanara Tribes

The colonisation and settlement of the South could not proceed without a fierce struggle with the Rakshasas, hostile tribes which opposed Brahmanical rituals and institutions. But in the struggle the Vanaras, representing another group of tribes, proved a valuable ally to the Indo-Aryan cause. The Rakshas or Rakshasas are mentioned by Panini as a tribe along with the Parsus (Persians) and Asuras (Assyrians); while in respect of the Vanaras of Kishkindha, D.R. Bhandarkar refers to an inscription that mentions a ruling family in Dharwar described as "of the Bali race", "lords of Kishkindha", "best of towns". and "bearing the device of an ape (kapi) on their banner". Kishkindha is modern Bellary in Karnataka. One of the homes of the Rakshasas is Janasthana in the Godavari valley. Their connection with Lanka suggests that they were a sea-going people, while the Puranic tradition indicates their descent from the royal line of Vaisali-Paulastya Rakshasas or cruel Brahma Rakshasas, as these were called. The Rakshasa culture of the South was in no way inferior to the Indo-Aryan culture of the North. AS Ramachandra leaves the Ganges Valley he comes across, according to the *Ramayana,* vast forests extending across the Vindhyas into the Dakshinapatha with Brahmana ascetics living here and there in the region between Chitrakuta and the Pampa (tributary of the Tungabhadra), whose rituals and sacrifices were hindered by the Rakshasas, at the instance of the ascetics in the Dandaka forest, brought about the intervention of their guardian and lord, Ravana of Lanka. To wreak his vengeance on Rama he stole Sita. South Indian in the Ramayana is largely covered by the dense jungle of Dandakaranya, and no civilisation is encountered before Ramachandra reaches Kishkindha which constitutes the intermediate bastion of Aryan civilisation. Ramachandra and his consort and brother are probably deities of a certain Aryan Ikshvaku clan of Kosala that after some court intrigue in Ayodhya, started out on a colonisation enterprise in Daksinspatha, and having safeguarded against Dravidian depradations the sporadic colonies of Brahmanas in the trackless forests south of the Vindhyas, reached as far as Lanka which it conquered from the Dravidian king with the assistance of the Vanara tribes. Both Rakshasas and Vanaras are names of actual tribes of South India. In that original Ramayana, Lanka was a town, as pointed out by Jacobi. In Indian astronomy Lanka stands on the equator, where it is intersected by the meridian of Ujjayini. The identification of Lanka with Ceylon came much later and is generally attributed to Buddhist sources. The alliance between the Princes of Kosala and the Dravidian Vanara tribes of Kishkindha could be easily cemented because the former by marriage in the royal house of the Videhas of Mithila went definitely against Brahmanical orthodoxy, the kings of Magadha, where the Dravidian elements were dominant, being regarded as Sudras in the Vedic period. Finally, Ravana, as Pargiter suggests, is a title of kings derived from the Tamil Iraivan. In the puranas there is more than one Ravana or Dravidian prince. One of the Ravanas was captured and imprisoned at Mahismati by Arjuna Kartavirya. In respect of the ten heads of the king of Lanka (Dasanana) the explanation may be that Ravana's personal Dravidian name when Sanskritised accounted for this monstrosity. Ravana is spoken of sometimes as having two arms and being otherwise beautiful, adept in the Vedas and devoted to Siva.

The pioneer of Southern colonisation, however, was not Ramachandra, but Agastya who humbled the pride of the Vindhya and obtained the right of access the South, including Java and Sumatra. It is significant that the Indian Archipelago, comprising" the seven flourishing realms of Yava-dvipa, Suvarna-dvipa and Malaya-dvipa, first finds mention in literature along with the Dakshinapatha in the *Ramayana* (IV, 40,36), and that Agastya is regarded as the patron saint of both South India and South-east Asia as Siva-Guru. In Tirunelveli, there is Agastya's Hill, where the missionary saint finally retired as an anchorite after finishing his mission of Brahmanising the South.

Traces of Early Economic History

Another significant fact is that like Krishna of the Mahabharata, Ramachandra is described as dark and blue, the colour of the non-Aryan people, although both are incarnations of Vishnu, the God of the blonde Aryans. Both the epics fuse present with past history. Rama's conquest of Lanka under the guidance of Agastya, the Brahmanic sage of Southern colonisation, who gave him the weapon and the mantra for overpowering Ravana in the final encounter, and the invaluable aid he obtained from hosts of Vanara tribes of the forests, where cannibals were also encountered, led by Hanuman and Sugriva, no doubt preserve the memory of a momentous phase of Indo-Aryan history.

Primitive races and peoples of the forests have their half-human, half-beastly guardians. The five chief monkeys on the mountain Risyamukha that saw Sita being carried away by Ravana and Jatayu, king of the eagle-tribes, and his brother Sampati are leaders of the less advanced early folks of the jungle, won over to Aryan friendship and co-operation. The alliance between Aryan Rama and non-Aryan Sugriva is cemented by Hanuman making fire in primitive fashion with two pieces of wood and passing sunwise round it. That the Ikshvaku Princes played a leading role in the Aryan settlement of the far South is indicated by the *Vayu Purana* which mentions two Ikshvaku princes, Asmaka and Mulaka, living in the Dakshinapatha. The capital of the former was Potana or Paudanya and that of the latter was Pratisthana, according to Pali literature. The Suttanipata specifically mentions Bavarin, a Brahman teacher of the king of Kosala, having settled in the territory of Asaka (Asmaka) on the godavari, south of Paithan (Pratishthana). Ikshvaku kings find also prominent mention in the Nagarjunikonda and Jagayyapeta inscriptions of the South; they lived in the third or fourth century AD. But as the epic now stands the traces of early economic history that formed the nucleus of the Ramayana are completely overshadowed by heroic and elegant poetry and the inculcation of the *Dharma* of man that penetrates into every happening.

The Epic Deification of Man

It is remarkable that in both the epic Rama and Krishna are represented not as deities but as ideal men or supermen. The wicked Ravana obtained the boon from the progenitor Brahma that he cannot be slayed by either god or Gandharva, Yaksha or Rakshasa. As Ravana oppressed the gods, the Supreme Being desired that he should be slayed by man. This is the mythical genesis of the humanity of Rama. It is true that as the story unfolds, gods and sages stand before Rama in reverence urging him to remember that he was the Supreme Being himself. But Ramachandra seldom deviates from the position that he is nothing more and nothing less than man. In fact, the stress of the Ramayana is that of men becoming god-like or divine through discipline, self-restraint and the practice of *Dharma* that constitute the code of obligations of every man. These are episodes in the Ramayana where Valmiki indeed makes Rama share the helplessness of every mortal before a superior enemy, as for instance, Indrajit. Vishnu's vehicle, Garuda, rescues both Rama and Lakshmana from the peril and as he departs ovserves: "By nature the Rakshasas have cunning shifts in fight, whilst thou, who art heroic and of pure spirits, reliest on thy simplicity alone for strength. Thou should'st never trust these Rakshasas in the field of battle, for they are deceitful. And allow me to depart, O, Raghava, and do thou entertain no curiosity, as to our friendship." Garuda, who is the servant of Vishnu yet leaves Rama, who does not recollect nor takes advantage of his incarnation, after assuring him succour in need. Similarly Krishna of the Mahabharata is not the deity but the ideal man, seer and friend, and though now and then he slaughters demons, slays the king of the snakes, kills Kamsa and Hiranyakasyapa, the stress is always on the human rather than the divine attributes. Krishna himself says in the epic:" whatever I shall accomplish is due to my own will and power (*purusakara*), nothing which is in any manner divine I can undertake". But Krishna worship is established and promulgated in the Mahabharata, and there is no more dramatic scene in the epic than the one in which Sisupala grudges Krishna the chief rank and precedence in the coronation sacrifice of Yudhisthira, angrily protesting that he is neither a ruling monarch nor a Brahman seer or teacher, and summons him to battle until Krishna, for a long time forbearing and serene, kills him to the relief of the entire assembly.

There is a mythopoeic descent of the gods in the epics—both Rama and Krishna are incarnations (*avatars*) of Vishnu, the beneficent deity who rescues mankind through his rebirths from age to age whenever righeousness is overpowered by unrighteousness. But, as in the Ramayana, so in the Mahabharata, the divine incarnation is laid aside and Ramachandra and Krishna are presented as god-man, ideal man or super-man. The epics have captured the mind and soul of India because they rever along with the Supreme Being Narayana, the Superman or the ideal man (*Narottama*) as well as the common man (*Nara*). "This is the holy mystery", unequivocally asserts the Mahabharata, "there is nothing nobler than humanity." Man, absolutely every common man, is God.

The Rise of Krishna-Bhagavatism as Reform Movement

The Mahabharata strikes a significant contemporary note as it gives a symbolical meaning to sacrificial offerings against which Asceticism, Jainism and Buddhism launched their emphatic protest. The delineation of the exploits of the Pandavas led by Arjuna and Krishna Devakiputra, later on aptheosised into *Nara* and Narayana; in the annals of the Bharatas (Bharati-katha) sung in Ayodhya, Naimisharanya and Hastinapura developed into the scripture of the Bhagavata cult what the epic really is. Devakiputra Sri Krishna of Mathura must have been an outstanding spiritual leader, seer and reformer, who preached a theistic faith stressing the almighty, worshipful (Bhagavan) character of the deity before the time of the Buddha, The image of Heracles that Quintus Curtius mentions as being carried in front of the army of Porus arrayed against Alexander's forces was that of Sri Krishna, the worship of the "Indian Heracles" being associated with the Surasenas and the city of Mathura. There were three outstanding features of this new cult that from the fifth to the first century B C was developing an all-India importance. Panini refers to Vasudevakas and Arjunakas, cults of worship of Sri Krishna and Arjuna, and Udaipur inscription of the second century BC mentions the worship of Samkarsana and Vasudeva; while Patanjali who lived about the same time quotes a sentence, "May the power of Sri Krishna, accompanied by Samkarsana, increase," and also refers to the dramatic recitals of Kamsavadha and Balivadha. The same sect was also early known as the Arya Satvata sect, practising a special type of yoga meditations of Vamadeva according to the four-fold nature of the Divine. According to Yamunacarya, those who worship the Supreme God in purity of spirit are called Satvatas and Bhagavatas.

First, the new religion vies with Buddhism in replacing the ancient sacrifice of animals by the sacrifice of the desires and passions of life establishing a profound serenity of self. The Mahabharata observes: "Engaged in the sacrifice of peace, possessed of self-control and employed also in the sacrifice of Brahman, the sacrifices I shall perform are those of speech, mind and deed. How can one like me celebrate an animal sacrifice which is full of cruelty? How can one endowed with wisdom perform, like a ghoul, a sacrifice of destruction after the manner of the Kshatriyas—a sacrifice which brings only transitory rewards? I am born of my own self, O father, and without progeny I shall seek my own spiritual welfare. I shall offer the sacrifice of self, I require no children to buy my saviours. " "No animal should be sacrificed in the Krta age", we read in the Santiparva of the epic. In another place the epic speaking of the merit of Vaishavism, mentions of performance of a horse sacrifical rite in which however, no animal is killed. The emphasis of a simple, compassionate code of morality in the epic is also an answer to the Buddhist call to the law of altruism, to the noble eight-fold Aryan path. When Krishna says in *Mahabharata,* ``Know that *Dharma* is my beloved, first-born mental son, whose nature is to have compassion on all creatures: In his character I exist among men, both present and past, through many varieties and forms of existence for the preservation and establishment of righteousness,'' the epic effects a striking reconciliation between the Buddhist law of compassion and the new Bhagavata faith and incarnation and immanence of the deity. It is significant that the simple, basic principle in which *dharma* is epitomised in the Mahabharata are inscribed in the Garuda column of Heliodorus, the Greek convert to Bhagavatism, in the second century BC at Besnagar near ancient Vidisa, the capital of the Sungas. "There immortal precepts, when practised will lead to Heaven-self-restraint, renunciation and vigilance." The very words of the epic are repeated in the column.

The Stress of the Immanence of Deity

The second fundamental principle of Bhagavatism, embodied in the Mahabharata is its re-interpretation of *Dharma* from both the metaphysical and moral side. *Dharma* as the primordial norm, sustaining the universe in Rigvedic and Buddhist thought and underlying and harmonising all differences, becomes transformed in the Mahabharata into the realisation of the immanence of the deity. Dharma's eternal root principle becomes the knowledge that the Supreme Deity dwells in the hearts of all living beings. God, says Krishna in the Asvamedha Parva, takes his birth and lives among men in his infinite love for man. The incarnation of the divine is for the good of mankind (*Jagatam upakarakam*).

The third principal flows from the second, viz., the divinity of Man. This is the kernel of the teaching of the Mahabharata. In the *Bhagave Gita* as Krishna unfolds to Arjuna's wondering gaze his Universal From, all-creating and all-devouring, gracious and terrible, transcendent and immanent, the latter is struck with both ecstasy and terror. God, who is impersonal and transcendental, then assumes his gracious human form (*manusam rupam.*). Arjuna now obtains his bearings and is himself again. The transformation of the historical Krishna, the seer and friend of Arjuna, into the deity is nothing new in India. For according to the Brhadaranyaka Upanishad, " the worshipper becomes one with the god he truly sees". Thus, formerly had the sage Vamadeva, after realising the Supreme Truth felt, " I am Manu, I am Surya", and Indra himself said, " I am Prana, I am the conscious self. Know me and worship one as life and as breath." Besides, the doctrine of the descent of God (*avatara*) that found its first dramatic formulation in the fourth chapter of the *Bhagavad Gita* facilitated the identification of the historical individual with the Absolute, which" though eternal and immutable in essence passes through many births for the good of mankind." The apotheosis of Krishan-Vasudeva is completed when he is called Kesava or Lord of Brahma (Ka) and Siva (Isa) in the *Mahabharata* and Govinda or Lord of Indra in the Harivamsa. The *Bhagavad Gita* clinches the point by observing that the worship of Krishna leads to Brahma-bhava and salvation. The *Mahabharata* finds and proclaims the Deity intimate, visible, human are personal. God in the *Mahabharata* is the Mother, Father, Friend or Beloved, the counsellor, friend and guide of the Pandavas in their war of righteousness—the battle of Bharata-the protector of the honour of outraged Draupadi, the call of conscience of Dhratarastra and Drona on the eve of the great battle and the protective father of the forlorn Vrsni women of Dvaraka.

Besides Krishna-Vasudeva is the ruler of Mathura and Dwaraka, the Samghamukhya (president) of the confederation of the republican tribes, the Vrsnis, Yadavas, Andhakas, Kukuras and Bhojas which he saves from internal disruption due to the party politics of Babhru, Ugrasena, Ahuka and Akrura, the political seer, prophet and builder of United India, the Pandavan empire (Mahabharata) held by Yudhisthira for about thirty-six years. The epic has lost definite recollections of the great migrations and settlements of the Rigvedic Aryans. In the Vedic literature we find the Ganges-Jamuna Doab occupied by the Kuru-Panchalas of whom the Bharatas were the leading tribe. The epic takes up as its focus of interest, the northern doab for which rival Aryan clans fight: the tribes of Southern Madhyadesa, the Panchalas and the Srnjayas against the Kurus. It has utilised tales and lays, referred also in some Upanishads and Brahamanas relating to the hostility between the Srnjayas and the

Kurus and the downfall and expulsion of the latter from the "Field of the Kurus" (Kurukshetra). The defeat of the Kurus and the establishment of paramount sovereignty of the Pandava kings under the aegis of Krishna Vasudeva at the Kuru capital of Hastinapura situated on the Ganges (Anugangam Hastinapuram, says Patanjali) are gloriously depicted. The scene of the Battle of Bharata is laid near Thanesar not far from another ancient capital Indraprastha on the Jamuna (Indapatta or Indapattana, according to the Guttila and Maha-sutassoma *Jatakas*) and the epic makes all the Kshatriya princes and people of ancient India from the Himalayas to the Dravidian states of the south and from Dvaraka to Kamrupa participate in the both the battle and the imperial coronation ceremony. The Kuru-Panchala country had long ago lost the political importance it had at the time of the Bharata warrior kings, but became instead the most celebrated seat of Brahmanical leaning, humming with hermitages and parsads where the great bulk of literature of the Upanishads, the Brahmanas and the Aranyakas was composed and Buddhism could never have any foothold But the epic restores its political importance through the victory of the Pandavas over their Kinsmen and proclamation of the imperial suzerainty of Yudhisthira. The sacred land which was *par excellence* the cradle of Vedic learning and culture should be, in the eyes of the epic. The natural political focus of the empire of the Bharatas. The "Tale of the Victory" (Jayanama Itihasa) reflects the ideas and achievements of Mauryan imperialism. Historians find in the epic references not to Emperor Chandragupta Maurya but to the "unconquerable" Ashoka and to the Yavana overlord of the lower Indus valley and his compatriot, Dattamitra, possibly Demetrios of Sakala. Krishna, the inspirer of the Rajasuya sacrifice of the Pandavas, was fully alive to the danger of foreign conquest and the need of political integration of vast numbers of kingdoms stretching from Badari in the north, the hermitage of Nara-Narayanaa, to Kanyakumari in the extreme south. The superman of the epic is *par excellence* the builder of Bharatavarsa.

The Dominant Cult of Sri Krishna-Narayana

The Mahabharata achieves a synthesis of the superhuman attributes of Sri Krishna as the seer and speaker of the Bhagavad Gita, the counsellor of Emperor Yudhisthira, the prince of Mathura and Dvaraka, the associate of the cowherds of Gokula or Vraja, the pastoral country, and the Purusottama of the Yogis.The non-Aryan folk elements in the Sri Krishna-Narayana cult are fully revealed not only in Krishna's name as Govinda, the god of the cowherds or "cow-finder," his association in early life with Bakadeva or Halayudha, the god of husband-men in his destruction of demons and many marvellous exploits such as the lifting of the Mount Govardhana (depicted in Gupta sculpture) to offset the devastation threatened by the Indo-Aryan God Indra in his wrath against the agricultural and pastoral folks but also in his dark complexion, yellow apparel and the peacock feather in his headgear. Krishna's non-Aryan filiation is shown by his marriage to the fair Chandala girl Jambhavati according to the *Mahanamagga Jataka*. Jambhavati later on became transformed in the Puranas into Jambavati, the daughter if the king of Bears, But the Krishna-Narayana cult achieves a most significant religious synthesis between Indo-Aryan vedic worship and the non-Aryan Dravidian puja. The Vedic sacrifices. the epic warns, are not for the aspirants after the highest. "Those who offer sacrifices to the various gods go to the gods. the worshippers of the manes to the manes, and the worshipper of the elemental powers and spirits go to them. So my (Krishna's) devotees will come to me." And the Krishna cult gives the message of hope of deliverance to the non-Aryans by adding that not only the Vedic sacrifices (*yajnas*) ultimately reach the Lord alone through the Vedic path but the offering with devotion of a leaf, a flower, a fruit, or water as in the non-Aryan ritual is also acceptable (The *Bhagavad Gita, 9, 25.25*). According to Mark Collins *'puja'* is a Dravidian word (pu meanining flower, and *gey* meaning to do).S.K. Chatterji translates *puja* as flower ritual or *puspa-karma* which he contrasts with the Vedic fire oblation or *puspa-karma*. The cleansing of Vedic ritualism through the omission of animal slaughter and the four-fold metaphysical re-interpretation of sacrifices and *daiva-yajna, jnana yajan* and *indriya yajna* and the cleansing of the Dravidian puja ritualism through the emphasis of love and purity of heart are the great achievements of Sri Krishna of the epic. But the epic clearly indicates that the new dispensation was not accepted without serious opposition. Reinforcing the childhood legends of Krishna as the slayer of Putana, the epic here and there deifies the prophet of the new Bhagavata cult, identifying him with Vishnu-Narayana of the Vedic religion and stresses religious bhakti in such dramatic incidents as the outraged Draupadi's cry to Sri Krishna for the protection of her honour and Bhism's final absorption in Him. For the Mahabharata above all expound the doctrine of Bhakti which could rally round various sections of orthodox Brahmans and wean them from the heresies of Buddhism and Jainism. The *Bhagavad Gita*, the Narayaniya, the Visvopakhyana and other parts of the *Mahabharata* equally emphasise the conception of a personal deity, immanence, bhakti, reverence and grace. The Krishna-cult has inspired some of the best examples of Gupta art in the form of images. Some of the earliest Krishna images are those of the forth century AD at Mandor, near Jodhpur, depicting beautiful Krishna-scenes including the raising of Mount Govardhana. Near Udayagiri at Patli there is a colossal Gupta relief (about 5th century AD) on the nativity of Krishna lying by the side of Devaki, watched by five attendants. Reference may also be made to Krishna-Narayana placed by Skandagupta on the top of the Bhitari Lat (about 460 AD) commemorating his victory over the Huns "which he reported to his mother who listened with tears of joy in her eyes, as Krishna reported his victories to his mother Devaki" For the Imperial Guptas, fighting for the honour of the land and of Kula-Lakshmi that was being "shaken" and "overwhelmed" by the demoniac barbarians, Krishna, "the slayer of Putana", was the special object of devotion and worship. In the age of the *Mahabharata* along with the Krishna-Bhagavatas other theistic cults such as the as Pasupatas and the Sauras, worshipping Siva and Sirua respectively, rose. There were also worshippers of Skanda, Visakha, Vaisravana and Manibhadra. The more ancient folk deities such as Kuvera, the Nagas and the Yakshas were also objects of devotion of the common people. Fissiparous religious trends were combated in the Maḥabharata by the doctrine that Vishnu and Siva are identical and that the Supreme Being is one, the Ordainer who lives in the heart of everybody. The *Mahabharata* speaks of the Triune (Trimurti) Creator in the manifestation of Brahma, Preserver in that of Vishnu and Destroyer in that of Siva and also of Satya Naryana as the one Supreme Being or Truth. Such are the attempts in the Mahabharata to integrate a theistic faith with the earlier Upanishadic speculation, and rehabilitate Brahmanism after a few centuries of Ajivika, Jain and Buddhist demolition of devas and emphasis of personal development as the aim of spiritual life.

The Emphasis of Universalist Morality in the Mahabharata

On the social side the Mahabharata similarly combats the emphasis of asceticism in the new heresies, and finds no justification for persons abandoning their homes and families for the cloister of forests. Virtues can be achieved or lost in household and social life and relations. The true spirit of India is embodied in the following:

"the household (*grhastha*) shall have his life established in Brahman, shall pursue the eternal varieties, and in all activities of life dedicate his works to Brahman". Thus the epic posits the doctrine of self-less action (niskama karma) with a detachment of spirit. This, and not homelessness, opens the avenue to a virtuous and adequate life. Says the Mahabharata, "Self-restraint, charity and vigilance—these are the three horses of Brahman. He who rides on the car of his soul, having yoked (three horses) with the help of reins of right behaviour, goes, O King, to the realm of Brahman, shaking off all fear of death. He who assures to all beings freedom from fear goes to the highest of regions, the blessed abode of Vishnu".

Again, the Mahabharata accepts the criticism of Buddhism against the emphasis of heredity, race or colour in the status system, and reiterates like the latter the ancient norm, the meta-physical principle of *varna* or social gradation according to spiritual status and moral responsibility. The epic stresses that the highest sacrifices that man can undertake—the Sraddhayajnas, sacraments of devotion, are open to all including the Sudras."Even gods do not disdain to share the offerings of sacrifices of Sudras when performed in such spirit. Therefore, all the four *varnas* are equal". Finally, the Mahabharata is a compendium of the Indo-Aryan philosophies of state, law, morality, *dharma* and salvation, of ancient lore adjusted to the changing times and circumstances (*yugadharma*). The Santiparva gives a brilliant exposition of the duties of the king and of his relations to the various orders of the people, groups and institutions that have stood in good stead the monarchs of the later ages in the establishment of a sound polity. The King's ministers in the Mahabharata comprised four Brahmanas, eight Kshatriyas, twenty-one Vaisyas, three Sudras and one Suta—the inclusion of the latter being a recognition of the importance and dignity of the lower castes.

Parasikas, Hunas and Sakas

While not too apprehensive of, or intolerant towards, the hordes of outlandish Mlecchas or barbarians such as the Yavanas, Pahlavas, Hunas and Parasikas with their divergent customs, beliefs and ways of living, the epic is a challenge towards the realisation of the fundamental cultural and spiritual unity of Bharatavarsa and of political unification under a single suzerain. There is reference in the epic to the Yavana rule over Sauvira or the lower Indus basin and to another

Yavana Prince Dattamitra, sometimes identified with Demetrios. The epic prophesies that the Sakas and Yavanas will rule unrighteously in the evil age to come. Against such a national misfortune the Mahabharata steels the heart of the people. It formulates a universalist code of *dharma* for all social classes and communities that serves as the strong enduring binder in a fluent racial and political scene. The *Mahabharata* is the inspirer and builder of the unity of India amidst great, even baffling, diversity and complexity.

The *Mahabharata* is a growth of centuries that saw not merely the influx of vast numbers of Yavanas, Hunas, Sakas and other foreigners and racial admixture (*varnasamkara*), but also the spread of Aryan colonisation and settlement to the south beyond the Godavari and to the east beyond the Lauhitya or the Brahmaputra. The river hymn of the epic that replaced the ancient Rigvedic hymn clearly indicates the extension of the geographical horizon, and is even now repeated at the time of daily ablution: "O ye Ganga, Yamuna, Godavari, Sarasvati, Narmada, Sindhu, Kaveri, join ye in this ablution water". Yet the centre of Aryan civilisation was still the western portion of the Middle-land. Even the imperial capital of the Mauryas, viz., Pataliputra is not mentioned in the epic which refers, however to the more ancient capital of Girivajra where were kept in cinfinement many princes for slaughter "as mighty elephants are kept in mountain caves by the lion." There are many forests even in the Madhyadesa that are mentioned, such as Khandavavana, the Kamyakavana and the Dvaitavana. The burning of the Khandavavana in the valley of the Jamuna and expulsion of the Nagas with their ruler, Taksaka, who had to take refuge in the hills, represent episodes where the Indo-Aryan and non-Aryan peoples met in bloody conflict. On the other hand, the marriage of Arjuna with Ulupi, daughter of the Naga king, Vasuki, and of Bhima with Hidimbi, daughter of a Rakshasa, represents a significant step towards racial assimilation of the two great peoples in the Yamuna-Ganges basin.

The Mahabharata—an Epitome of the Indian Philosophy of Life

The *Mahabharata* brings in old and ancient gods and religions and philosophical doctrines, now to scrutinise and reject, now to accommodate or reconcile. It is a repository of forgotten gods and heroes and of abandoned creeds and faiths, Yet it is a living embodiment of the new cult of Bhagavatism and the philosophical doctrines of Bhakti and Karma—truly Krishna Veda, so significant for the social and religious history of the later ages—the from end to end of the moving drama interweave like warp and woof the tangled lives and fates of the various characters. The Mahabharata epitomises the philosophy of life of India.

In spite of its eclecticism and assemblage of diverse social custom, moral doctrines and philosophical speculations, it remains for the people of India as a whole the enduring bedrock on which their moral and spiritual values are rooted and practised; while the types of men and women it created such as Krishna, Bhima, Karna, Drona, Arjuna, Yudhisthira, Gandhari, Draupadi, Savitri and Damayanti are some of the noblest that can be found in any civilisation and perennial living symbols and models of goodness, love and righteousness. It is the epic religion of Man, the conception of immanence of the deity in man, of Hari the Ordainer, Censor and Guide of all "sacrifices" of mind, speech and activity in every human heart (antayami) that has been the fountain-head of the development of such heroic, tender, self-effacing and delicate personalities and of their "imitations" through the centuries. There is no blessing in which Indian womanhood rejoices more than this; Be like Savitri and Damayanti, no nobler exhortations to Indian manhood than act energetically like Arjuna respomding to the call of his Divine charioteer (Partjhasarathi); and no wiser counsel than pursue Truth and Justice like Yudhisthira, beloved of *dharma.*And yet the epic constitutes a profound appeal to the modern heart and conscience. The anger and indignation of Draupadi enslaved and outraged by the insolent Duryodhana, the voluntary blindfolding of Gandhari to share the perpetual disability of her royal husband, blindness, Karna's disobedience to his mother revealing to him the secret of his illegitimate birth on the eve of the Great Battle, Amba's frustrated love and fierce resolve to wreak her vengeance not upon the King of the Salyas but upon Bhisma's vow of celibacy to enable his father to marry that lady of his choice, his unfolding to Yudhisthira and Arjuna the secret of slaying him in battle and his poise as he lies on his bed of arrows watching for death on the turning of the sun to the north, and the strange procession of the dead Kaurava princes and troops issuing out in night from the dark waters of the Ganges in their full might and majesty before Dhrtarastra and Gandhari whose aching grief is lightened, Yudhisthira pleading before God not cast off the devoted dog in his ascent to heaven and his preference of hell where his presence may sooth his kinsmen and comrades—these are a few typical episodes that are thoroughly modern in tone and spirit, and have the same stirring perennial interest as the great richly human creations of contemporary literature. It is the tender and broad humanity of the *Mahabharata* that accounts for its universal appeal. No wonder that the legends of the Mahabharata were carried beyond the Indian Ocean to Kambuja (Indo-China) in the sixth century AD and to Mongolia in the seventh century and translated into the vernacular in Java by the tenth century. Even without their social and religious context the stories of the *Mahabharata,* recited and dramatised, still arouse enthusiasm among peoples in other lands.

The Mahabharata as the Focus of a National Renaissance

Yet the *Mahabharata* is intended not only for the common man of India, whom it educates and exhorts through numerous soul-stirring, didactic and narrative episodes, and for the Kshatriya prince, whom it teaches the life of valour and art of government, but also for the man of contemplation. The *Bhagavad Gita* is really the core and epitome of the voluminous *Mahabharata,* the concise formulation of the religious and practical principles of the epic into a system. It was the same *Risi* or poet who composed both. The epic is integrated out of various stuffs and strands; the *itihasa* or saga of the Bharatas and the Kshatriya tribes and princes sung by the bards; the various moral and religious folktales of different regions and peoples of India; the tales of sacredness of the holy places of pilgrimage recited locally; the myths and legends of the Risis oft repeated in their sylvan hermitages; the maxims and regulations derived from the current Puranas and Dharmasastras; and above all, the cult of Bhakti of the new Krishna-Bhagavatism. On the whole there is a remarkable unity in the whole composition, inspite of the opinions of Winternitz and Hopkins, who miss the basic design in their emphasis of the juxtaposition of the narrative and the didactic, and judge the Indian cultural product from the norms derived from Homeric criticism. In India *kavya,* painting and sculpture often have not pursued an exclusively aesthetic purpose, and the *Mahabharata* should be regarded at once as a narrative and a *Dharma-samhita* without imposing any limits on the Indian literary tradition or the creative genius of an Indian poet. Linguistically speaking, the epic establishes the supremacy of Sanskrit as the national language of India. Vittore Pisani observes in this connection:"It is the greatest exponent of a reaction to the use of Prakrit in the literature out of strictly Brahmanical circles, and of the successful attempt to give to profane India an over-regional and national language."

The *Mahabharata* is a rallying focus of the social and religious revival that ultimately culminates in the Gupta renaissance and imperialism. It is a defence of the Brahmanical society and scheme of life of the Vedic pattern against the inundation of exotic ideals due to foreign infiltration, invasion and conquest, and the spread of the heresies of Jainism and Buddhism that were threatening to dissipate the whole cultural heritage. The *Mahabharata* owes its power and popularity in India to two factors: first, it is the expounding of a new faith, an ardent and catholic neo-Hinduism that integrates the current metaphysical theories of the Sankhya and the Vedanta with a mystical, theistic emphasis of the Supreme Being; and second, it is the epitome and compendium of the ancient essential traditions of the Divine society that were threatened by foreign infiltration and conquest. The Mahaabharata, cognizant of the egalitarian spirit of Jainism and Buddhism and their vehement protest against sacerdotalism and caste, reformulates the vedic metaphysical ordering of Varna as well as the spiritual principle of fire rituals. In the epic the Vedic ritual and sacrifices are not rejected but invested with a new symbolic significance. The sacrifices now extolled are those of speech, mind and action. The more recent philosophical speculations of the Sankhya and the Vedanta are reconiled with the sweeping current of Bhakti, the new religious manifestation assumed by Krishna and Siva-Bhagavatism and Mahayana Buddhism. But the reconciliation is on the lines of the ancient mystical and philosophical tradition, as represented by the Svetasvatara Upanishad. The Brahman of the Upanishad and the Purusa of the Sankhya become identical with Purusottma and Mahesa in the Yoga of the *Mahabharata*. But all derive their *raison d'etre* from the Supreme Cosmic Being, Brahman or Truth, who appears in myriad forms according to the level and stage of social and individual culture. And the Supreme Deity lives in the heart of man, eliciting his love, devotion and self-surrender. The resuscitation of the Divine society takes place in the *Mahabharata* in the fervour of devotion to the personal deity, Krishna-Vasudeva, which instills into the Indian, man an undying faith in his inalienable spiritual destiny, and protects him against both the denationalisation by foreign influences and the disruptive monastic creed of the Buddha.

Asceticism, renunciation and compassion that have become the basis of the religious reform of Jainism and Buddhism are not discounted. but given their place in a revised, flexible scheme of the duties and stages of Varnasrama and the reorientation of the heroic and moral traditions of the people. The withdrawal of the elite of the people to the monastery and the forest has been a national danger in an era of foreign invasion and subjugation. The Mahabharata fights the battle against the foreigners as it sets forth the ideal of Sri Krishna, the supreme man of action, the happy warrior for Dharma's sake to whom victory is assured (yato Krishnas yato dharma yato dharmastato jayah). The epic sings the deeds of courage, enterprise and sacrifice of the Bharatas and other famous ancient kings and warriors in a manner and context calculated to invigorate the Indian nation in the grim fight against the hordes of the dangerous (daruna) Sakas and Hunas that had invaded and conquered large parts of the Indus valley, Kathiawar and Malwa. The composer of the *Mahabharata* is at once a social reformer, a prophet of nationalism and a seer of a universal religion. The epic is a perennial reservoir of moral and spiritual strength and inspiration which has never failed the people of India in the crises of individual life and the vicissitudes of history.

8 | Ancient Indian Tribes

The Prāgjyotiṣas

If the story of Krsna's fights with the demons, Muru and Naraka, as told in the Viṣṇu Purāna,[1] the Mahābhārata[2] and the Harivamsa[2] can be interpreted to have any ethnological significance, then undoubtedly the Prāgjyotisas were a people of non-Aryan extraction. The Epics definitely describe the country of the Prāgjyotisas as an *asura or dānava* kingdom ruled over by the demons, Naraka and Muru, with whom the leaders of Aryanism were in frequent conflict. The Puranic description of Naraka, the asura leader, attributes to him immense power and strength that baffled and perplexed even Indra. The environs of his capital city, called Prāgjyotisapura, were defended by nooses, the Puranic description states, constructed by the demon, Muru.[6] Of course the Aryan leader, Kṛṣṇa, is described to have got the better of his fight with the demons which may be interpreted as one of the exploits of the history of the spread of Aryan influence in the east.

The Mahābhārata[5] in other places refers to Prāgjyotisa as a Mleccha kingdom ruled over by a king named Bhagadatta 'who is always spoken of in respectful and even eulogistic terms'. Bhagadatta is styled as a Yavana,[6] probably denoting that he did not belong to the Aryan fold. The Udyoga Parva of the Great Epic describes him as the son of Naraka, the Prāgjyotisa king, vanquished by Kṛṣṇa, and as an ally of Duryodhana.[7] Among his retinues Bhagadatta counted the Cīnas (the people of China),[8] and if the Kālayavana of the Viṣṇu Purāna refers to the same king, as Wilson seems to think,[9] he also 'assembled many myriads of Mlecchas and barbarians' among his followers. The Mahābhārata mentions him as a king of boundless might (*aparyanta-bala*) and ruling over (the country of) Muru and Naraka.[10]

According to the Mahābhārata, Prāgjyotisa was situated in the northern region of Indian[11]; but the Mārkandeya Purāna places it in the eastern region, once along with the Bradmottaras (a misreading for Suhmottaras), the pravijayas (perhaps Prāvrseys), the Bhārgavas the Jñeyamallakas, Madras, the Videhas, the Tāmraliptakas the Mallas and the Magadhas, and at another place with the Candreśvaras, the Khaśas, the Magadhas and the Lauhityas.[12] The mountainous regions called Antar-giri, Vahir-giri and Upa-giri in the Great Epic[13] appear to comprise the lower slopes of the Himalayas and the Nepalese Terai; and it is not unlikely that Prāgjyotisas lived contiguously as Bhagadatta is called Sailālaya.[14] His country was also probably contiguously situated to those of the Kirātas and Cīnas who formed his retinue.[15] According to the Abhidhāna-cintāmani, the Prāgjyotisa was the same as Kāmarūpa,[16] though in the Raghuvaṁśa, the Prāgjyotisas the Kāmarūpas are described as two different people. Generally speaking the two countries came in latter times to be regarded as the same. In the Kalikā Purāna,[17] for example, the capital of Kāmarūpa is called Prāgjyotisapura which has been identified with Kāmākhyā or Gauhātī. The Raghuvaṁśa seems to locate Prāgjyotisa beyond the Brahmaputra,[18] but Kālidāsa's knowledge about distant geographical locations is not always very satisfactory. For all practical purposes Prāgjyotiṣa may, therefore, be identified with the whole of Assam proper along with northern Bengal as far as Rangpur and Cooch Behar which is the territory comprised by Kāmarūpa, according to the Yoginitantra.[19]

Bhagadatta, as we have seen was a *mleccha,* and his people also *mlecchas or yavanas,* i.e. non-Aryans, but the Rāmāyana ascribes the foundation of the kingdom to Amūrtarajas, one of the four great sons of the great King Kuśa,[20] which is a significant. Aryan name.

According to the Brahmāṇḍa Purāṇa and the Rāmāyaṇa, there seems to have been another Prāgjyotisapura on the river Vetravatī or Betwa.[21]

The later kings of Kāmarūpa, who claimed to have been descended from the lineage of Narakāsura and Bhagadatta, figured prominently in Indian history. Most important of them was Kumāra Bhāskaravarman, an ally of Harsavarddhana Śilāditya, and referred to by both Bāṇa in his Harṣacarita and Yuan Chwang, the celebrated Chinese pilgrim.

King Prālamba of Kāmarūpa (C . 800-825 A.D.)[22] is described in the Tezpur plates of his grandson as Prāgjyotiṣeśa. His grandson

Vanamāla Claims to belong to the line (anvaya) of the lords of Prāgjyotiṣa, and so also does Balavarman, another king of the same dynasty (C. 975 A.D.). During the earlier half of the eleventh century A.D. the capital city of Prāgjyotisa seems to have attained a great eminence under the kingship of Ratnapāla. In the Bargaon grant of the king the city is referred to as an impregnable one and rendered beautiful by the Lauhitya.[23]

The Kamauli grant of Vaidyadeva[24] (C. 1100) refers to the Maṇḍala of Kāmarūpa and the Viṣaya of Prāgjyotiṣa which implies that the latter was the bigger administrative division including Kāmarūpa.

Rājyamatī, a daughter of King Harṣavarman Prāgjyotiṣa (according to the stray plate of King Harjara),[25] is described as Bhagadattarākjakulajā.[26]

The Pāriyātras

It is doubtful whether the Pāriyātras, or Pāripātras as they were also called,[27] can be, ethnologically speaking, designated as a tribe or people, to be distinguished from the Vindhyas with whom they lived contiguously or from other peoples who had their habitat in and around the same locality. The Purāṇas however always enumerate them as a distinct people associated with the Pāripātra mountains which evidently gave their name to the people.

As already noticed, there are two variant forms of the mountainous region inhabited by this people as given in the Purāṇas: Pāriyātra and Pāripātra; but Pāripātra seems to be the more usual form of reading, though Pāriyātra occurs not unfrequently. In the topographical list of the Purāṇas, the Pāriyātra or Pāripātra hills are mentioned as the one of the seven hill range together forming what is called *Kulācalas* or *Kulaparvatas,* family mountains, or mountain ranges or systems. They are the Mahendra, Malaya, Sahya, Śuktimat, Rkṣa, Vindhya and Pāripātra.[28] The Bhāgavata, Vāyu, Mārkaṇḍeya and Padma Purāṇas and the Bhīṣmaparvan of the Mahābhārata also add a list of inferior mountains to these seven.[29] The principal seven hill ranges are similarly enumerated in all the Puranic authorities, and their situation is easily determined by the rivers which are listed to flow from them.[30]

Pāripātra in particular is always associated with the Vindhyas which, it is well known, is the general name of the chain of hills that stretches across Central India dividing India into its well-defined and natural north and south divisions; but it is evident from the Puranic list and the situations of the hils mentioned in it that the name Vindhyas, in the Purāṇas, is restricted to the eastern division of long range of hills. According to the Vāyu Purāṇa, however, it is the part south of the river Narmada, or the Sātpurā range of hills. Pāripātra is the northern and western portion of the Vindhyas, and may be said to include the range of hill now known as the Aravalli.

The Purāṇas, for example, the Viṣṇu, mention another Pāriyātra or Pāripātra as situated on the west, associated with the semimythical mount Meru, 'Nisadha and Pāriyātra are the limitative mountains on the west (of Meru), stretching, like those on the east, between the Nila and Niṣadha ranges.[31] But there is hardly any reason to confound the Pāripātra of the *Kulācalas* situated in the centre and south of India with this Pāripātra or Pāriyātra associated with the semi-mythical Meru of the extreme north.

The list of the seven Kulācalas seems to have been known, in some form or other, to Ptolemy, as early as the first half of the second century A.D.; he also specifies seven ranges of hills although his list does not correspond with the Puranic list, with the exception of the Ouindion, identical with the Vindhyas, and the Ouxenton, identical with the Rkṣa (Vant).[32] Wilson thought that Adeisathron might be identified with the Pāriyātras,[33] this has been found to be untenable, and modern research tends to connect the range more with the Western Ghāṭs, more properly, 'that section of the Western Ghāts which is immediately to the north of the Coimbatore gap as it is there the Kāverī rises'.[34]

According to Rājaśekhara, all the seven *Kulaparvatas* were comprised within the Kumārī dvīpa who we southern-most limit, according to the Skanda Purāṇa, was the Pāriyātra.[35] In the period of the Brahmanical and Buddhist sūtras too Pāriyātra was the southern-most limit of contemporary Aryandom or Āryāvarta, while the eastern and western boundaries were formed by Kālakāvana (probably near Allahabad) and Adarsana and Thūna (on the Saraswatī) respectively.[36]

The Purāṇas refer to a number of rivers issuing from the Pāriyātra: the Varṇśā, the Siprā, the Carmanvatī, the Sindhu and the Vetravatī. The Mahi is well known; Varṇśā or Parṇśā has been identified by Pargiter with the modern Banās, a tributary of the

Carmanvati identical with the Chambal. Sindhu is Kāli Sindhu, a tributary of the Chambal and Vetravati is the same as modern Betwa. Śiprā is the famous river immortalized in Sanskrit classical poetry. The Viṣṇu Purāṇa mentions still another river as issuing from the Pāripātra mountains, namely the vedaṣmṛti on Vedasmṛta, according to the Mahābhārata.[37]

The Vāyu Purāṇa mentions the Kārusas and the Mālavas as dwelling along the Pāripātra mountains.[38] The Nasik Praśasti of Gautamiputra Śātakarṇi seems to associate the Kukuras also with the Pāriyātra.[39] This is also probably the earliest epigraphic mention of the mountains. But a more elaborate mention is made in the Mandasor inscription of Yaśodharman and Viṣṇuvardhana,[40] where a large tract of land is described as containing many countries, which lie between the Vindhya (mountains), from the slopes of the summits of which there flows the pale mass of the waters of (the river) Revā, and the mountain Pāriyātra, on which trees are bent down in (their) frolicsome leaps by the long-tailed monkeys (and stretches) up to the ocean.

The Lāṭas

The name of the Lāṭas as a people must have been known as early as the beginning of the Christian era, if not earlier still, and their country Lāṭa or Lāṭaviṣaya was well known in Indian history till as late as the seventh and eighth centuries. It is however curious that neither the country nor its people are ever mentioned in any of the earlier or authoritative Purāṇas or even in the Epics.

The earliest definite mention of the country seems to have been made by Ptolemy, the celebrated Greek geographer and astronomer. According to his description of Indian within the Ganges, Lārike lay to the east of Indo-Skythia along the sea-coast.[41] It was Lassen who first established identity of Lārike with Sanskrit Rāsṭrika in its Prākrit form Lāṭika which is easily equated with Lāāta Lāṭadeśa in its Prākrt from Lārdeśa in its Prākrt form Lārdeśa (the country of Lār) also seems to have been a very early name for the territory of Gujarat and northern Konkon,[42] and McCrindle conjectured that Lārike might therefore be a formation from Lār with the Greek termination *ike* appended'.[43] The name Lārdeśa probably survived the Hindu period, 'for the sea to the west of that coast was in the early Muhammadan time called the sea of Lār, and the language spoken on its shores was called by Mas'ūdi Lāri' (Yule's Marco Polo, II, p. 353 n).[44]

In ptolemy's Lārike lay the mouth of the river Mōphis which is identical with the Mahī, a village named Pakidare which is difficult to be identified, and the cape Maleo which 'must have been a projection of the land somewhere between the mouth of the Mahī and that of the Narmadā, but nearer to the former if Ptolemy's indication be correct'.[45]

The two great cities of Baryagaza and Ozene were also within the political division of Lārıke. In Ptolemy's Gulf of Barygaza lay Kammane, doubtless identical with Kamonone of the Periplus which places it to the south of the Narmadā estuary while Ptolemy locates it to the north; north of the river Namados identical with the river Narmadā; Nausaripa which is the same as modern Nausāri on the coast and Sanskrit Navasārikā, and finally Poulipoula which in Yule's map is located at modern Sanjam on the coast south from Nausārī. Barygaza itself is the same as Sanskrit Bhraguksetra or Bhṙgukaccha, Pāli Bharukaccha, modern Broach; the same form of the name is repeatedly found also in the Periplus.

Lāṭa is mentioned twice in Vātsyāyana's Kāmasūtra; in one passage characterristics of ladies of the Lāṭa country are described while in another those of men.[46] He does not however give any clue as to the location of the country.

The Ceylonese chronicles, the Dipavamsa and the Mahāvamsa refer to the country of Lāla in connection with the first Aryan immigration to Ceylon led by Prince Vijaya. Lāla has been sought to be identified with both Lāta or Lāḍa in Gujarat and Rādha in Bengal and both countries seem to claim the honour of the first Aryanization of the island. Prince Vijaya is described in the chronicles to have been the great-grandson of the princess of Vanga, and hence one school of scholars mainly depending on historical evidence proposes to equate Lāla with Rāḍha, while the other school mainly resting their argument on philosophical grounds finds Lāla to be philologically more closely akin to Lāṭa or Lāḍa. It is not impossible that the tradition of two different streams of immigation, as Dr. Barnett thinks, came to be knit together in the story of Vijaya.

The Lāṭa country in the days of the early Imperial Guptas came to be constituted into an administrative province as Lāṭa-viṣaya along with Tripuri-viṣaya, Arikiṇa-viṣaya, Autarvedi-viṣaya, Vālavī-viṣaya, Gayā-viṣaya, etc. These *viṣayas* or *pradeśas* seem to have been subordiante to the administrative division of *bhukti.*

It is likely that the Lāṭa country was the same as the Lāteśvara country mentioned in one or two early Gujara and Rāṣṭrakūṭa records. In the Barroda copperplate inscription, the capital of the kingdom of Lāteśvara is said to have been at Elapur (verse II). The inscription also gives the genealogy of the kings of Lāteśvara. That the Lāṭa country was distinguished from Saurāṣtra is proved by a grant dated 812 A.D. when the Rāṣṭrakūṭa Karkarāja of Lāteśvara recorded a grant of land (C. 800-825 A.D.).

—*B.C.Law*

REFERENCES

1. 5, XXIX, Wilsou's edn., 88ff.
2. Vana P., xii. 488; Udyoga P., xlvii. 1887-92.
3. Hari V., cxxi. 6791-9; cxxii. 6873, etc.
4. Prāgjyotiṣapurasyāsitsamantācchatayojanam
   ācita Mauravaiḥ pāśaiḥ kṣurāntirmurdhijotam
5. Sabhā P., xxv. 1000-1; *ibid.*, L. 1834; Udyoga P., clxvi.5804; Karṇa P., 104-5.
6. Sabhā P., xii. 578-80; *ibid.*, L. 1834-6.
7. Chap. IV.
8. Udyoga P., xvii. 584-5.
9. Wilson's Visṇu P., Book V., pp. 54-55.
10. Muruṁ ca Narakaṁ caiva śāsti yo Yavanādhipaḥ
    aparyantabala rājā praticyāṁ Varūṇo yatha
    Bhagadatto mahārājo vṛddhastava pituḥ sakhā
    sa vācā praṇatastasya karmaṇā ca viśesataḥ
    Sabhā P., i. 578-9.
11. Sabhā P., xxv. 1000; Vana P.,cclii. 15240-42.
12. Pargiter's Ed., pp. 327-330 and 357.
13. Sabhā P., xxv. 1000-xxvi. 1012.
14. Strī P., xxiii. 644.
15. Sabhā P., xxv.1002; xxxiii. 1268-9; Karṇa P., v. 104-5.
16. Prāgjyotiṣah Kāmarūpaḥ, IV. 22. The name Kāmarūpa seems to have been later.

17. Chap. 38.
18. IV. 8I.
19. Imp. Gaz. India, xiv. p. 331.
20. Ādi K., xxxv. I-6.
21. Chap. 27, and Kiṣkindhyā K., Chap. 42 respectively.
22. J.A.S.B., 1840, ix. 2, pp. 766ff.
23. *Ibid.*, 1898, LXVII, pp. 115-118.
24. Ep. Ind. XII, pp. 37ff.
25. I.H.Q., Dec. 1927, p. 841, f.n.I.
26. Ind. Ant., 1880, IX,p. 179; J.R.A.S., 1898, pp. 384-5.
27. Mārk, P., 58.8.
28. E.g., Viṣṇu Purāṇa, 2. III. Wilson's edn., Bk. II. Ch. III, pp. 127-28; also *Mārk.,* 57. 10; Mbh., vi. 9. 11.

    Mahendrra Malayaḥ Sahyaḥ Śuktimān Rkssaparvataḥ

    Vindhyaśca Pāripātraśca saptaivātra Kulācaleḥ.
29. Bhāg., V, 19, 16; Mārk., LVII, 13, etc.; Mbh. Bhiṣma P.,śl. 317-378.

    As subordinate portions of them are thousands of mountains; some unheard of, though lofty, extensive and abrupt; and others, better known, though of lesser elevation, and inhabited by people of low stature.
30. Rai Chaudhuri Studies in Indian Antiquities, 2nd Edn.
31. Viṣṇu, 2, II. Wilson edn., p. 123.
32. Ptolemy's Ancient India by McCrindle, S.N. Majumdar's edn., pp. 75-81.
33. Wilson 's edn. of the Viṣṇu Purāṇa, 2. III, p. 128.
34. Skandha Purāṇa Kumārika-khaṇḍa, ch. 39, 113. Pāriyāṭrasya chaivārvāk khaṇḍam Kaumārikam smritam.
35. Dharma-sūtra of Bodhāyana, I. I.25. *Prāgadarśanāt pratyak Kālakavanād dakṣiṇena Himavantan udak Pāriyātram elad Āryāvariam.*
36. III, Wilson's edn., p. 130.
37. Bhīsmaparvan, *op. cit.*
38. *Op. cit.*, 2. III, Wilson's edu., p. 133. Mālukas and Mārukas are variant readings for Kārūsas. See also Kūrma p., Purva ch. 7. which seems to include the countries of Aparānta. Saurāṣṭra, Śūdra, Mālapa (Mālava). Malaka and others within the Pāriyātra area.
39. See also Br. Samhitā, XIV, 4.

40. C.I.I. Vol. III, p. 154.
41. Ptolemy's Ancient India by McCrindle, Majumdar's ed., pp. 38,152-53.
42. Marco Polo, Vol. II, p. 302 n.
43. *Ibid.*, p. 38.
44. *Ibid.*, p. 153.
45. *Ibid.*, p. 38.
46. Kāmasūtra, pp. 103 and 126.

9 Buddha, Kautalya, and Krishna

The critical period of ancient Indian history was the age that spanned the Upanishads and the fullest development of Mauryan administration under Ashoka. In these formative years, roughly from the seventh to the middle of the third century B.C., the dimensions of Indian philosophical and social thought were established. All subsequent speculation was embellishment, the logical development of ideas, and the transformation of philosophy into ideology. Our study has attempted to indicate certain relationships between social organization, styles of thought, and prevailing ideas and values. Within these four centuries new modes of economic production evolved, which threatened the old tribal organization and made possible experimentation with new forms of social integration and, ultimately, the achievement of empire.

The connection between economic surplus and political systems capable of co-ordinating large territories has often been observed, but the tie between such institutional developments and the philosophical ideas and psychological states that seem to accompany them—namely awareness of the self, moral consciousness, and monotheistic religious conceptions—is still somewhat obscure. Among the most promising attempts to explain this connection are the psychologies that account for types of mental functioning in terms of the destruction of the original unity of emotional and intellectual processes. Expanding on the Hegelian distinctions of subject and object, Marx made the concept of *Entfremdung* central to his early social analysis, and today these youthful humanistic writings are considered by many to be among the most important in the body of Marxian literature. In the foregoing chapters such concepts as alienation have been employed in the attempt to account for the psychological consequences of the deterioration of tribal culture with its strong ethnic ties and communal ownership of property. The details of that culture remain uncertain, and conjecture necessarily; has a prominent role in our reconstruction of Vedic society. We glean what we can from the epics, the Budhist records, and like, and occasionally in the pages above the methods and theories of modern social science have been introduced in the effort to understand ancient Indian civilisation.

But it is not only the need to fill historical lacunae that leads us to supplement the institutional approach and that of the history of ideas with a psychological-cultural method. Any analysis of the dynamics of social systems must concern itself with the motivational processes of human beings. The centuries that culminated in the imperial state of the Mauryas are of interest precisely because they were productive of so many ideals, life-styles, and elaborations of symbolism—the study of which calls for techniques that go beyond the traditional textual dissection and chronicling of institutions.[1] In a recent study of the nature of symbolism, a psychologist has remarked that man "*experiences himself as a self* in terms of symbols which arise from three levels at once; [symbols which have their source in] those archaic and archetypal depths within himself, symbols arising from the personal events of his psychological and biological experience, and the general symbols and values which obtain in his culture." We shall probably never know more than the barest particulars of the symbolic experience of early Indian culture, and in the summation that follows we shall do no more than compare the most significant responses to a world that could no longer be interpreted and manipulated through the sacrifice, or understood as inexorably given.

Economic change and the incorporation of indigenous people into the Aryan community had rendered the traditional agencies of social integration inadequate. When old values and institutions are challenged, old certainties are gone, and new social relationships demand new justifications, men are faced with the need to articulate that which earlier could have been left unsaid. In such a time many men must have become acutely aware of differences between their own needs and purposes and those of the collectively to which they belonged. Such questions as how to live with pose and integrity began to arise. The Buddha is the most famous of those who questioned the old ways, and the answer he proposed was in essence psychological. It involved a discipline that aimed at no less than the transcendence of the dichotomy of subject and object.

The two other solutions proposed at this time were basically organisational—the bureaucratic state designed for the efficient mobilization of social resources, and the more or less self-regulating society based on clearly-define status groupings among which different social functions would be distributed. The first of these is best described in the *Arthashastra* of Kautalya, in which society is politically organised to meet the security and welfare needs of its people. The adaptive requirements of the community are stressed in the theory, and politics as administration tends to replace politics as interaction.[2] Caste, on the other hand, emphasizes the integrative imperative of society. It is no less than a priofessionalizing of society, the freezing of actions in the mould of role. Historically, caste represented in part the attempt to preserve status based on birth from the threat of status based on wealth; but in the *Bhagavad Gita* (Which Radhakrishnan places in the fifth century B.C., though it is doubtful that it attained its present form until several centuries later), caste achieves its most sophisticated rationale as the social reflection of a philosophy of self-realization through the pursuit of inherited duty.

The earliest sources reveal a society dominated by a warrior aristocracy. The chieftain was *primus inter pares* and rarely acted simply on his own volition. Tribal religious beliefs were symbolized in the sacrifice, the manifest function of which was to sustain the universe, to win the favour of the gods and their support for the various objectives of the tribe. It also provided a mechanism of adjustment to social and psychological strains, the though Vedic man understood the sacrifice as a propitiation of and gods and the ceremonial reproduction of the cosmic order, he was in fact reading the social structure of the tribal community into his belief about the sky-gods he worshipped. The sacrifice thus served to maintain the pattern of social relationships under the guise of preserving the universe. But it did contain an important truth: our intentions toward the world are what constitute that world, the object of our consciousness. Man was not yet alienated from his gods—or rather he had not yet come to feel the need to project his feelings of estrangement upon them.

Probably only the very few who, because of their role in the performance of the sacrifice were looked upon as representing the tribal community, had any sense of individual distinctiveness. Vedic man was, for the most part, submerged in the group and in nature.[3] This is not to say that there was no active political life. Scattered references in the texts point to popular assemblies and tribal councils; power appears to have been dispersed among the members of the community to an extent that was rare in Indian history. The close identification of the individual with the social unit made possible such political life—as it had in the ancient polis before the internecine wars of the later fifth century and before the influences of the great teacher whom Hegel was to describe as the first "self-conscious" man. In this world where gods and men are still on familiar terms the historical manner of viewing the sequence of events was as yet unborn. Nature provided the model and, like nature, social life renewed itself with comforting regularity. But the process was not automatic. The sacrifice was of crucial significance in this periodic regeneration.[4]

The sacrificial rite served to exalt those who officiated and those who, in the name of the tribe, sponsored the increasingly elaborate ceremonies. Eventually, as these roles became stabilised in the offices of Brahman and king, tension developed between the two authorities—the priesthood of the sun and the imperium of the moon as the problem was sometimes summarized in medieval European theory. Perhaps Buddhism must be explained as a reaction to Brahman controls, but such an explanation seems less than adequate: we know that Brahmanism was not fully developed in the Himalayan foothills where the Shakyan people lived. We are equally justified in viewing Buddhism, in its original expression, as the search for a way of life that would make possible the reintegration of personality.

As long as instinctive responses to the environment had provided an adequate basis of social activity man had not even the experience of a "self." At best the Vedic warrior had seen himself revealed only in his failures to live up to the heroic ideal that had inspired the tribal community. But now, in the more complex social environment of the sixth century B.C., the instinctive and reflexive aspects of the self had diverged to a degree unknown in the lusty, combative Aryan culture of the Vedic era. Guilt and moral consciousness began to emerge us the basis of an internalized authority. In this "birth of tragedy" the self made its appearance as a burden to be suffered. The teaching of the Buddha can be understood as a technique for coping with the demands of the instinctual life (the free expression and satisfaction of which may no longer be tolerated by civil society)[5] by bridging the unconscious and conscious aspects of the mental processes. By removing the causes of personality dissociation, the Buddha hoped to overcome the sense of alienation that had served to define the self. He saw the problem as rooted in man's seemingly inexhaustible cravings. It is desire that produces consciousness of the self; desire is the cause of alienation. And the sense of alienation is conquered only insofar as man succeeds in recognizing himself in objects exterior to his body. This recognition would be possible only when man emancipated himself from the wish to possess these objects as his own.

Employing the vocabulary of modern psychology, we might say that the Buddha sought anxiety-free ego functions by means of a technique which did not disregard the self but rather freed it for the realization of its purposes by eliminating the interpsychic conflict that impedes this pursuit. Conduct would cease to be the anxiety-generated action (as analyzed in psychoanalysis), or the alienated act motivated by the desire for the products of a system made possible by the worker's estrangement from himself (as analyzed by neo-Marxian theorists), or the action that seeks to establish the identity of the actor by making of the self a thing (as analyzed in existentialist writing). We are told that the Buddha rejected the extreme asceticism that was directed toward the destruction of the self, that he himself remained active in the world of men, and that he established a community in which men could live together amicably with only those few possessions absolutely necessary to survival and health. The sangha was an association of equals, which operated on the assumption that unanimous agreement on policy questions would be possible, given this reintegration of personality.

If truth is not readily apparent in phenomena as they are revealed to the senses, there must be present in man an active faculty capable of discovering truth. This view would seem to provide the basis for an epistemology compatible with a democratic political theory, but in Buddhism this comprehension demanded a rigorous training of the mind(which in turn presuppose leisure)—and this must have seemed to the average man as remote from practical possibility as the esoteric technical knowledge of the Brahman. Democracy, for the larger community, would have to await the romantic identification of truth with the subjective feeling available to all men.

The Buddha sought a standard for the proper functioning of the organism—which might also have serve as the basis for a critical evaluation of the society of the time (in contrast to the brahman theory of the sacrifice which made of the cosmos a mirror reflecting the existing social order). But the philosophy and technique of the Buddha's teaching were never intended to inspire a movement of reform. The psychological ideal was itself a rejection of attempts to find security in an established identity that forces perception and experience into stereotypes and systems. The mystic sought a freedom from customary modes of understanding and action; the relationship with the environment must acquire a directness and an immediacy that diminished the distinction between self and other. Only in this sense is the self "destroyed." The Buddhist attack on the fixed identities established in the caste system, which substitutes ascription (the individual as objects) for performance (the individual as actor), reflects this aspect of Buddhist philosophy.

Buddhism might also be understood as a challenge to the new, more abstract, political arrangements of the time (but not as a return to the more immediate political relationships of the tribal polity, i.e., to politics as the direct resolution of conflict—a form of interaction that was being replaced by the administrative systems necessary to the governing of large territories). The tribal organization had been "political" in something of the sense understood by the Greeks; it represented the common life of its members, even though actual political activity was confined to those who represented the familial groups that compose the tribes. Politics as the expression of that which is common to the members of a group implies by definition a certain homogeneity of culture. Never of course, in the poleis, constructed as they were on a slave economy, did all men participate in these activities. The Aryan tribal collectivities were generally of an aristocratic nature, but those who participated in political life enjoyed a relative equality. What is important is that the *res publica,* insofar as it was capable of being distinguished from other aspects of tribal life, was viewed as the means for realizing those purposes shared by the whole community.

The Buddhist sangha was not an attempt to recapture a political life rendered obsolete by new modes of production and the organizational requirements of ever-expanding territorial units, the consolidation of royal power, and the incorporation of dasa peoples. Buddhism, though perhaps not the quiescent philosophy it is frequently made out to be, supplemented the *vita activa* with a new emphasis on contemplation.[6] In discounting the claims of caste and the state, it turned (as did the Hellenistic philosophies) to the private experience as the ultimate vehicle of fulfilment. The individual was reunited with the species by virtue of his humanity—that which is more fundamental than his membership in a specific group. The spiritual had come to replace the political as the highest expression of human purposes. "Compare with the attitude of quiet," as Arendt says of a similar development in European civilization, "all distinctions and articulations within the *vita activa* disappear."[7]

The second challenge to the heroic ideal provided an alternative to the communal polity in the form of hierarchical organization—empire based on the bureaucratic rationalizing of areas of conflict. As political life become increasingly abstract, the need for political symbolization become more acute. We find new attention to questions of authority and legitimacy, and political theory begins to take on a systematic and sophisticated form. One might almost say that with the failure of politics (in the sense of face-to-face political relationships), political and moral philosophy flourish. Justifications and explanations are needed for the new social relationships that appear, or these new forms are decried in the name of traditional values—or the attempt is made to diminish the importance of these institutions and relationships by encouraging self-sufficiency.

Just as the invasions of Alexander introduced the Greeks to the organizational techniques of the Persians, so may the intercourse between Persia and India have served to familiarize Indians with large-scale political structures and administrative processes. Kautalya best represents this application of rational thought to the problems of social organization. By the time of the Buddha the Gangetic valley was divided among a number of kindoms, the most important of which was Magadh. Tribal elements were still present in this transitional period before the establishment of a central authority capable of effective control. It was still common for power to be conceived in terms of what we would today call a scarcity (conflict) model, which sees power as essentially power over others rather than as a resource for achieving the desired goals of the collectivity. Conflict in such societies tends to be resolved directly—either by violence or in the more or less intimate political associations of clan and tribe. The growth of political units and the consequent dilution of the kinship ties that had characterized the earlier Aryan communities had produced what Banfield, in another context, has referred to as "amoral familism".[8] Custom and the natural bonds of the tribal "nation" were no longer sufficient to the needs of ordered life and it remained for the kings of Magadha to superimpose the artificial bonds of the state on a situation moving toward anarchy. New types of law were required for resolving disputes, and the royal edict came to be increasingly emphasized.

The remaining centres of tribal power, such as the kshatrya military associations, constituted a threat to be emergent states, and a major concern of the monarch was to subvert those tribal institutions that remained potentially capable of impeding the purposes of the state or dividing the loyalties of the people.[9] One device for promoting ill will among the members of a tribal group was the use of agents to encourage the humbler segment of society to insist on equality of treatment and status. Those of higher position (the descendants of the original Aryan tribes, or the kshatriya aristocracy) were to be dissuaded from intermarriage and eating at common table with those of lesser rank. Thus were caste values introduced as a competing mode of organization. The Magadhan ruler Ajatashatru systematically undertook to create dissension among the Lichchhavi tribesmen. The master agent in his employ was reputed to be a shrewd brahman minister. Pretending to be *persona non grata* in the Mahadh court, he gained the confidence of the tribal nobles and began circulating stories of his own invention designed to create bad feeling among them. Ultimately he was successful in sabotaging the assembly of the republic. But the real menace to the tribal community was less Magadhan imperialism than the new modes of production that called for new agencies of control and sharpened consciousness of the class divisions underlying the old societies.

The great Mauryan minister Kautalya and, later, the emperor Ashoka were at least indirectly concerned with expanding the categories of Political speculation to meet the needs of empire and the realities of the age. Kautalya wished his king to represent the political unity of the people—a unity that transcended the particular interests and varying status of the different sectors of society.[10] The person of the king is distinguished from that of his subjects not simply because the king represents the collective purposes of society (this is true also of the tribal leader) but because he is that which the diverse elements of society share. The new and positive functions of the king are reflected in such statements as "the king is maker of his age," which begin to appear in the Brahman literature of the time. For the Brahman, the state represented a means of ensuring his own social position. He had as much, if not more, to gain from the substitution of a caste hierarchy for aristocratic tribal values. In the older society his status had never been secure. From the vantages point of the state, caste made possible social integration along functional lines, thoroughly rationalized through the elaboration of the idea (already present in tribal society) of inherited guilt.

The "individualizing" of anxiety was the product of the changes we have mentioned in our discussion of the Buddha, but it is perhaps worth remarking on the beginnings of a sense of the distinction between the goals of society and those of the individual, which encouraged the development of the concept of the private individual, —an idea that appears to have been related to the appearance of the bureaucratic state in other cultures as well. When kinship could no longer provide the basis of social regulation, legal insitutions evolved to supplement the communal bonds of the tribe. Functional differentiation requires the recognition of private areas of interest legitimate in their own right—goals not necessarily those of the larger society. If these are to be effectively implemented, private sectors must enjoy institutional rights. Such claims are, in effect, a restriction on the exercise of public authority.

We have thus far considered two efforts to cope with the problems of an age of great social change. The first took the form of an attempt to overcome the separation of the perceiving subject from the perceived object. But Kautalya's state, in its dependence on the hierarchical division of labour, must itself contribute to this feeling of alienation. New controls over the environment sharpened the distinction between physical necessity and necessity that is created by man. We may surmise that men began to conclude that remaking the world was within the realm of possibility. The ancient belief in the cyclical periodicity of time, the eternal return, was modified or displaced altogether by a sense of continuity and development approximating a historical attitude. Accumulated wealth and the military power and administrative efficiency it made possible could now be used for achieving ambitious, long-range political and social goals. The great man is, in fact, the great organizer. He creates the very conditions that make the hero obsolete, for he imposes an order that limits the unpredictable contingencies against which the hero struggles. The hero was made by his age; the organizer is the maker of his age. Men can now do things that earlier could be accomplished only by the gods.[11]

Possibly the most basic of all political problems concerns the extent to which conflict may be permitted in a society. It was the practical necessity to integrate different tribal, linguistic, and religious backgrounds that was the most immediate concern of Ashoka Maurya. Like the Romans confronted with the tasks of imperial administration, he was compelled to find a set of universalistic principles that could be the basis of governmental policy and social coordination. (When the state was consolidated, this coordination could be based on the functional differentiation of the Brahmanical caste theory). For this reason Ashoka sought, in a sense, to combine the Buddhist ethic with the administrative system of Kautalya. He was not primarily concerned, as his grandfather had been, with the mobilization of power resources. Most of India acknowledged his suzerainty. Ashoka wished to establish what might be called an educative state—a state that would take an active role in inculcating certain ethical tenets in its subjects. The dangers implicit in this caesaropapism have been commented upon. The illustrious emperor probably understood that, as a jurist has put it, "transpersonalized power is economical of the use of force," and that Brahmanism was too closely linked to the caste structure to be able to inspire a sense of social responsibility and the common conviction capable of transforming power into authority by relating it to ethical principles. The ambitions of the imperial Guptas were more modest; the Gupta kings were generally content to see themselves as mediators of the various interests that composed society. The task of integration was left to the castes.

Caste was the third response to what we have elsewhere called the tribal trauma. The most positive expression of the values basic to the caste structure is to be found in that bible of Hinduism, the *Bhagawad Gita.* In one sense the poem may be understood as an attempt to retain the purity of the act—to prevent the kshtriya heroic ideal from developeing into a conception of egoistic man. Though it seems to teach that actions are not to be transformed into objects (the "fruits of action"), it does in fact fuse act and object in that what one does in related directly to what one is. A man who is a warrior by birth must find his fulfillment in the battle. The demands of duty are foremost. Part of the difficulty of interpretation lies in the fact that the *Gita* concentrates on kshatrya obligation and thus emphasizes the risk that are implicit in life (i.e., in the warrior's role). In action man become a "subject," rather than the object of someone else. Krishna, the "divine charioteer," is concerned with easing the conscience of a knight whose disgust at the seemingly pointless ravages of war causes him to hesitate on the eve of battle. But he is a kshatriya; his identity in this life is fixed. He is the object of his past. Conduct is made the expression of a preordained mode of life.

The changes in social organization, the increase in economic opportunities, the new conceptions of personal responsibility, and the like, would be expected to affect the manner in which that most basic of human problems, the problem of suffering, is articulated and evaluated. The unrighteous prosper: why should this be? Suffering found its explanation in the belief that no man in innocent, for if he were he would not exist as an earthly being. He caries the weight of the transgressions of his earlier lives, and his sinful actions in this life will be punished in the next. There was at least the cold comfort of knowing that the wicked could not escape punishment. And in the ancient tribal solidarities each man, though never so preoccupied with the question of sin, was made to bear the burden of the actions of *all* the members of the clan. The concepts of the individual and history had taken a peculiar turn to leave man answerable for actions committed in the earlier lives of the soul. And he was rendered powerless by the belief that social institutions existed as the only possible remedy for man's sin. It would appear that religious, philosophical, and ideological symbolization, complex and "total" as it was, allowed man no flexibility in self-and social-image, no opportunity to break out of the cultic pattern and create a symbolism detached, in part at least, from this mythical, religious, or historical reality, a symbolism that is the work of the free imagination and it capable of projecting new combinations of images.[12]

One historian of Indian social thought has remarked that "India has always displayed an emotional flow and vibration which, on the whole, militates against rigidity of discipline and organization. If in one or two spheres organization was attempted on a scale unknown in the West, there were whole departments of life that were left unorganized. Here culture was embodied in institutions to a far lesser degree than in Europe. Social thought is more diffuse and less exact and systematic than in the West." We find much the same assessment of Indian Polity in the writings of Aurobindo, who maintained that it reflects the vigorous and natural communal life freely incorporated into the large political structures that had emerged by the fourth century B.C.

This spontaneous principle of life was respected by the age of growing intellectual culture. The Indian thinkers on society, economics, and politics, Dharmashastra and Arthashastra, made it their business not to construct ideals and system of society and government in the abstract intelligence, but to understand and regulate by the communal mind and life, and to develop, fix, and harmonize without destroying the original elements and whatever new element or idea was needed was added or introduced as a superstructure or modifying but not a revolutionary and destructive principle.

Accordingly, India has not been productive of experiments involving the overthrow of traditional social devices, and the great cornerstone of the modern West—the idea of progress—has not taken a similarly idealistic and social form. Change was conceived in terms of a gradual evolution of custom "conservative of the Principle of settled order, of social and political precedent, of established framework and structure."

These evaluation have been included to help balance the record; they represent interpretations not usually found in studies by Western writers. They have much to commend them and they point up the limitation of a strictly political analysis, but a description of the more positive aspects of Indian cultural life in terms of "emotional flow and vibration" must not be allowed to obscure the limitations imposed on expression by the caste system and the consequent stifling of opportunities for social advancement on the basis of talent and achievement. To say that culture finds its embodiment more commonly in other than institutional forms is to ignore, with slim justification, the pervasive influence of caste and to give too much emphasis to individual forms of religious expression and commitment. Law became a system of detailed status—differentiated prescriptions and prohibitions based on these differing capabilities. The legal code, which depended on the coercive power of the king for its enforcement, was rationalized as the safeguard of the moral order; it insured the hierarchy of social duties—duties which, if performed faithfully and effectively, ultimately qualified men for those disciplines leading to spiritual emancipation.

We look in vain for ethical universalism in "official" legal and social theory: Hindu monarchy was government under law in a certain sense but this was not law as the Western tradition has come to know it. At the apex of the structure, enshrined in immunities and privileges protected by the law codes and by tradition, was the Brahman. This authority, according to the theory, could not be considered an encroachment on the freedom of the other orders to society. For it is through the exercise of Brahman authority that the individual is established in those modes of life that make possible his ultimate salvation—which is more highly valued than freedom as such.

Studies of African political organizations in transition from relatively homogeneous tribal organization to centralized administrative systems appear to indicate that economic and cultural heterogeneity (an increasingly prominent feature of India society in the period that has concerned us here) is frequently associated with a statelike form of political organization. Centralized authority provides a framework for the accommodation of diverse peoples, and if economic and cultural differences are considerable, a class system will usually result. Where class is combined with an ideology that rationalizes completely the hierarchy of status, different groups may live in peaceful proximity without the need for a strong central authority to ensure order and arbitrate differences arising among them. For all the criticism of the system, implied and otherwise, it was caste and the village, rather than the political and administrative organization, that during most of India's history preserved that integrity of her culture and made possible the absorption of alien elements. A remarkable and, indeed, almost unmatched attribute of early Indian society was the toleration shown by the Hindu to diverse traditions and outlooks.[13] Most traditional societies have been characterized by an aversion to that which varied from the orthodox, and even in secular societies it is difficult to find greater powers of cultural absorption than India possessed. Such hospitality has been her strength as well as her undoing. Respect for and delight in differences are still the charm of India.

Rarely in India history was there a concentration of authority at the centre; authority was located in caste, custom, guild, religious tradition, the teaching and example of the sage, and the village council as well as in provincial and central governments. Throughout Indian history, the basic unit of administration was the village. Hindu law exhibits great respect for local variance in custom and tradition, allowing a remarkable autonomy to the village and the corporation. This is the virtue that Aurobindo and others have justly emphasized.

Intervention by the central government might be necessary when these organizations were unable to settle internal disputes or problems arising from contact with other associations. Communal self-government was, as a rule, successfully combined with political stability, and the structure flourished for a longer period than any other.

Two of the three responses to the disintegration of tribal values emphasized types of coordination more appropriate to cultural heterogeneity and large territories. One of these may be described as social. Integration is based on social duty, rigidly defined and hierarchically arranged. A man is born into a set of obligations; he knows his place in the total scheme of things and will hold to his duties—for their performance is the key to his salvation. The problem of conflict, for all practical purposes, is solved. This type of authority Max Weber called "Traditional."

The second answer was political. Bureaucratic organization—a corps of officials with defined political roles, whose offices are arranged in a clear chain of command—enables the state to take an active part in social regulation. In such a system rules become basic. The assumption here is that there must be an agency of special competence to resolve the conflicts that constantly arise in society. The state represents a more dynamic organization than the caste structure; in essence it is a set of procedures for dealing with problems, mobilizing resources, and formulating goals. It may exist to ensure that each man is permitted to find his salvation in his own way, it may dictate the form this salvation takes, or it may subordinate individual purposes to those of the state itself. Coordination comes from "outside" the community; the sate may take whatever steps are necessary to presersve society and regulate the groups that compose it. Weber termed this type of authority "bureaucratic." This central concepts of bureaucratic authority imply a distinction of the political from other social functions. Of course political roles exist in "traditional" societies, but integration is accomplished by religion and custom. Weber was thinking primarily in terms of the rational bureaucracy of the modern state when he developed this category. But there are other types of bureaucracy that we may mention in passing because they provide a transition to the third type of authority, charisma, which we have earlier described as "leadership." These charismatic bureaucracies may take patrimonial or totalitarian forms. Loyalty is to the person of the leader as well as to office. The rule is both *dux* and *rex*.

The third solution is psychological and spiritual. It may involve a turning away from the world, as in Buddhism, for man cannot find his salvation in the things of this world. Or it may seek to transform the world in order to make it more amenable to that salvation. The former, the more passive "learning" process, is the more common in the East. In Western history prophecy took more active forms and has thus had more significant implications for political life. But although it could be argued that the Buddha has no place in a history of political thought, he is in one sense very important. For this withdrawal from the political is one of the first expressions of protest, and marks the birth of critical philosophy. In the case of the Buddha and of Lao-tse in China[14] this protest took the form of reducing life to its simplest statement, detaching oneself from the world in order to attain union with the all-embracing impersonal One.

This questioning of the legitimacy of the old order is often an attempt to return to an original purity that had existed before social institutions appeared or before they became corrupt. But the basis of legitimacy may be no more than the uncommon personal characteristics that are believed to qualify a man to lead or instruct. The prophet or savior "has set his personal charisma against [the traditional hierocratic powers of magicians or of priests] in order to break their power of force them to his service." The word charisma means, literally, "gift of grace." It is, in fact, the source of *all* authority—rooted in that which is extraordinary, which is removed from institutional routine.

The ritual and initiation possess much that is charismatic; they lift men from the commonplace world and transport them to the sacred. It is this sacred element in tradition that gives it authority. Chance and the unpredictable may find a place among the traditions, as for example in the symbolic game of dice played between the king and his ministers, in which the sacred wager was the wealth of the humblest member of society.[9] The dice game, or any of a number of rituals, dramatises the fact that charisma has become objectified and inhabits an office as well as the person who has inherited charisma. The role has been established. Authority refers to such established roles; leadership to the creating or expanding of roles. Charisma is the mysterious quality of leadership, the magnetism, heroism, or saintliness that inspires a following, the magical element that the Brahman sought to institutionalise in the sacrifice, that the Mauryan monarchs hoped to locate in the office of the king, that Indra personified for the Vedic warrior and that the divine avatar represented for the Hindu believer. Our story is ultimately the story of this force—which is, at once, power and authority.[15]

In this study we have observed the extend to which religion, law in its several forms, and political speculation were interwoven and served to reinforce one another. Indeed, political and social thought can be comprehended only in the light of prevailing belief and religious practice. Analyses dealing exclusively with ideas—which most commonly are found in the brahman literature of mythology, ritual, and religious philosophy, or in manuals intended primarily for the instruction of the prince—cannot provide the impression of social life that is needed if we are to have more than a catalogue of concepts and theories. We have therefore been led to consider social institutions and ideologies, economic developments and political structures, as well as religious values, in an effort to arrive at a more complete picture of Indian society and a realistic appraisal of Indian thought about man, his obligations to himself and his fellows, and particularly the authorities to which he submits himself. It has been a journey down a Ganges—its upper reaches the ancient heroic myth, the waters deepening as we reach the elaborate systems of the Brahmans. Many tributaries join the sacred river; its surface becomes rough. We pass the great city of Pataliputra, and at length find ourselves in the broad marshland of Hinduism. The shore is indistinct and we are at times in danger of losing our bearings.

Now that this expedition is completed, a few concluding remarks may be useful in bringing together the major ideas that have appeared and reappeared along the way. Whether the people of ancient India were consistently guided by these principles is not our immediate concern. We are interested primarily in the ideals of conduct of king and subject and of the ordering of social relationships that were thought to be most worth attaining.

The brahmacharin ashrama was intended to instruct man in the discipline of his senses and to give him an awareness of the values that transcend worldly experience with its deceptions and material goals. It was not the preparation for a life devoted to social melioration. Nor was it an atmosphere to encourage the skeptical and analytical frame of mind. And yet because the spiritual ideal could be realised only after obligations had been met, and because these duties implied a social life that must be protected against the predatory and anarchical bent of human nature, the body of social speculation is not as slight as might be supposed. The forces operative in Indian social life produced institutional forms that have no exact counterpart in the West, but these forces were by no means unique in historical experience and we discover an appreciation of the role of economic factors and the general phenomenon of power. Religious belief lent a high colour to social commentary, but this does not justify the argument of so many European observers that the Indian spirit was insensitive to the more prosaic requirements of human existence and provided no secular treatise comparable in any way to those produced in the West.

There is, as I have sought to indicate, a thorough rationale of society and the state, though religion often hinders the development of a systematic philosophy of government. The great bulk of social thought was meant not to challenge the existing order, but only to justify and explain. Whereas Western theory has been interlaced with utopian philosophies inspired by the wish to bring the kingdom of God to earth or by the wish for a more equitable distribution of the world's goods, the peculiar complex of Indian thought, with karma and samsara securing the values that legitimated institutions, impeded any thoroughgoing reconsideration of the bases of authority and obligation. Neither Buddhist thought nor Mauryan administrative theory succeeded in establishing alternative norms capable of challenging Brahmanism.

Political speculation is essentially Aryan; by comparison the contribution of non-Aryan peoples to the corpus of political ideas is small. This theory is concerned almost exclusively with the monarchical form of government. Rarely do we find an attempt to evaluate the relative merits of kingdom and republic. The ancient theorists comprehended many of the elements that compose the state and are central to a definition of sovereignty. But we cannot assume that such a term as "rastra" is the equivalent of the abstract idea of the state that we employ.

The state in early India was believed to be instrumental to the attainment of the spiritual goal. This ultimate purpose was itself so conceived as to presuppose an elite responsible for defining and interpreting the values that ordered the world and regulated even the actions of the king. This elite maintained its purity by remaining more or less apart from political life, which was tainted by the sin inherent in political and military roles. But the brahman might serve as the king's adviser and involve himself indirectly in governmental functions, for the state represented a concentration of power that could too easily become its own justification. This general aloofness of the priests and the jealous guarding of their own purity may help account for their toleration of the moral ambiguities that characterised the institutions that governed lesser men—institution themselves dictated by the imperfection of the lower orders. It was Soma who was the *true* king of the brahmans.

The king's function was not simply negative. He must seek to translate the dharmic code into terms appropriate to the age. This relativism has its most dramatic expression in the powerful figure of the sinful Indra and the seemingly self-contradictory Krishna. The dharma of the individual, as the sacred texts reiterate, is linked with rajadharma the king's own duties are the keystone of the system. But the king is compromised by the nature of this very duty; only by giving to the brahman and performing the sacrifice is he cleansed. As early as the period of the Upanishads the prosperity of the people implied moral as well as material welfare. In the *Chandogya Upanishad* a king remarks on the righteousness of his subjects and appears to take personal credit for the virtuous behaviour that distinguishes his realm. Jayaswal sees in this an early statement of the axiom that the king is the maker of his age, responsible for the moral condition of his subjects. His task of preserving dharma committed him to maintaining the caste order, which was itself based on the moral authority and spiritual supremacy of the brahman. Though the king assumed a moral function, he was himself subject to the sacred tradition. And the spokesman for this sovereign tradition was the brahman.

In Hindu political speculation, duty occupies the central position that in European liberal thought belongs to conceptions of natural rights and freedom. The psychological sensationalism at the root of Locke's theory of individualism would not find much encouragement in a philosophical setting that limited the validity of sense experience and stressed the importance of escape from personality through the renunciation of desire and the fruits of action. The essential weakness in the Hindu theory of the state is its failure to provide any very searching analysis of the relation between government and the governed. One explanation for the infrequent reference to the rights of subjects is the fact that most of the political literature was composed expressly for the governing class. More important, the relation of the state to the stratified dharmic order per-emptied any consideration of human rights as the West understands the problem. The doctrine of transmigration and karma and the devaluation of mundane experience could result only in the subordination of the individual. Rights in this world were as nothing when measured against the requirements of eternal salvation, and freedom, which was conceived as the escape from the cycle of birth, death, and rebirth, could be attained only through the faithful discharge of duties. There was no sanguine faith in a natural identity of interests. Caste was the means for reconciling individual self-interest with broader social needs. Without the institutions of caste and state, human life would be like that of the animals of the jungle, the strong devouring the weak. In positing self-interest as the basic psychological fact, and in constructing authority as a negative restraint on antisocial expression, Hindu theory may be likened to several schools of Western political thought.

The egalitarian ideal, save possibly for Buddhist thought, never asserted itself in Indian thought as it did in the West. As in the case of civil rights, so also with the more specific rights of the citizen: the concept of "citizenship" had little meaning in Hindu society. For all practical purposes we are justified saying that civil obligation rather than civil right formed the basis of the relation of state and subject. We must never look past the fact, however, that there always exist for the Hindu, as for the Western liberal, criterion above the state by which its actions could be judged. It was not the idea of the sanctity of the individual personality or the association; it was sacred law and tradition.

Though not concerned with the rights of men, except the right to pursue that which is necessary to salvation, Hindu political thought does share with the natural rights theory the idea of contract and the belief that power must be limited. The contract theory is never elaborated beyond the most basic statement and the people are rarely party to the contract, but that it played a key role in Hindu polity cannot be denied. Authority was based on both function and status—the former finding its symbolic expression in the contractual exchange of allegiance for protection or in the differentiation of roles in the performance of the sacrifice, the latter in such images as the division of the primeval person of Purusha to form the various order of society from the different parts of the body of this original man. This division of the organism suggests the close relation of status to function. Though the hymn does not stress this, the creation of the warrior from the arm of Purusha indicates as much about the function of the warrior as creation from the feet tells us about the status of the shudra. It is this intimate relation of status and function that keeps the theory conservative. Hindu thought assumes that there is a peculiar brahman mentality, a shudra mind, and so forth, and that the basic social group is composed of those of similar mental configuration. The caste system-the fundamental sociological context of Hindu polity—aimed at providing the individual with a milieu of like minds in which to fulfil the obligations of his social station. There is in, Brahmanical theory, the rationale of status in terms of character, and we are told that before the fall from grace all men were brahmans. The ethical life is dependent on knowledge of the Veda, and men whose energies are devoted exclusively to material pursuit have neither the opportunity nor the ability to pursue this sacred learning. Thus was the brahman intelligentsia able to establish itself in an almost impregnable position at the summit of the social hierarchy.

Still, the brahmans were themselves restricted in the creative use of their intellectual abilities. They were the interpreters of the sacred tradition; only indirectly did they exercise a legislative function. In certain important respects brahman theory recalls the political philosophy of Thomas Aquinas, although in relating the origin of political institutions to man's sinful nature it more closely resembles earlier medieval political ideas. For both St. Thomas and orthodox Indian thinkers, society is constructed on the fundamental differences in the practical telents of men. The political relationship is justified in terms of these differences a *subjectio civilis* necessary for the attainment of the common good.[16]

In both theories the state was charged with maintaining security, promoting a minimum standard of morality, and protecting religion. The task of positive law, where it was recognized in brahman theory, was to realize in concrete terms the higher moral law. The sacred law of the brahmans, however, was not based on a universal ethic of the type we find in Christian thought, nor do we find the emphasis on the need to administer higher law in the interest of the common good that is a feature of Thomistic theory. The actions of the ruler were circumscribed by objective moral law. Because government existed to fulfil a trust, the deposition of a tyrant might be legitimate. As in the argument of Aquinas the spiritual goal of man is higher than his temporal ends. For this reason the spiritual sword, though coordinate with the secular, is the more exalted. Because man's purpose is ultimately spiritual, the temporal sphere of authority can never be completely independent of the representatives of religion.

The peculiar distribution of wealth, fighting power, and intellectual eminence obstructed the growth of the type of aristocracy common to many ancient polities. The power of the brahman class was due more to its control over culture than to its material position or its influence exercised through the ministries. To term the Hindu state a theocracy would be to suggest its sectarian foundation on dogma and an identification of magistrate and priest. This was not the case, though a strong bond existed in theory between the brahman and kshatriya classes. Prosperity could result only if the two classes cooperated closely with one another. If the alliance should break, eternal confusion would be the result.

The great Mauryan empire of Chandragupta and Ashoka was reincarnated under the Guptas, and from time to time in the history of ancient India power was consolidated according to the grand design of Kautalya. At length the peninsula succumbed to the Sultanate, but Hindu culture survived in the apparently invincible institutions of caste and village. From the point of view of the modern world, the price of this strength was high. The tragedy of India is that it became a land where tragedy and had become irrelevant. The depoliticizing of society through the penance ideology of caste subverted that most human of all urges the wish for a better life in this world. The image of Utopia, the earthly kingdom of God, had no place in a culture resigned to an imperfect world. Aspiration and anticipation were relevant only to the future life of the soul. Thus was hope diverted.

Today the Indian state is as new as it was in Kautalya's time. And it is as old as all states must be in an age when sovereignty has proven an inadequate answer to the organizational requirements of security and peace. A solution as creative as that put forth in the *Arthashastra* is needed if the amoral tribalism of our century is not to end in the mutual destruction of peoples. At least in the struggle of the fishes, the image beloved of brahman theorists, the big fish survived. Now the big will be the first to go. But the political answer must be accompanied and reinforced by such truly radical programes as that of the Buddha, which would free the individual from the alienation that tortures the self and makes of freedom a mockery.

REFERENCES

1. In the last decade or two a school of political analysis, inspired by logical positivism, has taken upon itself the task of purifying the language of political discussion. Obviously these attempts to point up the ambiguities of argument and clarify the terms we use should have a salutary effect on the development of political theory. If, however, we should become preoccupied with the fine points of definition to the exclusion of a concern with the ends of government (because we cannot get beyond the posing of the question), then the very life of political philosophy is threatened. It is an easy victory to bring the instruments of modern social inquiry to bear on the ideas of theorists who lived and wrote in ages less congenial to the critical spirit or who were sometimes contradictory because they saw farther than their fellows and lacked the means to express accurately their vision. But we may be the real losers if we deprive ourselves of the insights of a Plato or Rousseau because we insist on equating departures from consistency with deception, or epistemologies that differ from our own with fatuity. It is our responsibility to apply the refinements of methodology and the social sciences in searching out the intended or latent sense of the ideas that confront us. The discovery of meanings that might otherwise remain hidden to us is a nobler employment for our newer knowledge than its restriction to the essentially negative tasks of controverting and deriding.

2. "Every social process may be divided into a rationalized sphere consisting of settled and routinized procedures in dealing with situations that recure in an orderly fashion, and the 'irrational' by which it is surrounded." (Karl Mannheim, *Ideology and Utopia* [New York, 1949], p. 101. Mannheim sees the distinction as the difference between administration and "politics."

3. The dominance of tradition in the communal society provides "a basis for self-relatedness, rather than a source of self-alienation. In the second place, adherence to tradition favors group-centered attitudes, rather than self-centered orientations. That is, the traditional man conforms in order to fulfill his obligations to the group, to avoid shame, whereas the [members of a mass society] conforms for the purpose of overcoming the diffuse *anxiety* which accompanies the lack of self-confidence." (William Kornhauser, *The Politics of Mass Society* [Glencoe, Ill., 1959], pp. 110f.) The variety of principles that organized ancient Indian society at different times discourages the use of broad characterizations like "communal" or "traditional" in describing Indian civilization without mention of such refinements as the distinction between the heroic "shame-culture" of the Vedic warrior and the penitential "guilt-culture" of the later Brahmanic age, or the distinction between types of cosmological symbolization.

4. Our definition of freedom does not exhaust the possible views of what constitutes freedom. We tend to convince ourselves that men can and do make history, and we differ from "archaic" man in that we see freedom as the relative independence from normative controls. The cyclical conception of time encourages the belief that man can annually begin life afresh. No small freedom this—and how far removed from the later ideology that placed man in bondage to his past, the deeds of his previous lives. When caste came to be the dominant social institution, based on the theory of karma, history was understood in terms of regressive cycles. Once men were virtuous, but as a consequence of a fall (which is never really explained), law and agencies of its enforcement became essential to social life. Theories that justify strong social controls put the golden age in the past. But Vedic man had faith in his capacity to manipulate the sentiments of the gods. He was master of his destiny. (It is instructive to compare the Oedipus of the heroic culture depicted in the *Iliad* with the tortured soul portrayed by Sophocles. *Vide* Dodds [98], p. 36.)

5. I have in mind here a distinction between immediate discharge of tension in action and the social need to inhibit action. *Vide* Parsons, *et al.* [319], p. 82.

6. *Vide* pp. 89f. above—Weber's distinction between the emissary phophecy (more familiar to the West) as typified by Jeremiah or Isaiah, and the exemplary prophecy of such teachers as Gautama Buddha.

7. In the earlier discussion of Buddhism I have suggested certain parallels with modern psychological theories and techniques aimed at attaining an effective integration of personality. In a recent study of Freudian analysis, Philip Rieff remarks of psychoanalysis that "it undercuts the whole problem of the freedom of the individual in any society, emphasizing instead the theme of the anti-political individual seeking his self-perfection in a context as far from the communal as possible. All politics are corrupt, in the democratic community as well as in the totalitarian state. Since freedom is a psychic condition (residing essentially in the individual, not in him as a member of a group), the possibility of freedom exists in all societies." (*Freud: The Mind of the Moralist* [New York, 1959], p. 256.)

8. Speaking of modern Montegrano in southern Italy, Banfield remarks that "it is tempting to compare the ethos of the Montegranesi with that of their very early ancestors as described by Fustel de Coulanges in *The Ancient City.* The early Indo-Europeans were amoral familists too, but their families consisted of thousands of persons and the bonds within the family were immensely strong." (*The Moral Basis of a Backward Society* [Glencoe, Ill., 1958, p. 164, n.2.)

9. Often the kings lacked the legitimacy that kshatrahood provided and it was necessary for them to establish a new basis of authority, itself a

departure from tribal values. From this time on, kings were "shudra-like" according to the puranas. And at least a few of them *were* shudras. We might speculate that in some instances the Brahman was able to establish a position for himself by providing legitimation for kings who did not possess kshatriya pedigree.

10. "A multitude of men are made *one* person, when they are by one man, or one person, represented.... For it is the *unity* of the representer, not the *unity* of the represented, that maketh the person *one.*" (Hobbes, *Leviathan,* Part I, chap. 16.)

11. This rudimentary historical consciousness, which is suggested in the *Arthashastra* of Kautalya, would later disappear with the ascendance of the village economy, practically self-sufficient and mirroring the natural cycle. Only the occasional merchant with the need to keep accounts bothered himself with dates that went beyond the year itself.

12. Erich Kahler calls this "ascending symbolism" and distinguishes it from the symbolism that descends "from a prior and higher reality, a reality determining, and therefore superior to, its symbolic meaning." ("The Nature of the Symbol," in May [261].)

13. This toleration is related to caste organization in interesting ways—one of which was noted by Alexis de Tocaqueville in a manuscript on India that occupied him intermittently 1840 and 1843. (The draft of the projected book, edited by André Jardin, will be included in the collection of Tocqueville's works and papers now being prepared for publication by J.P. Mayer and others.) In this study Tocqueville remarks that "Brahmanism is at the same time the most absorptive and the most tolerant religion. This is easily explained when one notes that it is a religion of privileges.... One belongs to it by right of birth; it is impossible to enter it unless one is born within it. So it is impossible to feel hatred towards those whom Brahma has left outside." The implication of this, as Mayer has noted (*Encounter,* May, 1962), is that proselytism and persecution are closely linked with religious conceptions of the common nature of all men and their equality before God.

14. Though his conception of government was far more positive than that of the brahmans who sponsored the caste theory, Confucius' teachings may be compared with the brahman "solution" in that he emphasized standardized conduct: man must do what is proper to his station. Kautalya has his counterpart, broadly speaking, in the Chinese Realists (or Legalists, as they are usually called). In the classical world the same dimensions of authority may be found in Plato, in imperial Rome, and in the withdrawal philosophies of the Epicureans. But Greek experience also indicates that politics may be based on persuasion, just as the excesses of the Ch'in state suggest that domination is at times based only on naked power.

15. This distinction may provide the major clue to the reconciliation of Machiavelli's *Discourses* with *The Prince*. The former is concerned with the preservation of civil society once it is established, whereas the latter is preoccupied with the founding of the state and the creation of authority.

16. The two summas differ in that Brahmanism conceives of this subordination as crucial to the salvation of the individual.

Appendix

BATTLE OF KURUKSHETRA
(MAHABHARATA BATTLE)

The Battle of Kurukshetra, as described in the epic 'Mahabharata', is an incident of the greatest singular importance in the panorama of Indian history. It occurred long before the Christian era. View of historians and other authorities vary widely on the year of its occurrence. Some of the probable dates indicated by various authors are given below:

B.C.

3201 D.R. Mankad: 'Puranic Chronology'.

3137 M.M Krishnamachari: 'History of Classical Sanskrit Literature'.

3127 A.N. Chandra: 'The Date of Kurukshetra War'.

3110 As per the age of Manu Vaivaswata.

3102 Aryabhatta.

Brahmagupta.

C.V. Vaidya: 'History of Sanskrit Literature' (Vedic Period).

3101 As per Aihole inscriptions of Raja Pulakesin II (609 A.D.-655 A.D.) of Chalukya dynasty of Maharashtra, based on astronomical calculations of Aryabhatta.

3067 By application of modern astronomical methods based on the data available in Mahabharata. The battle is supposed to have been fought in November-December.

3016 V.B. Athvale.

2449	Probodh Chandra Sen Gupa; 'Indian Chronology'.
2448	Brahamihir: 'Brihat Samhita'.
	Kalhan: 'Rajatarangini'.
1450	Meghnath Saha.
1432	Tarakeswar Bhattacharya.
1424	A. Cunnigham: 'Archaeological Survey, First Report, 1864, Vol. I. Page 131'.
	K.P. Jaiswal.
	Most of the historians accept this year as the most probable one. In this book also, this year is taken as the base.
1416	Girindra Shekhar Basu: 'Purana Pravesh'.
1400	Bankim Chandra Chattopadhyaya: 'Krishna Charitra'. Balgangadhar Tilak: 'Gita Rahasya'.
1400	Swami Vivkeananda.
	A.D. Pusalkar: 'History and Culture of India People'.
	H.C. Deb: First all India Oriental Conference.
	Jogesh Chandra Vidyanidhi.
1267	B.B. Ketkar: Oriental Conference.
1197	K.L. Daptary: 'Astronomical Chronology of Ancient India'.
	K.G Shanker: Annals of Bhandarkar Institute.
1191	Sri Aurobindo: 'Vyasa and Valmiki'.
1151	Sitanath Pradhan: 'Chronology of Ancient India'.
1000	L.D. Burnett.
950	F.E. Pargiter: 'Ancient Indian Historical Tradition'.
900	Hem Chandra Roy Chowdhuri 'Political History of Ancient India'.

DIFFERENT PERIODS

Based on 1424 B.C. as the year of the Battle of Kurukshetra

A. *Pre-Vedic Period* (Before 3100 B.C.)

B.C.

6100 to 5500	Aditi Rishi era.

5500 to 4400	Daksha Rishi era.
4400 to 3102	Birabhadra era.
	B. *Vedic Period* (1st Phase 3100 B.C.-2550 B.C.)
3102	According to Aryabhatta, the Battle of Kurukshetra took place in this year, which ushered in the 'Kali Yuga' era on February 18.
	Nabhanedistha Rishi era.
	Sharbani Atri Rishi era.
3102 to 3100	There was the devastating flood which is the most important landmark of the world's history. It has its references in Indian, Hebrew and Babylonian scripts. "Satapatha Brahmana" mentions that Manu Vaivasvata was the Saviour of mankind. This may also be the reason for considering this time as the beginning of the 'Kali Yuga' era of February 18.
3100 2750	Yayati era.
2750 to 2550	Mandhata era.
	C. *Vedic Period* (2nd Phase 2550 B.C.-2150 B.C)
2550 to 2350	Viswamitra, I, contemporary of king Harishchandra
	Viswamitra II, originator of 'Nakshatra System' (celestial study) and contemporary of Bharata, son of King Dusyanta.
	The era of Kartyavirya Arjuna, Jamadagni and Parasuram.
2350 to 1950	Ramachandra and Sita of Ramayana.
	Garga I and his son Gargya, the great astronomers, Viswamitra III.
	Aryans started coming to India.

D. *Vedic Period* (3rd Phase 2150 B.C.-1400 B.C.)

1895 Bamdeva.

1630 Vagambhrini.

1466 Birth of Krishna (of Mahabharata) at Gokul.

1439 The Crystal Hall was constructed by the Pandavas at Indraprastha for Yudhisthira's Coronation and the 'Rajasuya Yajna'.

1424 Battle of Kurukshetra (Mahabharata battle) took Place during November-December.

1423 Bhisma Pitamaha died. He initiated 'Pitamaha Siddhanta' Method of celestial study, which became the basis of Vedanga Jyotish.

Also the era of Parashara ane Garga II, who made reasonably accurate observations of celestial study. Parikshita was born.

1421 The first edition of Mahabharata was composed by Vyasa Deva, perhaps at Kurukshetra, and was titled 'Jaya'(See 1390 B.C. and 1316 B.C.)

1410 In a Philosophical conference Yajnavalkya, the author of Brihadaranyak Upanished, was acknowledged as the supreme authority on philosophy.

E. Vedanga Jyotish Period (1400 B.C.-1200 B.C.)

1403 Krishna (of Mahabharata) died at Dwarka in Gujarat.

1390 The Second edition of Mahabharata was composed and recited by Vaishampayana to Janamejaya at Taxila during Janamejaya's 'Sarpayajna' to celebrate his victory over the Takshaka Nagas. It was titled as Bharata Samhita. (See 1421 B.C. and 1316 B.C.)

1316 The sages held a conference in Naimisaranya, under the Presidentship of Saunaka. In this conference the third edition of Mahabharata was composed and recited by Ugrashrava Shauti to Saunaka, and was titled 'Mahabharata'. Additions and alterations continued till about 300 B.C.

(See 1421 B.C. and 1390 B.C.)

1300 Ashwalayana and Patanjali I noticed the Pole Star (Dhruva Tara).

Hastinapur was abandoned by Kauravas.

1270 End of Upanishad Period.

1250 Dark age of India protohistory began. The unaccounted for gap continued till 642 B.C. i.e. untill Sisunaga dynasty was established in Magadha. Perhaps a new horde of unknown people invaded and completely devastated the North Western part of India.

642 Sisunaga started to rule Magadha with Rajgir as his capital. He was the founder of Sisunaga dynasty, the earliest dynasty which has a historical base.

618 the oldest Indian sculptures were made, whose dates could be determined with some certainty. These are Parkham statue now in Mathura museum and Yakshi status in Calcutta museum.

598 Mahavira Vardhamana Jnataputra, founder of Jainism, was born as a prince at Vaisali. (d 525 B.C.)

569 Mahavirra renounced his worldly possessions to seek spiritual bliss.

544 Gautam Buddha, founder of Buddhism, was born in a noble family in Lumbini Garden, now in Nepal (d. 461 B.C.)

535 Jain saint Mahavira died on April 24. (b. 598 B.C.)

520 Darius, King of Perrsia, crossed the Indus with a large army and brought Gandhar, Kamboj and the Indus region under his control.

519 Skylax, a Greek General of Persian emperor Darius, sailed down the Indus on a peaceful mission on his way back to Persia across the Persian Gulf.

Bimbisara, sat on the Magadha throne and established the real imperial power. He built the new Rrajgir.

469 Bimbisara, the Buddhist ruler of Magadha, was put to death by starvation by his son Ajatasatru, for restoration of Hindu religion. Ajatasatru became the Magadha ruler. (See 490 B.C.).

490 Ajatasatru converted himself to Buddhism. (See 494 B.C.).

461 Buddha died at Kushinara. (b. 544 B.C.)

459 Ajatasatru expired and was succeeded by Darsaka.

434 Udayan succeeded Darsaka on Magadha throne. He built the city Kusumpura on the Ganga near Pataliputra.

414 There was a formation of Tamil Confederacy, which was unique at that time, for the purpose of defence. (See 174 B.C.)

377 A Buddhist Council was held at Vaisali.

369 King Gopaditya built the original temple of Jyesthesvara on the top of Gopadri hill in Srinagar, Kashmir. The hill is also known as Sivjee hill or Sankaracharya hill. Sankaracharya's statue was put up there only in 1962.

361 Mahapadmananda, said to be the son of the last Magadha ruler Mahanandin, born out of a woman belonging to a lower caste, usurped the Magadha throne. He was hostile to Brahmins and Kshatriyas and established Nanda dynasty which lasted till 321 B.C.

361 Mahapadmananda, said to be the son of the last Magadha ruler Mahanandin, born out of a woman belonging to a lower caste, usurped the Magadha throne. He was hostile to Brahmins and Kshatriyas and established Nanda dynasty which lasted till 321 B.C.

350 Panini, the great Sanskrit grammarian, was born.

327 Alexander the Great arrived at the banks of the Indus around end June at the age of only 33. He defeated Porus (Puru) and captured Punjab.

Chandragupta Maurya met Alexander and joined his army perhaps to seek his assistance to captured Magadha.

325 Alexander left Karachi in October for Pesia. He died in Babylon in June 323 B.C.

324 Chandragupta attacked Macedonian garrison and captured Punjab.

321 With the support of Chanakya (Kautilya) Chandragupta captured Magadha. His Maurya dynasty lasted till 184 B.C.

317 Eudemos, the Geek Governor of Punjab, treacheously murdered Porus (Puru) and took possession of his Empire which was earlier returned to Porus by Alexander.

305 Seleucus Nikator, King of Syria and a general of Alexander, crossed the Indus and fought an indecisive battle with Chandragupta, who forced Seleucus to surrender Kabul, Kandahar, Herat and Baluchistan.

302 Megasthenes, a Greek emissary, visited India. His writing 'Indika' gives a valuable picture of life and customs of India in those days.

297 On Chandragupta's death Bindusara Amitraghata, father of Ashoka, started to rule Magadha and continued till 272 B.C.

272 Ashokavardhana or Ashokapriyadarshin, commonly known as Emperor Ashoka, ascended the throne of Magadha after his father Bindusara's death and ruled till 232 B.C. That was a golden period in India's history. (See 269 B.C.).

269 Ashoka's coronation took place. The coronation was delayed since his accession was perhaps contested by an elder brother Susima. (See 272 B.C.).

261 Ashoka captured Kalinga (Orissa) after a sanguinary battle near Bhubaneswar. The great devastation and miserable suffering of the people after the bitter fight brought profound remorse in Ashoka's mind. Since then he took refuge in the Law of Duty and Piety.

259 Ashoka abolished royal hunting of animals, it being contrary to the Buddhist teaching not to take the life of a man or a beast.

251 On the initiative of King Dewanampiya Tissa of Ceylon, Ashoka sent a mission of Buddhism to Ceylon, led by his son Mahendra and daughter Sanghamitra.

250 The third Buddhist Council was held in Pataliputra.

249 Ashoka made a pilgrimage to Lumbini, the birth-place of Buddha, alongwith his preceptor Upagupta and daughter Charumati and erected a 11-metre high monolithic pillar to mark the birth place. His journey was marked by five monolithic pillars on the way.

242 Ashoka made the seven pillar edicts laying down the code of regulations.

240 Emperor Ashoka became a monk and started wearing yellow robe.

232 Ashoka died after a very long reign in the history of India.

220 Simuka established Satavahana (Satakarni) dynasty in Andhra, which ruled till 236 A.D. After a few years he became very wicked. He was dethroned and killed.

209 Kharavela, King of Kalinga, was born. (d. 172 B.C.)

206 Antiochus the Great of Syria invaded North-Western India.

204 Ashoka's son Arahat Mahendra died in Ceylon.

203 Ashoka's daughter Sanghamitra died in Ceylon.

185 Coronation of Kharavela took place as the King of Kalinga.

184 Pushyamitra Sunga usurped the Magadha throne and started Sunga dynasty which ruled Magadha till 72 B.C. Pushyamitra was the Commander-in-Chief of the Maurya King Brihadratha, whom he killed while reviewing the army. Pushyamitra was perhaps as Iranian, but with Brahmin orthodoxy. Patanjali II, the celebrated grammarian, was possibly Pushyamitra's contemporary and witnessed the 'Ashwamedh Yajna' performed by Pushyamitra.

180 Menandar, a Greek King, invaded North-Western India and became the Indo-Greek ruler there till 160 B.C.

174 Kharavela anihilated Pithunda and broke the Tamil Confederacy. (See 414 B.C.).

173 Kharavela invaded Magadha.

172 Kharavela convened a council of Jain monks, which met on Mt. Kumari of Udaygiri Hill in Orissa, and was attended by nearly 3,500 monks.

Kharavela died. (b. 209 B.C.).

140 Antialkidas, a Greek, became the King of Taxila and ruled till 130 B.C.

80 Malles became the first Saka King of Western India.

72 Devabhuti, the last Sunga King, was killed in an intrigue of his Brahmin Minister Vasudeva, who founded a shortlived Kanya dynasty of Magadha. (ended 27 B.C.)

65 The teachers sent to India by the Chinese Emperor Ming-ti went back to China and Buddhism was introduced there.

57 Vikramaditya, the famous King of Ujjain, ascended the throne by repelling the Saka invaders who earlier overthrew Vikramaditya's father Gardhabhilla. Vikram era started from that date. He built the famous Mahakala Temple in Ujjain which was destroyed by Altamas (Iltutmis) in 1234 A.D.

27 Susarman, the Kanya King of Magadha, was probably killed by Sata Satkarni belonging to Satavahana dynasty. Thus ended the Kanya dynasty of Magadha.

21 The joint Indian mission from mighty kingdoms of Pandya, Chola, and Chera, which sailed from Broach in 25 B.C., was presented to Emperor Augustus in Rome on terms of equality. (See 138 A.D.).

Bibliography

(EPIC CULTURE)

Acharya, P.K., *Elements of Hindu Culture and Sanskrit Civilization.* Mehar Chand Lachhman Das, Lahore, 1939.

Acharya, P.K., *Glories of India.* On Indian Culture and Civilization. 2nd Edn. Jay Shankar Brothers, Allahabad, 1952.

Adidevananda, Swami, *Yatīndra-mata-dīpikā.* Text and translation. Ramakrishna Math, Madras.

Aiyangar, T.R. Srinivasa, and Murti, G. Srinivasa, *Śaiva and Śākta Upaniṣads.* Translation. The Adyar Library, Madras.

Aiyangar, T.R. Srinivasa, and Sastri, S. Subrahmanya, *Sāmānya Vedānta Upanisads,* Translation. The Adyar Library, Madras.

Aiyangar, T.R. *Ten Major Upanisads.* Translation. The Adyar Library, Madras.

Aiyangar, T.R. *Vaiṣṇava Upaniṣads.* Translation. The Adyar Library, Madras.

Aiyangar, T.R. *Yoga Upaniṣads,* Translation. The Adyar Library, Madras.

Aiyar, K. Narayanaswami, *Laghu-Yogovāsiṣṭha.* Translation. Madras

Altekar, A.S., *Sources of Hindu Dharma in its Socio-religious Aspects.* Institute of Public Administration, Sholapur, 1952.

Alterkar, A.S., *State and Government in Ancient India.*3rd Edn. Motilal Banarasidas, Banaras, 1958.

Apte, V.M., *Social and Religious Life in the Gṛhya-Sūtras.* Popular Book Depot, Bombay, 1954.

Arnold, Edwin, *The Song Celestial or Bhagavad-Gītā.* Translation in verse. Jaico Publishing House, Bombay, 1957.

Arnold, Edwin, *The Song Celestial,* Allahabad.

Atreya, B.L., *The Philosophy of the Yogavāsiṣṭha.* The Adyar Library, Madras.

Atreya, B.L., *Yogavāsiṣṭha and Its Philosophy.* Indian Bookshop, Banaras.

Atthalye, Y.V., and Bodas, M.R. *Tarkasungraha* (witth *Dāpikā and Nyāya-bodhinī*). Text and translattion with notes. *Bombay Sanskrit Series.*

Aurobindo, *Essay on the Gītā.* Sri Aurobindo Ashram, Pondecherry, 1959.

Aurobindo, Sri, *Bases of Yoga.* Arya Publishing House Calcutta.

Aurobindo, Sri, *Essay on the Gītā* (2 Vols.). Arya Publishing House, Calcutta.

Aurobindo, Sri, *The Synthesis of Yoga,* Arya Publishing House, Calcutta Coster, G., *Goga and Western Psychology.* Oxford University Press.

Aurobindo, *Vyāsa and Vālmīki.* Aurobindo Ashram, Pondecherry, 1956.

Avalon, Arthur (Sir John Woodroffe), *Shakti and Shakta,* Ganeṣh & Co. Ltd., Madras.

Avalon, Arthur (Sir John Woodroffe), *The Great Liberation (Mahānirvāṇa Tantra).* Text and translation. Ganesh & Co. Ltd., Madras.

Avalon, Arthur (Sir John Woodroffe), *The Principles of Tantra* (2 Vols.), London.

Avalon, Arthur (Sir John Woodroffe), *The Serpent Power Ṣaṭ-cakra-nirūpaṇa* and *Pādukāpancaka*). Ganesh & Co. Ltd., Madras.

Avalon, Arthur (Sir John Woodroffe), *The World as Power* (6 Vols.). Ganesh & Co. Ltd., Madras.

Avalon, Arthur (Sir John Woodroffe), *Varṇamālā* (*Garland of Lettters*). Studies in the *Mantraśāstra.* Ganesh & Co. Ltd., Madras.

Bagchi, P.C., *Studies in Tantras* (Part I). Calcutta University.

Baij Nath (Trans.), *The Adhyātma Rāmāyaṇa: or, the Esoteric Rāmāyaṇa.* Panini Office, Allahabad, 1913.

Ballantyne, J.R., *Bhāṣā-pariccheda* (with *Siddhānta-muktāvatī).* Text and translation. Calcuttta.

Ballantyne, J.R., *Lecturers on Sāṁkhya Philosophy.* With text and translation of *Tattvasamāsa* and *Tattvasamāsa-sūtravṛtti* (*Sāṁkhyakramadīpikā*). Calcutta.

Ballantyne, J.R., *Nyāya System of Philosophy* (with the Ontology of Vedānta), London.

Ballantyne, J.R., *Sāṁkhya-Sūtras* of Kapila. Translated with extracts from Vijnāna Bhikṣu's commentary. Asiastic Society, Calcutta.

Ballantyne, J.R., *Vedāntasāra* of Sadānanda. Text and translation. Allahabad.

Banerjee, K.M. (Trans.), *Mārkaṇdeya Purāṇa.* Author, Calcutta, 1851.

Banerji, N.C., *Kautilya: or an Exposition of His Social Ideal and Political Theory* (2 Vols.). R. Cambray & Co., Calcutta, 1927.

Banerji, Satish Chandra, *Sāṁkhya Philosophy (Sāṁkhya-kārikā* with Gauḍapāda's scholia and Nārāyaṇa's gloss). Text and translation. Calcutta.

Barnett, L.D., *Paramārthasāra* of Abhinavagupta (with Yogarāja's commentary). Translated in *Journal of the Royal Asiatic Society.*

Barth Auguste, *The Religions of India.* Trans. by J. Wood. Kegan Paul, Trench, Trubner & Co., London, 1921.

Barth, A., *Religions of India.* Trans. by J. Wood. Kegan Paul, TTrench, Trūbner & London, 1921.

Barua, B.M., *A History of Pre-Buddhistic Indian Philosophy.* Calcutta University.

Basham, A.L., *The Wonder that was India.* A Survey of the Culture of the Indian Sub-Continent before the coming of the Muslims. Sidgwick & Jackson, Lodnon, 1954.

Basu, Manindramohan, *Post-Caitanya Sahjajiyā Cult of Bengal,* Calcutta University.

Belvalkar, and Ranade, *History of Indian Philosophy.* Poona, 1927 *Cambridge Ancient History,* Vols. I & II. 1922-24.

Belvalkar, S.K. *Śrīmad Bhagvad-Gita.* With English Translation. Hindu Visvavidyalaya, Varanasi, 1959.

Belvalkar, S.K., and Ranade, R.D., *The Creative Period,* Poona.

Belvalkar, S.K., *Four Unpublished Upanishads.* Text and translation. Poona

Beni Prasad, *Theory of Government in Ancient India* (Post-Vedic). Indian Press, Allahabad, 1927.

Besant, Annie, *Śrī Rām Candra, the Ideal King.* Theosophical Publishing Society, Banaras, 1901.

Besant, Annie, *Avatāras.* Theosophical Pub. Society, London, 1900.

Bhagavan Das, *Science of Social Organisation or the Laws of Manu in the Light of Ātmaviidyā.* 2nd Edn. Theosophical Pub. Society, Madras, 1932.

Bhandarkar, R.G., *Vaiṣṇavism, Śaivism, and Minor Religious Systems.* Strassburg. Germany.

Bhattacharya, Asutosh, Sastri, *Studies in Post-Śankara Dialectics.* Calcutta University.

Bhattacharya, K.K. (Trans.), *Institutes of Parāśara.* Asiatic Society, Calcutta, 1887.

Bhattacharya, Satish Chandra, *Hindu Philosophy.* Calcutta.

Bose, Atindranath, *Crossroads of Science and Philosophy.* Calcutta.

Brahma, Nalini Kanta, *The Philosophy of Hindu Sādhanā*. Kegan Paul, London.

Briggs, G.W., *Gorakhnāth and the Kānphata Yogīs*. Calcutta.

Bühler, Georg (Trans.), *The Law of Manu with Extracts from Seven Commentaries*. The Sacred Books of the East Series No. XXV. Clarendon Press, Oxford, 1886.

Bühler, Georg (Trans.), *The Sacrred Laws of the Āryas as Taught in the Schools of Āpastamba, Gautama, Vaiṣṭha, and Bandhāyana* (2 Vols.). The Sacred Books of the East Series Nos. II & XIV. Clarendon Pess, Oxford, 1897.

Burrard, Sir S.G., and Heron, A.M., *The Geography and Geology of the Himalaya Mountains*. Delhi, 1932.

Carpenter, J.E. *Theism in Mediaeval India*. Constable & Co. Ltd., London.

Chakravarti, P.C., *Sakti in Indian Literature*, Calcutta.

Chandrasekharan, K., *Rāmāyaṇa Triveṇī*. Comparative study of Vālmīki. Kamba, and Tulasī *Rāmāyaṇa*. S. Viswanathan, Madras, 1954.

Chatterjee, S.C., and Datta, D.M., *An Introduction to Indian Philosophy*. Calcutta University.

Chatterjee, Satish Chandra, *The Nyāya Theory of Knowledge*. Calcutta University.

Chatterji, Hiralal, *Internaitonal Law and Inter-State Relations in Ancient India*. K.L. Mukhopadhyaya, Calcutta, 1958.

Chatterji, J.C., *Kashmir Śaivism*. Srinagar.

Chatterji, J.C., *The Hindu Realism*. Indian Press. Allahabad.

Chatterji, Mohini Mohan, *Ātmānātmaviveka* and *Ātmabodha* of Śaṇkarācārya. Translation. Bombay.

Chaudhuri. Mrs. Roma, *Doctrine of Nimbārka and His Followers*. Asiatic Society, Calcutta.

Chaudhuri, Mrs. Roma, *Vedānta-pārijāta-saurabha* of Nimbārka and *Vedāntakaustubha* of Śrīnivāsa. Text and translation. Asiatic Soviety, Calcutta.

Chitale, M.P., *Bhagvad-Gītā and Hindu Dharma*. Continental Publishers, Poona, 1953.

Colebrooke, H.T. (Trans.), *The Law of Inheritance According to Mitākṣarā*. Hindusthanee Press, Calcutta 1869.

Colebrooke, H.T. (Trans.), *Two Treaties onthe Hindu Law of Inheritance*. Translation of *Dāyabhāga* of Jimūtavāhana and *Mitākṣarā* of Vijnāneśvara. Hindustanee Press, Calcutta, 1810.

Colebrooke, H.T., and Wilson, H.H., *Sāṁkhya-kārikā* (with the bhāsya of Gauḍapāda). Text and translation. Bombay.

Cowell, E.B., and Gough, A.E., *Sarva-darśsana-saṅgraha* of Mādhavācārya. Translation. Kegan Paul, London.

Cowell, E.B., *Hastāmalaka* of Śaṇkarācārya. Translated in *The Indian Antiquary*. Bombay.

Cowell, E.B., *Nyāya-kusumānjali* of Udayana (with the commentary of Haridāsa). Text and translation. Calcutta.

Cowell, E.B., *Tattvamuktāvalī* of (Gauḍa) Pūrṇānanda. Translated in *Journal of the Royal Asiatic Societty*.

Cox, G.W., *The Mythology of the Aryan Nations*. Kegan Paul, Trench & Co., London, 1882.

Cunningham, A., *The Ancient Geography of Indian*. Ed. by S.N. Majumdar. Calcutta, 1924.

Das, Bhagavan, *Mystic Experiences or Tales of Yoga and Vedānta from Yogavāsiṣṭha*. Indian Bookshop, Banaras.

Das, Bhagavan, *The Concordance Dictionary to the Yoga-Sūtra and Bhāṣya*. Indian Bookshop, Banaras.

Das, R.V., *The Essentials of Advaita* (*Naiṣkarmyasiddhi*). Translation. Calcutta.

Das, S.K., *A Stury of the Vedānta*. Calcutta University.

Das, Sudhendukumar, *Sakti or Divine Power*, Calcutta University.

Dasgupta, Ramaprasad, *Crime and Punishment in Ancient India*. Book Co., Calcutta, 1930.

Dasgupta, S. N., *A History of Indian Philosophy* (5 vols). Cambridge University Press.

Dasgupta, S.N., and De, S.K., *A History of Sanskrit Literature*. Classicial Period. Vol. 1, Calcutta University, Calcutta, 1947.

Dasgupta, Sasibhusan, *Obscure Religious Cults*. Calcutta University.

Dasgupta, Surendranath, *A History of Indian Philosophy* (4 Vols.) Cambridge University Press.

Dasgupta, Surendranath, *The Study of Patanjali*. Calcutta Univesity.

Dasgupta, Surendranath, *Yoga as Philosophy and Religion*. Kegan Paul, London.

Dasgupta, Surendranath, *Yoga Philosophy in Relation to Other System of Indian Thought*. Calcutta University.

Datta, Bhupendra Nath, *Dialectics of Hindu Rituals* (2 Vols.). Gupta Press, Calcutta, 1951-56.

Datta, D.M., *The Six Ways of Knowing*. London.

Datta, K.N., *The Bhāgavata: its Philosophy, its Ethics, and its Theology* Gaudiya Math, Madras, 1959.

De, S.K., *Aspects of Sanskrit Literature,* K.L. Mukhopadhyay, Calcutta, 1959.

De, S.K., *Early History of the Vaiṣṇava Faith and Movement in Bengal,* Calcutta.

Deussen, Paul, *Outlines of the Vedānta System of Philosophy according to Śaṇkara*. Translated by J.H. Woods and C.B. Rrunkle. New York.

Deussen, Paul, *The Philosophy of the Upaniṣads.* Translated by Rev. A.S. Geden. Edinburgh.

Deussen, Paul, *The System of the Vedānta.* Translated by C. Johnston. Chicago.

Dey. N. L., *The Geographical Dictionary of Ancient and Mediaeval India.* 2nd Edn. London, 1927.

Dhar, Somnath, *Cānakya and the Arthaśāstra.* Indian Institute of World Culture, Bangalore, 1957

Dhole, N., *Pancadasī* of Vidyāraṇya. Translation. Calcutta.

Diehl, C.G., *Instrument and Purpose: Studies on Rites and Rituals in South India.* Gleerup. 1956.

Dikshitar, V.R. Ramachandra, *Hindu Administrative Institution.* Madras University, Madras, 1929.

Dikshitar, V.R. Ramachandra, *The Gupa Polity.* Madras University, Madras 1952.

Divanji, P.C., *Siddhāntabindu.* Translated with the commentary of Purusottama. Baroda.

Dixit, V.V., *Relation of the Epics to the Brāhmaṇa Literature.* Oriental Book Agency, Poona, 1950.

Dutt, M.N. (Trans.), *Agnipurāṇa.* Prose Translation, Elysium Press Calcutta, 1903-04.

Dutt, M.N. (Trans.), *Dharma-sāstrra* (2 Vols.). Ed. with English translation. Elysium Press, Calcutta, 1906-08.

Dutt, M.N. (Trans.), *Mārkandeya Purāna.* A prose English trans, Elysium Press, Calcutta, 1896.

Dutt, M.N. (Trans.), *Viṣṇupurāṇam.* A prose English trans. based on H.H. Wilson's translation. Elysium Press, Calcutta, 1894.

Dutt, M.N., *Bhāgavata Purāṇa.* Translation. Calcutta.

Dutt, Manmathanath, *The Rāmāyaṇa* (7 Vols.) Translated into English Prose. Printed by G.C. Chakravarty, Calcutta, 1891-94.

Dutt, N.K., *Vedānta: Its Place as a System of Metaphysics*. Calcutta University.

Dutt, R.C., *Ancient India*, Longmans Green & Co., London, 1893.

Dutt, R.C., *Ancient India*. Longmans, Green & Co., London, 1893.

Dutt, R.C., *History of Civilisation in Ancient India, based on Sanskrit Literature* (3 Vols.). Thacker, Spink & Co., Calcutta, 1889-90.

Dutt, R.C., *History of Civilization in Ancient India*. London, 1893.

Dutt, R.C., *The Great Epics of Ancient India*. Condensed into English Verse. J.M. Dent & Co., London, 1900.

Dvivedi, M.N., *Vākyasudhā*. Translation. Bombay.

Edgerton, F., *Mīmāmsā-nyāya-prakāśa* or *Āpadevī*. Text and translation. Oxford Univesity Press.

Edgerton, Franklin, *The Bhagvad-Gītā* (2 Vols.). Translation and Interpretation. Harvard University Press, Cambridge (Mass), 1952.

Elliot, *Climatological Atlas of India*. Calcutta, 1906.

Faddegon, Barend, *The Vaiśeṣika System*. Described with the help of oldest texts. Amsterdam.

Farquhar, J.N., *An Outline of the Religious Literature of India*. Oxford University Press, London, 1920.

Farquhar, J.N., *An Outline of the Religious Literature of India*. Oxford

Farquhar, J.N., *An Outline of the Religious Literature of India*. O.U.P., London, 1920.

Fausboll, V., *Indian Mythology*. According to the *Mahābhārata* in outline, Luzac, London, 1903.

Frazer, R.W., *A Literary History of India*. T. Fisher Unwin, London, 1898.

Garbe, R., *Die Sāmkhya Philosophie*. Translated by R.D. Vadekar. Poona.

Garbe, R., *Sāṁkhya and Yoga*. Strassburg, Germany

Garbe, R., *Sāṁkhya-Sūtras* of Kapila (with Aniruddha's commentary). Text and translation. Calcutta.

Gharpure, J.R. (Trans.), *The Smṛrticandrikā, Śrāddha Kāṇda*. An English translation with notes. office of the Collections of Hindu Law Texts, Bombay,1954.

Gharpure, J.R. (Trans.), *The Subodhinī*, Being a commentary, by Viśveśvara Bhaṭṭa on the Vyavahāradhyāya of the *Mitākṣarā* of Śrī Vijnāneśvara of the *Yājnavalkya Smṛti*. Author, Bombay, 1930.

Ghate, V.S., *The Vedānta*. Poona.

Ghosh, J., *Sāṁkhya and Modern Thought*. Calcutta.

Ghoshal, U.N., *A History of Hindu Public Life* (pt. I). Calcutta, 1945.

Ghoshal, U.N., *A History of Political Ideas*. Rev. Edn. of *A History of Hindu Political Theories*. O.U.P., Bombay, 1959.

Giri, Mahadevananda, *Vedic Culture*. Calcutta University, Calcutta, 1947.

Gode, P.K., *Studies in Indian Literary History* (2 Vols.). Singhi Jain Shastra Shikshapith, Bombay, 1953.

Gokhale, D.V., *Arthasaṇgraha* of Laugākṣi Bhāskara. Text and translation. Poona.

Goswami, Bhakti-siddhanta Saraswati, *Relative Worlds*. Gaudiya Math, Calcutta.

Goswami, Bhakti-siddhanta Saraswati, *Vedānta: Its Morphology and Ontology*. Gaudiyya Math, Calcutta.

Gough, A.E., *Advaitamakaranda* of Lakṣmīdhara Kavi. Translated in *The Pandit*. Banaras.

Gough, A.E., *Vaiśeṣika-Sūtras* of Kaṇāda (with comments from Śaṇkara Miśra's *Upaskāa* and Jayanārāyaṇa's *Vivṛti*). Text and translation. Banaras.

Griffith, Ralph T.H., *The Rāmāyaṇa of Vālmīki* (5 Vols.). Translated into English Verse. E.J. Lazarus. Baranas, 1870-74.

Guénon, Rene, *Introduction to the Study of Hindu Doctrines*. Translated by Macro Pallis. London.

Gurumurti, D., *Saptapadārthi* of Śivādiya. Translation. The Adyar Library, Madras.

Hamsa Yogi, *Saṁskāras: the Genius behind Sacramental Rites*. Suddha Dharma Office, Madras, 1951.

Hastings, J. (Ed.), *Encyclopaedia of Religion and Ethics* (13 Vols.). T. & T. Clark, Edinburgh, 1925-52.

Hastings, J. (Ed.). *Encyclopaedia of Religion and Ethics*(13 Vols). New York.

Hastings, James, *Encyclopaedia of Religion and Ethics* (13 Vols.). New York.

Hayden, H.L., 'Relation of the Himalayas to the Indo-Gangetic Plain and the Peninsula'. *Rec. Geol. Survey of India*, XLIII. Pt. 2, 1913.

Hazra, R.C., *Studies in the Purāṇic Records on Hindu Rites and Customs*. Dacca University, Dacca, 1940.

Hazra, R.C., *Studies in the Upapurāṇas*. Sanskrit College, Calcutta, 1958.

Held, G.I., *The Mahābhārata: an Ethnological study*. Kegan Paul, London, 1935.

Hiriyanna, M., *Outlines of Indian Philosophy*. George Allen & Unwin, London.

Hiriyanna, M., *Outlines of Indian Philosophy.* George Allen & Unwin. London.

Holditch, T. H., *India.* Religions of the World Series. Oxford, 1905.

Hooper, J.S.M., *Hymns of the Alvars.* London.

Hopkins, E. W., *The Religions of India.* Ginn & Co., Boston. 1902

Hopkins, E.W., *Epic Mythology.* Karl J. Trubner, Strassburg, 1915.

Hopkins, E.W., *Indian Inheritance* (3 Vols.). Bharatiya Vidyabhavan Series, Bombay, 1955-56.

Hopkins, E.W., *The Ethics of India.* Yale University Press.

Hopkins, E.W., *The Great Epic of India: its Character and Origin.* Charles Scribner's Sons, New York, 1902.

Hopkins, E.W., *The Religions of India,* Ginn. & Co., Boston, 1902.

Houghton, G.C. (Ed.), *Mānava-Dharma-śāstra, or the Institute of Manu* (2 Vols.), Vol. 1: Sanskrit text; Vol. 2: English trans. London, 1925.

Hume, R.E., *The Thirteen Principal Upanishads.* Oxford University Press.

Ingalls, D.H.H., *Materials for the Study of Navya-Nyāyya Logic. Harvard Oriental Series,* Cambridge (Mass.)

Iyengar, K.V. Rangaswamy, *Rājdharma.* Adyar Library, Madras, 1941.

Iyengar, K.V. Rangaswamy, *Some Aspects of the Hindu View of Life According to Dharma-śāstra.* Baroda University, Baroda, 1952.

Iyengar, K.V. Rangaswamy,*Considernation on Some Aspects of Ancient Indian Polity.* 2nd Edn. Madras University, Madras, 1935.

Iyengar, K.V. Rangawamy, *Considerations on Some Aspects of Ancient Indian Polity.* 2nd Edn. Madras University Press. Madras, 1935.

Iyengar, P.T. Srinivasa, *Śivasūtravimarśinī.* Translated in *Indian Thought.* Allahabad.

Iyengar, Venkatesa, *The Poetry of Vālmiki.* A Literary appreciation of the best parts of the *Rāmāyaṇa.* Bangalore, 1940.

Jagadananda, Swami *Upadeśasāhasrī* of Śaṇkarācārya. Text and translation. Ramakrishna Math, Madras.

Jayaswal, K.P., *Manu and Yājnavalkya—a Compaison and a Contrast.* A treatise on the basic Hindu Law. Butterworth, Calcutta, 1930.

Jayaswal, Kasi Prasad, *Hindu Polity* (2 Vols). A Constitutional History of India in Hindu Times. Bangalore Printing and Publishing Co., Bangalore, 1955.

Jha, Ganganath, *Śabara-bhāṣya.* Translation. Oriental Institute, Baroda.

Jha, Ganganath, *Śloka-vārttika* (with extracts from *Kāṣikā* and *Nyāyartnākara*). Translation, Allahabad.

Jha, Ganganath, *Advaitasiddhi* of Madhusūdana Sarasvatī. Translated in *Indian Thought*. Allahabad.

Jha, Ganganath, *Khaṇḍana-khaṇḍa-khādya*. Translated in *Indian Thought*. Allahabad Madhavananda, Swami, *Bṛhadāraṇyaka Upaniṣad*. Text with translation of Śaṇkara's commentary. Advaita Ashrama, Calcutta.

Jha, Ganganath, *Nyāya-Sūtas* (with *Bhāṣya* and *Vārttika*). Translated in *Indian Thought*. Allahabad.

Jha, Ganganath, *Padārtha-dharma-saṇgraha* (with the *Nyāya-kandalī* of Śrīdhara). Translated in *The Pandit*. Banaras.

Jha, Ganganath, *Pūrva-Mīmāṁsā in its Sources*. Banaras.

Jha, Ganganath, *Prābhākara School of Pūrva-Mīmāṁsā*. Allahabad.

Jha, Ganganath, *Tarka-bhāṣā* of Keṣava Miṣra. Translation. Poona.

Jha, Ganganath, *The Nyāya Philosophy of Gautama* (Sadholal Lectures). Allabahad.

Jha, Ganganath, *The Pūrva-Mīmāṁsā-Sūtras* of Jaimini. Text and translation Panini Office, Allahabad.

Jha, Ganganath, *The Sāṁkhya-kārikā* of *Iśṛṣṇa (with* Tattvakaumudī of Vācaspati Miśra). Text and translation. Bombay.

Jha, Ganganath, *Vedāntaparibhāṣā*. Text and translation. Advaita Ashrama, Calcutta.

Jha, Ganganath, *Vivekacūḍāmani*. Text and translation. Advaita Ashrama, Calcutta.

Jha, Ganganath, *Yogadarśana* (with the *sūtras* of Patanjali and the *bhāṣya* of Vyāsa with notes from Vācaspati's *Tatttva-vaiśāradī*, Vijnāna Bhikṣu's *Yoga-vārttika*, and Bhoja's *Rājamārtāṇḍa*). Text and translation. Bombay.

Jha, Ganganath, *Yogasāra-saṇgraha* of Vijnāna Bhikṣu. Text and translation. Bombay.

Jha, Ganganatha (Trans.), *Manu Smṛti: The Laws of Manu with the Bhāṣya of Medhātithi* (5 Vols.). Calcutta University, Calcutta, 1920-26.

Jhavery, M.B., *Comparative and Critical Study of Mantraṣāstra*. Sarabhai Manilal Nawal, Ahmedabad.

Jnaneshvara, *The Gītā*. Explained by Dnyaneshwar. Trans. by Manu Subedar. 2nd Edn. Bombay, 1941.

Johnson, J.J., *Vedānta-tattvasāra* of Rāmānuja. Translated in *The Pandit*. Banaras.

Jolily, J., and Schmidt, R. (Trans.), *Arthaśāstra of Kautilya*. A new Edn. Punjab Oriental Series, Lahore, 1923.

Jolly, Julius (Trans.), *Nāradīya Dharma-śāstra; or Institutes of Nārada.* Trūbner & Co.,

Jolly, Julius (Trans.), *The Institutes of Viṣṇu.* The Sacred Books of the East Series No. VII. Clarendon Prress, Oxford, 1880.

Jolly, Julius (Trans.), *The Minor Law-books* (pt. I); *Nārada Bṛhaspati,* The Sacred Books of the East Series No. XXXIII. Trnaslation of Nārada and Brhaspati. Clarendon Prress, Oxford, 1889.

Jones, Sir William (Trans.), *Institutes of Hindu Law; or the Ordinance of Manu.* India Government. Calcutta, 1794.

Kane, P.V., *History of Dharma-śāstra* (5 Vols.). Ancient and Mediaeval Religious and Civil Law. Bhandarkar Oriental Research Insitute, Poona, 1930-58.

Karmarkar, A. P., *Religions of India,* Vol. I. Mira Publishing House, Lonavala, 1950.

Keay, F.E., *Kabir and His Followers,* Calcutta.

Keith, A.B., *Classical Sanskrit Literature,* 4th Edn. Y.M.C.A., Calcutta, 1947.

Keith, A.B., *History of Sanskrit Literature,* O.u.P., London, 1956.

Keith, A.B., *Indian Logic and Atomism.* Oxford.

Keith, A.B., *The Karma Mīmāṁsā.* Oxford Uniesity Press.

Keith, A.B., *The Religion and Philosophy of the Veda and Upanishads* (2 Vols.). *Harvard Oriental Series,* Cambridge (Mass.)

Keith, A.B., *The Sāṁkhya System.* New York.

Kingsbury, F., and Philips, G.D., *Hymns of the Tamil Saivite Saints.* London.

Krishna Rao, M.V., *Studies in Kautilya.* 2nd Rev. Edn. Munshi Ram Manohar Lal, Delhi, 1958.

Krishnamachariar, K., *History of Classical Sanskrit Literature.* T.T. Devasthanams Press, Madras, 1937.

Krishnamacharya, V., *Vedānta-kārikāvalī* of Venkaṭācārya. Text and translation. The Adyar Library, Madras.

Kumarappa, B., *The Hindu Conception of the Deity as culminating in Rāmānuja.* London.

Laby, R.L., *Holy Land of the Hindus.* Robert Scott, London, 1913

Law, B.C., *Historical Geopgraphy of Ancient India.* Société Asiatique de Paris, 1954.

Law, B.C., *Rivers of India.* Calcutta, 1944.

Law, N. N., *Studies in Ancient Hindu Polity Based on the Arthaśḥstra of Kautilya* (2 Vols). With an introductory essay on the age and authenticity of the *Arthaśāstra* of Kautilya, by Radha Kumud Mukherji. Longmans Green & Co., London, 1914.

Liedecker, K.F., *Pratyabhijnāhṛdaya.* Translation with notes. The Adyar Library, Madras.

Lin Yutang, *The Wisdom of India.* Includes translations of passages from the *Bhagavad-Gītā* the *Rāmāyaṇa* and other Classical Works. Jaico Publishing House, Bombay, 1955.

Macdonell, A.A., *History of Sanskrit Literature,* William Heinemann, London, 1928.

Macdonell, A.A., *History of Sanskrit Literature.* London, 1913.

Macdonell, A.A., *India's Past: A Suvey of Her Literatures, Religions, Languages, and Antiquities.* Clarendon Press, Oxford, 1927.

Macdonnell, A.A., *Vedic Mythology.* Verlog Vonkarl of Trübner, Strassburg, 1897.

Mackinder, H.J., *Eight Lectures on India.* London, 1910.

Macnicol, N., *Psalms of Maratha Saints.* London.

Madhavananda, Swami (Trans.) *Last Message of Śrī Kṛṣṇa.* Chapters Six to Twenty-nine of the Eleventh *skandha* of the *Bhāgavata.* Text with English translation. Advaita Ashram, Almora, 1956.

Madhavananda, Swami, *Bhāṣā-paricaheda* (with *Siddhānta-muktāvalī*). Text and translation. Advaita Ashrama, Calcutta.

Madhavananda, Swami, *Mīmāṁsā-paribhāṣā.* Translated and annotated Ramakrishna Mission Sarada Pitha, Belur Math.

Mahadeva Sastri, A., *The Bhagvad-Gītā with the Commentary of Śrī Śankarācārya.* Text and Translation with Commentary. V.Ramaswamy Sastrulu & Sons. Madras, 1918.

Mahadevan, T.M.P., *Gauḍapāda: A Study in Early Advaita.* Madras University.

Mahalingam, T.V., *South Indian Polity.* Madras University, Madras, 1955.

Maitra, Sushil Kumar, *Madhva Logic.* Calcutta University.

Maitra, Sushil Kumar, *The Ethics of the Hindus.* Calcutta University.

Maitra, Sushil Kumar, *The Ethics of the Hindus.* Calcuttta University, Calcuttta, 1925.

Majumdar, and Pusalker, *The History and Culture of the Indian People:* Vol. I—*The Vedic Age;* Vol. II—*The Age of Imperial Unity.* Bharatiya Vidya Bhavan, Bombay, 1951, 1953.

Majumdar, R.C., and Pusalker, A.D., *The History and Culture of the Indian People* (6 Vols.). Bharatiya Vidyabhavan, Bombay, 1951-60.

Majumdar, R.C., *Corporate Life in Ancient India.* Surendranath Sen, Calcutta, 1918.

Majumdar, Sridhar, *The Vedānta Philosophy of the Basis of the Commentary by Nimbārkācārya*. Bankipur.

Majumder, J.C., *Ethics of the Mahābhārata*. Author, Calcutta 1953.

Mallik, P.N., *The Mahābhārata as it was, is and ever shall be*. Pioneer Press Calcutta, 1934.

Mandalik, V.N. (Ed.), *Vyavahārmayūkha*. English trranslation with notes. Bombay, 1880.

Mankad, D.R., *Purāṇic Chronology*. Author, Vallabhvidyanagar, Bombay, 1951.

Masson-Oursel, Paul, and Others, *Ancient India and Indian Civilization*. Routledge & Kegan Paul, London, 1951.

Max Müller, F., *Three Lectures on Vedānta Philosophy*. London.

Mayer, Johann Jakob, *Uber das Wasen der Altindischen Rechtsschriften und ihr Verhaltnis Zu Einander and Zu Kautilya*. Otto Harrassowitz, Leipzig, 1927.

Mayne, John Dawson, *A Treatise on Hindu Law and Usage*. 10th Edn. Ed. by S. Srinivasa Iyengar. Higginbothams, Madras, 1938.

Mazumdar, A.K., *The Sāmkhya Conception of Personality*. Calcutta University.

Mishra, Umesh, *Concepttion of Matter* (according to Nyāya-Vaiśeṣika). Allahabad.

Mitra, Rajendralala, *The Yoga Aphorisns of Patanjali* (with the commentary of Bhoja). Text and translation. Calcutta.

Mitra, Viharilala, *The Yogavāsiṣṭha-Mahārāmāyana of Vālmīki* (4 Vols.), Translation, Calcutta.

Modi, P.M., *Sidhāntabindu* of Madhusūdana Sarasvatī. Translation. Bhavnagar.

Modi, P.M., *The Bhagvad-Gītā a Fresh Approach with Special Reference to Śaṇkarācārya's Bhāṣya*. Text and Translation with Commentary. Baroda, 1956.

Monier-Williams, Monier, *Indian Wisdom or Examples of the Religious, Philosophical and Ethical Doctrines of the Hindus*. 4th Edn. Luzac, London, 1893.

Moti Chandra, *Geographical and Economic studies in the Mahābhārata*. U.P. Historical Society, Lucknow, 1945.

Motwani, Kewal, *Manu Dharma-śāstra*. A sociological and historical study. Ganesh & Co., Madras, 1958.

Müeller, Friedrich Max, *A History of Ancient Sanskrit Literature*, B.D. Basu, Allahabad, 1926.

Muir, J., *Metrical Translattions from Sanskrit Writers*. Trubner & Co., London, 1879.

Muir, J., *Original Sanskrit Texts on the Origin and History of the People of India* (5 Vols.). 3rd Edn. Trübner & Co., London, 1873-90.

Mukerjee, Prabhat, *Mediaeval Vaiṣṇavism in Orissa*. Calcutta.

Mukharji, Radha Kumud, *Ancient India*. Indian Press, Allahabad, 1956.

Mukherjee, C.C. (Trans.), *The Mārkaṇḍeya Purāṇam*. Trans. from the original Sanskrit in English Prose. P.G. Sen. Calcutta, 1893.

Mukherjee, Radha Kamal, *The Lord of the Autumn Moons*. Asia Pub. House, Calcutta, 1957.

Mukherji, Nalinimohan, Sastri, A Study of *Sankara*. Calcutta University.

Mukherji, Radha Kumud, *Local Government in Ancient India*. 3rd Edn. Delhi, 1958.

Narayanaswami Aiyar, K., *The Purāṇas in the Light of Modern Science*. Author, Adyar, Madras, 1914.

Navlekar, N.R., *A New Approach to the Rāmāyaṇa*. Jabalpur, 1947.

Nikhilananda, Swami, *Ātmabodha*. Text and translation. Ramakrishna Math, Madras.

Nikhilananda, Swami, *Dṛg-dṛṣya-viveka*. Text and translation. Ramakrishna Ashrama, Mysore.

Nikhilananda, Swami, *Māṇḍūkyopaniṣad* (with Gauḍapā *Karikā)*. Text with translation of Śaṇkara's commentary. Ramakrih. Ashrama, Mysore.

Nikhilananda, Swami, *The Bhagavad-Gītā*. Translation. New York.

Nikhilananda, Swami, *The Bhagvad-Gītā*. Trans. with notes, comments, and introd. Ramakrishna Vivekananda Centre, New York, 1952.

Nikhilananda, Swami, *The Philosophy of Advaita* (according to Bhāratī Tirtha Vidyāraṇya). Madras.

Nikhilananda, Swami, *Vedāntasāra* of Sadānanda. Text and translation. Advaita Ashrama, Calcutta.

Oldenberg, H., *Ancient India*, 2nd Edn. Chicago, 1898.

Oldenberg, H., *Ancient India: its Language and Religions*. Open Court Publishing Co., Chicago, 1898.

Oldenberg, Hermann (Trans.), *The Gṛhya-Sūtras; rules of Vedic Domestic Ceremonies* (2 pts.). The Sacred Books of the East Nos. XXIX-XXX. Clarendon Press, Oxford, 1886-92.

Oldham, R.D., 'The Structure of the Indo-Gengetic Plains'. *Memoirs of the Geological Survey of India*, XLII, 1917.

Oman, J.C., *The Great Indian Epics: The Stories of the Rāmāyaṇa and the Mahābhārata*. G. Bell & Sons, London, 1894.

Otto, Rudolf, *The Original Gītā: the Song of the Supreme Exalted One*. With copious comments and notes. Translation by J.E. Turner. George Allen and Unwin, London, 1939.

Pal, R. B., *The Gistory of Hindu Law in the Vedic Age and in Post-Vedic Time Down to the Institutes of Manu*. Calcutta University, Calcutta, 1958.

Pande, Raj Bali, *Hindu Saṁskāras, a Socio-religious Study of the Hindu Sacraments*. Vikrama Pub., Banaras, 1949.

Pandey, Kantichandra, *Abhinavagupta*. Banaras.

Panikkar, K.M., *The Geographical Factors in Indian Histoy*. Bharatiya Vidya Bhavan, Bombay, 1955.

Parekh, Manilai C., *Śrī Vallabhācārya: Life, Teaching, and Movement*. Rajkot.

Pargiter, F.E. (Ed.), *The Purāṇa Text of the Dynasties of the Kali Age*. O.U.P., London, 1913.

Pargiter, F.E. (Tans.), *The Mārkaṇḍeya Purāṇa*. Trans. and ed. with notes. Calcutta.

Patil, D.R., *Cultural History frrom the Vāyu Purāṇa,* Deccan College Post Graduate and Research Institute, Poona, 1946.

Paul, Manomatha Nath, *The Vedānta Tattvatraya* of Pillai Lokācārya. Translation. Panini Office, Allahabad.

Payne, E.A., *The Saktas of Bengal,* Oxford University Press, III-84.

Peter, I.S., *Beowulf and the Rāmāyaṇa, a study in Epic Poetry*. John Bale, London, 1934.

Pillai, Nallaswami, *Studies in Śaiva Siddhānta*. Madras.

Prabhavananda, Swami (Trans.), *Wisdom of God*. Trans. of *Śrīmad Bhāgavatam*. Vedanta Press, Hollywood, 1947.

Prabhavananda, Swami, and Ishewwood, Christopher. *Gītā*. Translation. Hollywood.

Prabhavananda, Swami, and Ishherwood, Christopher, *The Bhagvad-Gītā, the Song of God*. Translation in Verse. Ramakrishna Math, Madras, 1945.

Pradhan, Sitanath, *Vājasaneya Yājnavalkya and his Times (2 Vols)*. Calcutta, 1934.

Pt. 2: *Gṛhya-Sūtas* of Hobhila, Hiranyakesin, and Āpastamba.

Pt. I: *Gṛhya-Sūtras* of śāṅkhāyana, Āśvalāyana, Pāraskara, and Khadira.

Pusalker, A.D., *Studies in the Epics and Purāṇas*. Bharatiya Vidyabhavan, Bombay, 1951.

Radhakrishnan, S. (Ed.), *History of Philosophy: Eastern and Western* (Vol. I). Sponsored by the Ministry of Education, Government of India.

Radhakrishnan, S., and Others (Ed.), *History of Philosophy: Eastern and Western,* Vol. I. George Allen & Unwin London, 1952

Radhakrishnan, S., *Bhagavad-Gītā.* Translation. George Allen & Unwin, London.

Radhakrishnan, S., *Indian Philosophy* (2 Vols). George Allen & Unwin, London.

Radhakrishnan, Sarvepalli, *The Bhagvad-Gītā.* With an introductory essay, Sanskrit text, English translation, and notes. George Allen & Co., London, 1956.

Radharishnas, S., *Indian Philosophy* (2 Vols.). George Allen & Unwin. London, III—85.

Raghavan, V. (Trans.), *Śrīmad Bhāgavata.* Condensed in the poet's own words. Text and translation. G.A. Natesan, Madras, 1947.

Raghavan, V., *The Indian Heritage.* An Anthology of Sanskrit Literature witth detailed introduction. 2nd Edn. Indian Institute of World Culture. Bangalore, 1958.

Raghavendrachar, H.N., *Conception of Svatantra.* Mysore University.

Raghavendrachar, H.N., *Dvaita Philosophy and Its Place in the Vedānta.* Mysore University.

Raja, C. Kunhan, and Sastri, S.S. Suryanarayana, *Mānameyodaya.* Text and translation. The Adyar Library, Madras.

Rajagopalachari, *C., Bharat Milap from the Tamil Rāmāyaṇa of – Kamba,* Publication Division, Delhi, 1955.

Rajagopalachari, *C., Mahābhārata.* 5th Edn. Bharatiya Vidyabhavan, Bombay, 1958.

Rajagopalachari, *C., Rāmāyaṇa.* Bharatiya Vidyabhavan, Bombay, 1957.

Rajagopalachari, C., *The Bhagvad-Gītā.* Abridged and explained, setting forth the Hindu creed, discipline, and ideals. 4th Edn. Hindustan Times Press, Delhi, 1941.

Rajendra Singh, Thakur, *The Barbarians of Ancient India and the Story of TheirExtermination* (Story of the *Rāmāyaṇa*). Indian Express, Allahabad 1916.

Rajendra Singh, Thakur, *The Great War of Ancient India* (Story of the *Mahābhārata*). Indian Press, Allahabad, 1915.

Ram Gopal, *India of Vedic Kalpa-Sūtras.* A graphical portrayal of the social, economic, and religious life of India in the pre-Buddhistic times as depicted in the śrauta-, Gṛhya-,and Dharma-Sūtras. National Pub. House, Delhi 1959.

Rama Prasada, *Yoga-Sūtras* of Patanjali (with *Vyāsa-bhāṣya*). Text and translation. *Sacred Books of the Hindus*, Allahabad.

Ramanujachar, V.K., *Śrībhāgavatam* (3 Vols.). Being an analysis in English Author, Kumbakonam, 1933-34.

Ramanujachari, R., and Srinivasacharya, K., *Nītimālā*. Text with introduction and notes. Annamalai University.

Ramanujachari, V.K., *The Three Tattvas of Śrī Rāmānuja*. Translation. Kumbakonam.

Ramanujachari, V.K., *The Vedānta-Sūtra*. Translation of Rāmānuja's commentary. Kumbakonam.

Ramasubba Sastri (Trans.), Study or the true trans. in English of the Eleventh *shandha* in *Śrīmad Bhāgavatam* with text. Sridhara Power Press, Trivandrum, 1919.

Ramaswami Sastri, K., *Studies in the Rāmāyaṇa*. Dept. of Education, Baroda, 1944.

Ranade, R.D., *A Constructive Survey of Upanishadic Philosophy*. Poona.

Ranade, R.D., *Mysticism in Maharashtra*. Poona.

Ranade, R.D., *The Bhagvad-Gītā as a Philosophy of God-rrealization*. Being a clue through the labyrinth of modern interpretations. Nagpur University, Nagpur, 1959.

Rangacharya, M., and Aiyangar, M.B. Varadaraja, *The Vedānta-Sūtra*. Translation of Rāmānuja's commentary. Madras.

Rao, C. Hayavadana, *The Śrīkara Bhāṣya* (a Viraśaiva commentary on the *Vedānta-Sūtra* (in 2 Vols.). Text and translation. Bangalore.

Rao, P. Nagaraja, *Vādāvalī* of Jaya Tirtha. Text and translation. The Adyar Library, Madras.

Rapson. E. J., (Ed.). *Cambridge History of Indian*, Vol. I. 1922

Rapson. E. J., *Ancient India*. Cambridge, 1914.

Rau, C.V. Sankara, *Glossary of Philosophical Terms* (Sanskrit-English). Tirupati.

Rau, S. Subba, *Bhāgavata purāṇa*. Translation, Tirupati.

Rau, S. Subba, *Pūrṇaprajna-darśana* (*Vedānta-Sūtra* with the commentary of Śrī-Madhvācārya). Translation. Madras.

Ravi Tirtha, Swami, *Nyāya-kusumānjali* of Udayanācārya. Translaiton. The Adyar Library, Madras.

Ray, P.C., Revised Edition in being published by Oriental Publishing Co. Calcutta. 7 Vols. issued upto 1956.

Ray, P.C., *The Mahābhārata of Kṛṣṇa Dvaipāyana Vyāsa* (18 Vols.). Translated into English Prose. Bharata Press, Calcutta 1893-96.

Reed, Elizabeth A., *Hindu Literature,* Selections from Sanskrit Literature. Scott Foresman & Co., Chicago, 1907.

Renou, Louis, *Religions of Ancient India.* Trans, by sheila M. Fynn. The Athlone Press, London, 1953.

Renou, Louis, *Religions of Ancient India.* trans. by Sheila M. Fynn. Athlone Press. London, 1953.

Röer, E. (Trans.), *Hindu Law and Judicature, from the Dharma-śātras of Yājnavalkya.*In English. With notes, by E. Roer and W.A. Montrious. Calcutta, 1859.

Roy Chaudhury, Anl Kumar, *The Docrtine of Māyā.* Calcutta.

Roy, Anilbaran (Ed.), *The Message of the Gītā as interpreted by Sri Aurobindo,* George Allen and Unwin, London, 1946.

Roy, Dilip Kumarr, *Immortals of the Bhāgavat; or Nector of Immortality and Sri Ramakrishna's Parables.* Laxmi Narayan Agarwal, Agra, 1957.

Roy, S.C., *The Bhagvad-Gītā and Modern Scholarship,* Luzac, London, 1941.

Roychaudhrui, H.C., *Political History of Ancient india.* Calcutta University, Calcutta, 1953.

Sanyal., J.M. (Trans.), *The Śrīmad Bhāgavatam of Kṛṣṇa Dvaipāyana Vyāsa* (5 Vols.) Trans. into English prose from the original Sanskrit text. Datta Bose & Co., Dum Dum, 1936.

Sarkar, B.K., *Positive Background of Hindu Sociology.* 2nd Edn. Panini Office, Allahabad, 1947.

Sarkar, Benoy Kumar, *The Political Institutions and Theoies of the Hindus: a Study in Comparative Politics.* Chuckervertty, Chatterjee & Co., Calcutta, 1939.

Sarkar, G.C. (Trans.), *The Law of Inheritance as in the Vīramitrodaya.* With text. Thackar Spink & Co., Calcutta, 1879

Sarkar, K.L., *The Hindu System of Moral Science.* 3rd Edn. S.C. Majumber, Calcutta, 1912.

Sarkar, M.N., *Mysticism in the Bhagvad-Gītā.* Longmans Green & Co., Calcutta, 1929.

Sarkar, M.N., *The System of Vedantic Thought and Culture.* Calcutta.

Sarma, D.S., *The Bhagavad-Gītā.* Text and Translation with notes. Madras.

Sastri, A. Mahadeva, *The Bhagavad-Gītā.* Translation of Śaṅkara's commentary. Madras.

Sastri, Dakshinaranjan, *A Shortt History of Indian Materialism*. Calcutta.

Sastri, Dakshinaranjan, *Cārvāka-ṣaṣṭi*. The Book Company, Calcutta.

Sastri, Govinda Deva, *Sāṁkhya-tattva-pradīpa*. Translated in *The Pandit*. Banaras.

Sastri, Pashupatinath, *Introduction to he Pūrva-Mīmāmsā*. Calcutta.

Sastri, S. Kuppuswamy, *A Primer of Indian Logic*. Text and translation of *Tarkasaṅgraha*. Madras.

Sastri, S.S. Suryanarayana, *Siddhānta saṅgraha*. Translation. Madras University.

Sastri, S.S. Suryanarayana, *Vedāntaparibhāṣā*. Text and translation. The Adyar Library, Madras.

Sastri, S.S., Suryanarayana, *Śivādvaita-nirṇaya* of Appaya Dīkṣita. With introduction, translation, and notes. Madras.

Sastri, Suryanarayana, S.S., *The Sāṁkhya-hārikā* of Iśvarakṛṣṇa. Text and translation. Madras University.

Sastri, Suryanarayana, S.S., *The Sāṁkhya-kārikā* (with *Māṭharawṛtti*). Studied in the light of its Chinese version and translated into English from the French translation. Madras.

Schrader, F.O., *Introduction to Pancarātra and the Ahirbudhnya Saṁhitā*. The Adyar Library, Madras.

Seal, Brajendranath, *The Positive Sciences of the Ancient Hindus*. Longmans, London.

Sen, D.C., *The Bengali Rāmāyaṇas*. Calcutta University, Calcutta, 1920.

Sen, Dinesh Chandra, *Chaitanyc and His Age*. Calcutta University.

Sen, Kshitimohan, *Mediaeval Mysticism of India*. Calcutta.

Sen, R.N. (Trans.). *The Brahma-Vaivarta Purāṇam* (2 Vols.). The Sacred Books of the Hindus Series No. XXIV. Panini Office. Allahabad, 1920-22.

Sengupta, N.C., *Evolution of Ancient Indian Law;* Eastern Law House, Calcutta, 1953.

Sengupta, N.C., *Sourcs of Law and Society in Ancient India*. Art Press, Calcutta, 1914.

Shamasastry, R. (Trans.), *Arthaśāstra*. 4th Edn. Ranguveer Printing Press, Mysore, 1951

Sharma, D.S., *Lectures and Essays on the Bhagvad-Gītā*. 4th Edn. M.L.J. Press, Madras, 1945.

Sharma, R.S., *Aspecs of Political Ideas and Institutions in Ancient India*. Motial Banarasidas, Delhi, 1959.

Shastri, H.P., *Teachings from the Bhagvad-Gītā*. Translation with commentary. Shanti Sadan, London, 1949.

Shastri, H.P., *The Rāmāyaṇa of Vālmīki* (3 Vols.) Translated in Prose. Shanti Sadan, London, 1952-59.

Sidhanta, N.K., *The Heroic Age of India*, Kegan Paul., Trench, Trubner & Co., London, 1929.

Sindha, H.N., *Sovereignty in Ancient Indian Polity*. Luzac, London, 1938.

Singh, Mohan, *Gorakhnath and Mediaeval Hindu Mysticism*. Lahore.

Sinha, J.N., *Indian Psychology: Perception*, Kegan Paul, London.

Sinha, Nandalal, *Sāṁkhya-pravacana-sūtram*. Text and translation. *Sacred Books of the Hindus*, Allahabad.

Sinha, Nandalal, *Vaiśeṣika-Sūtras* of Kaṇāda (with *Vivṛti* and notes from Candrakānta's commentary). Text and translation. Panini Office, Allahabad.

Sinha, P.N. (Trans.), *Study of the Bhāgavata Purāṇa*. Text and translation. Theosophical Publishing House, Adyar, 1953.

Sinha, P.N., *A Study of the Bhāgavata Purāṇa, on, Esoteric Hinduism*. Freeman. Co. Ltd., Banaras, 1901.

Sivananda, Swamy, *Ethics of the Bhagvad-Gītā*. Yoga-Vedanta Forest University, Rishikesh, 1957.

Srinivasa Sastri, V.S., *Lectures on the Rāmāyaṇa*. Madras Sanskrit Academy, Madras, 1952.

Srinivasachari, P.N., *The Philosophy of Bhedābheda*. The Adyar Library Madras.

Srinivasachari, P.N., *The Philosophy of Viśiṣṭādvaita*. The Adyar Library Madras.

Stephen, Dorothea Jane, *Studies in Early Indian Thought*. Cambridge Univ Press, London, 1918.

Subba Rau, S. (Tans.), *Śrīmad Bhāgavatam* (2 Vols.). Trans. into English prose, embodying the interpretations of the leading schools of thought, Advaita, Viśiṣṭādvaita, and Dvaitta. Sri Vyasa Press. Tirpupati, 1928.

Subedar, Manu, *Bhagavad-Gītā Explained by Dnyaneshwar Maharaj*. Translation. Bombay.

Subramanya Aiyar, V.V., *Kamba Rāmāyaṇa: a Study*. Tamil Sanam, New Delhi, 1950.

Śukrācārya, *The śukranīti*. Trans. by B.K. Sarkar with an Index by kumar Narendranath Law. Panini Office, Allahabad, 1914.

Sukthankar, V.S., *Critical Studies in the Mahābhārata*. Edited by P.K. Gode. Sukthankar Memorial Edn. Committee, Poona, 1844.

Sukthankar, V.S., *On the Meaning of the Mahābhārata*. Asiatic Society of Bombay, Bombay, 1957.

Survey of India Maps: (I) *India and Adjacent Countries.* (2) *Southern Asia Series* (3) *Highlands of Tibet and Surrounding Regions.* 2nd Edn., 1943.

Swarupananda, Swami, *Śrīmad Bhagvad-Gītā*. Text and Translation. 8th Edn. Advaita Ashram, Mayavati, 1948.

Swarupananda, Swami, *Śrīmad-Bhagavad-Gītā*. Text and translation. Advaita Ashrama, Calcutta.

Tagore, Rabindranath, *One Hundred Poems of Kabir*. Macmillan & Co., London.

Tagore, Rabindranath, *The Philosophy of Our People*, Visvabhaati, Santiniketan.

Telang, K.T., *Bhagavad-Gītā* (with *Sanatsujātīya* and *Anugītā*). Translation. *Sacred Books of the East*, Oxford.

Telang, K.T., *The Bhagavad-Gītā with the Sanatsujātīya and the Anugītā*. The Sacred Books of the East Series No. VIII. Clarendon Press, Oxford, 1898.

Telang, K.T., *WasRāmāyaṇa copied from Homer? A Reply to Professor Weber*. Author, Bombay, 1873.

Thadani, N.V., *The Mystery of the Mahābhārata* (5 Vols.). Bharat Publishing House, Karachi, 1933.

Thibaut, G., *The Vedānta-Sūtra*. Translation of Rāmānuja's commentary. *Sacred Books of the East*, Oxford.

Tilak, Bal Gangadhar, *Śrīmad Bhagavad-Gītā Rahasya or Karmayoga-śāstra* (2 Vols.) Including an external examination of the *Gītā*, the original Sanskrit stanzas, their English translation, commentaries, and a comparison of Eastern and Western doctrines. Trans. by Bhalchandra Sukhtankar. Tilak Brothers, Poona, 1935.

Tridandi Swami Gosvami Maharaja, *The Bhāgavada, its Philosophy, its Ethics, and its Theology*. 2nd Edn. N.B. Bhaktibaibhava, Madras, 1959.

Ur. H., *The Vaiśeṣika Philosophy* (according to *Daśapadārtha-śāstra*). Chinese text with treanslation. London.

Vaidya, C.V., *Epic India, or India as described in the Mahābhārata and the Rāmāyaṇa*. India Litho Press, Bombay, 1907.

Vaidya, C.V., *The Mahābhārata: a Criticism*. A.J. Cambridge, Bombay, 1905.

Vaidya, C.V., *The Riddle of the Rāmāyaṇa*. Kegan Paul, Trench, Trübner & Co., London, 1906.

Vanamali, Vedantatirtha (Trans.), *Grhya-Sūtras of Gobhila.* In English with copious notes. Metropolitan Printing & Pub. House Ltd., Calcutta, 1940

Varadachari, K.C., *Rāmānuja's Theory of Knowledge.* Tirupati.

Varadachariar, S., *Hindu Judicial System.* Lucknow University, Luckonw 1946.

Varma, V.P., *Studies in Hindu Political Thought and its Metaphysical Foundations.* Motilal Banarasidas, Banaras, 1956.

Vasu, S. C. (Trans.), *Yājñavalkya Smrti.* Panini Ashram, Allababad, 1909.

Vasu, Srischandra, *Gheraṇḍa Saṁhitā.* Text and translaiton. Panini Office, Allahabad.

Vasu, Srischandra, *Haṭhayoga-pradīpikā.* Text and translaiton. Panini Office, Allahabad.

Vasu, Srischandra, *The Vedānta-Sutra of Bādarāyaṇa with the Commentarry of Baladeva* (including Baladeva's *Prameya-ratnāvalī*). Translation. Panini Office, Allahabad.

Venkataraman, *S., Select Works of Śrī Śaṇkara.* Text and translation. Madras.

Vidyabhushanga, S.C., *A History of Indian Logic.* Calcutta University.

Vidyabhushanga, S.C., *The Nyāya-Sūtras of Gotama.* Text and translation Panini Office, Allahabad.

Vidyarnava, S.C. (Trans.), *Yājniavalkya Smrti.* With the commentary of Vijnāneśvara. Panini Office, Allahabad, 1918.

Vijnanananda, Swami, *Śrīmad Devī Bhāgavatam.* Panini Office. Allahabad, 1954.

Vimuktananda, Swami, *Aparokṣānubhūti.* Text and translation. Advaiata Ashrama, Calcutta.

Vireswarananda, Swami, *Śrīmad Bhagavad-Gītā.* Text, translation, and the gloss of Śrīdhara Svāmin. Sri Ramakrishna Math, Mylapore, 1948.

Vireswarananda, Swami, *Bhagavad-Gītā.* Text with gloss of Śṛīdhara. Translation. Ramakrishna Math, Madras.

Vireswarananda, Swami, *Brahmasūtas.* Text and translation with notes. Advaita Ashrama, Calcutta.

Viswanathan, S.V., *International Law in Ancient India.* Longmans, Green & Co, London, 1925.

Vivekananda, Swami, *Rāja-yoga* (with the *sūtras* of Patanjali). Text with translattion and explanation. Advaita Ashrama, Calcutta.

Vivekananda, Swami, *The Complete Works of Swami Vivekananda* (8 Vols.). Advaita Ashrama, Calcutta.

Vivekananda, Swami, *The Complete Works of Swami Vivkananda* (8 vols.). Advaita Ashrama, Calcutta.

Walia. D.N., *Geology of India*. 3rd Edn. Macmillan, London, 1939.

Weber, A., *History of Indian Literature*. Trans. by J. Mann and Th. Zachariae. 2nd Edn. London, 1882.

Weber, A.F., *The History of Indian Literature,* Trans. from the 2nd German Edn., by John Maun and Theodore Zachariae. 3rd Edn. Kegan Paul, Trench, Trubner & Co., 1892.

Wilkings, C., and others. *The Glorious Upaniṣads of the Bhagavad-Gītā*. With *Śaṇkarācāyrya's readings*. Calcutta, 1902.

Wilkins, W.J., *Hindu Mythology*. Thacker Spink & Co., Calcutta, 1913.

Wilson, H.H. (Trans.), *The Viṣṇupurāṇa: a System of Hindu Mythology and Tradition*. Trans. from the original Sanskrit and illustrated by notes devived chiefly from other Purāṇas. John Muirray, London, 1840.

Wilson, H.H., *Purāṇas:* An account of their contents and nature. Society for Resuscitation of Indian Literrature, Calcutta, 1897.

Winternitz, M., *History of Indian Literature,* Vols. I & II. Eng. trans. by Mrs. S. Ketkar. Calcutta University, 1927, 1933.

Winternitz, Moriz, *A History of Indian Literature* (2 Vols.). Trans. by Mrs. Shilavati Ketkar. Calcutta University, Calcutta, 1927-33.

Wood, Ernest, and Subrahmanyam, S.V. (Trans.), *The Garuḍa Purāṇa*. The Sacred books of the Hindus, Series No. IX. Panini Office, Allahabad, 1911.

Woods, James Haughton, *The Yoga-system of Patanjali* (with the commentary of Vyāsa and the explanatiton of Vacaspati Miśra). Translation. *Harvard Oriental Series,* Cambridge (Mass).

Woods, James Haughton, *Yoga-Sūtra* of Patanjali (with *Maṇiprabhā*). Translated in *Journal of tthe American Oriental Society*.

Zimmer, Heinrich, *Philosophies of India,* Edited by Joseph Campbell. Routledge & Kegan Paul Ltd., London.

Zimmer, Heinrich, *Philosophies of India*. Routledge & Kegan Paul, London.